THE SOVIET
ACHIEVEMENT

1 The new revolutionary Red Army needs recruits

THE SOVIET ACHIEVEMENT

J. P. NETTL

with 144 illustrations, 19 in color

HARCOURT, BRACE & WORLD, INC.

АНДРЕИ ПЕТРОВНЕ

Lenin left two sealed envelopes when he died. One was marked 'To be opened when times are bad' and contained a sheet of paper which read: 'Blame me for everything'. The other was marked 'To be opened when times are *very* bad'. Inside it said: 'Do as I did'.

Party joke, originating in the indistinct area of East Central Europe where all good jokes come from

PICTURE RESEARCH: GEORGINA BRUCKNER

First American Edition 1967

6-10-71

Library of Congress Catalog Card Number: 68-10825

PRINTED IN GREAT BRITAIN BY JARROLD AND SONS LTD NORWICH

CONTENTS

Anyone should have serious doubts before adding to the mountain of literature on the Soviet Union. The fiftieth anniversary of the October revolution provides an occasion, perhaps, but no automatic excuse. My only justification for accepting the present commission is its format and approach. It is neither a history of the Soviet Union nor an original piece of research on any particular aspect, but a broad and highly selective interpretation. Opportunities for this kind of over-view are rare, and seldom taken on one's own initiative. Being asked is not only flattering but cathartic. This has been a good book to *write*.

In such a case an author necessarily postulates a certain type of reader. Mine would be familiar with the basic issues of international politics today, has been exposed to reportage of the Soviet Union in the press or on television, has at least a notion of who the main protagonists were and what the major historical issues were about. He is interested in politics, economics, social problems, art, literature – in every damn thing. He is endlessly curious and wants to understand things in the round. He is neither an expert nor a sensationalist. His roving mind is presently drawn to the Soviet Union because the fiftieth anniversary of one of the great events of the century may be a good moment to find out more about it.

The most crucial problem has been that of selection and emphasis. Claude Lévi-Strauss, one of our very few geniuses, writing on the subject of History and Dialectic, says: 'When one proposes to write a history of the French Revolution one knows (or ought to know) that it cannot, simultaneously and under the same heading, be that of the Jacobin and that of the aristocrat. *Ex hypothesi*, their respective totalizations (each of which is anti-symmetric to the other) are equally true. One must therefore choose between two alternatives. One must select as the principal either one or a third (for there are an infinite number of them) and give up the attempt to find in history a totalization of the set of partial totalizations; or alternatively one must recognize them all as equally real: but only to discover that the French Revolution as commonly conceived never took place.' If we substitute Russian for 'French' Revolution, Bolshevik for 'Jacobin' and government for 'aristocrat', we have a very clear description of the intellectual difficulties

7

◀ 2 Russian society in 1900, as caricatured by the Russian Social Democratic Party in writing about the Soviet Union. What all this means is that, looking back at 1917 and beyond, our interpretation is structured by our knowledge of later events; the history of the last decades of imperial Russia is necessarily the history of the coming Bolshevik revolution. It is best to admit this quite frankly. Many will not agree with my interpretation – either in detail or in general. We have to be clear just how little consensus over the history of the Soviet Union really exists, not only between Western and Soviet scholars, but even among ourselves – or them, for that matter.

I make one apology only. I have tried throughout to view the Soviet Union, and the process of its development, as a whole – to write about things rather than people. This produces an atmosphere of generality which knocks out most of the fascinating human drama. A few names tower above the history of their times: Lenin, Stalin, Trotsky, Khrushchev. If anything, I have under-emphasized their role; Lenin and Stalin are frequently used here more as shorthand notation for a system with which they are associated. I hope that the interest of the subject and its analysis will partially overcome the deliberate generality and its resultant dullness of style.

My colleague and former student, Lewis Minkin, did some of the detailed research for this book. He also acted as a severely critical filter for the ideas and facts put forward. Many contradictions and mistakes were eliminated as a result. Above all he helped to see the manuscript through its final stages, and prepared the charts and some of the maps. He therefore stands in part as co-author. Peter Frank kindly read the proofs. A book which integrates text and pictures raises special problems of production and control for the solution of which I had little useful to offer; the publishers have handled this magnificently.

Great events tend to obliterate the alternative possibilities existing in their immediate past. In the hands of historians/successful revolutions assume the mantle of the inevitable – for unexpected accidents are unscientific, disturbing and unmanageable. The period preceding the event is searched for signs of its coming, for evidence of why it was necessary and why it had to succeed. Clearly, any assessment of the fifty years since the Bolsheviks came to power must first of all come to grips with the 'great events' of 1917 and, by examining the Tsarist past, attempt to put them in historical perspective. The notion of a backward, decaying society involved in an intractable war and simply bursting asunder to enable an extreme sect of revolutionaries to emerge and capture the organs of state power, is oversimple. Particularly, it confuses two problems: the decay and overthrow of Tsarism under pressure of war and by a wide consensus of articulate people that the system had become insupportable, and the forceful action of one of a number of groups competing for power – and the most extreme group at that! – in capturing and holding control of society.

The Russia of 1917 was indeed a backward society but this description too can obscure more than it illuminates. At the end of the seventeenth century Peter the Great, only too conscious of his country's backwardness compared to the rest of Europe (backwardness and modernity are always relative concepts), had undertaken the most forceful programme of deliberate modernization that until recently had ever been known in the history of Europe. He was a self-willed autocrat in an autocratic environment, and his programme was enforced from the top downwards. Most affected were those socially nearest the Tsar – the aristocracy and the state officials, the bureaucracy which he himself helped to institute. His work was never entirely undone; the base he had created served his successors well – those who were able to make use of it. In the eighteenth century Russia had at least one great and modern Empress, Catherine, who matched her European contemporaries in finesse and ambition. During her reign Russia became as firmly part of the European scene as it had ever been. Perhaps the high point of Russian involvement in Europe was reached in 1815, when Tsar Alexander I and his allies in the victory over Napoleon played a crucial part in the resultant

European settlement. Even in the negative role of Europe's Gendarme, Nicholas I intervened, or threatened to, at various crucial moments in the nineteenth century to restrain and suppress the effervescence of revolutionary changes. Diplomatically, at least, Russia was a major European power from the eighteenth century onwards, and no statesman or revolutionary of consequence could afford to ignore her presence and ambitions.

Two major themes of Russian society in the nineteenth century need emphasis. The first is the growing ambivalence of educated Russians in their evaluation of themselves and their country's role. Russia had joined Europe relatively late, having only emerged from a barren and encapsulated subservience to Mongol rulers in the sixteenth century; the tradition of a wider mediaeval Christian community was lacking. Once Russia was drawn sharply into European affairs from the eighteenth century onwards, and subject to European influences at all practical and intellectual levels for two hundred years, consciousness of the relatively backward status of Russian society compared to the rest of Europe was balanced, and to some extent compensated by, an appeal to Russia's own past: the development of a unique society which had broken the domination of eastern Mongols and western Poles, and had evolved its own special institutions and distinct identity. This ambivalence between the foreign example of Europe and the unique potential of Russia's own past was never synthesized into a single world view, but remained a conflict between alternatives and the subject of endless debate. During much of the nineteenth century European and indigenous influences were viewed as alternatives, and policy swung like a pendulum between them.

The second theme is the authoritarianism of Russian society and its form of government. The gradual separation of church and state in Europe, the confining or shrinking of politics to a specialist sphere and its banishment from the area of economic activity, finally the subordination of formal power to some measure of popular control or at least a semblance of popular participation through elections – all these had passed Russia by. The French Revolution made its rationalist impact on a few intellectuals, it set – as we shall see – a revolutionary example, but its practical influence on Russian society and government was nil; it might never have happened. The Russian system of government depended on the Tsar and only on the Tsar, who was not just the political head but the social and religious apex of all power. An able Tsar was effective, a weak one merely froze the situation during the period of his rule. As the nineteenth century wore on, a dichotomy of progressiveness or reaction crystallized in European thinking and was reflected in turn by a number of 'European-minded' Russian intellectuals. In their view reactionary or backward Russia had two faces, both equally undesirable: that of an intelligent and determined Tsar like Alexander III, whose policies were a consistent negation of European influence, or the frozen incompetence and stagnation associated with weakness (or madness), typified by Paul at the beginning and Nicholas II at the end of the nineteenth century. The brightest hope for the 'European' reformers had been the first and longer portion of the reign of Tsar Alexander II. But already before his assassination in 1881 the pendulum had swung the other way and his successor Alexander III and his ministers merely plumped heavily for the known alternative – a policy of reaction coated with emphasis on the indigenous anti-European features of society. The retreat from reform from 1880 on was not only a decisive swing of the Russian-European pendulum, but a concession to fear: the survival of traditional Russian society or its complete disintegration. The rising wave of violence, of which Alexander II had only been the most distinguished victim, was laid at the door of dangerous foreign ideas, not of indigenous social evils.

For there was a symmetry between the authoritarianism of social life, the concentrated autocracy of government, and the widespread lawlessness in society – the violence of political action. These extremes often go hand in hand; the rigorous demand for unquestioning obedience, the total irrelevance

3 Nicholas I, the unpopular Gendarme of Europe, crushing the Polish revolution of 1830. An English view.

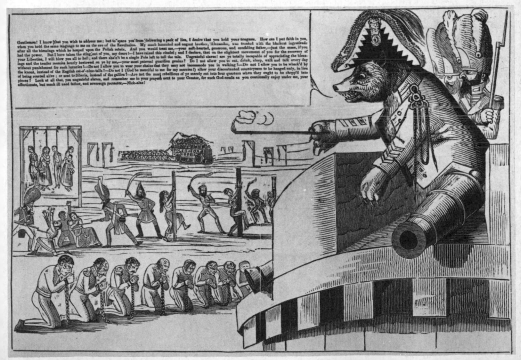

of law and order, the extreme claim of sovereign authority and its challenge with bomb or gun. Russia was a mass of polarized contradictions. As a recent historian writes in his introduction to *Russia in Revolution*, to understand the revolution we need 'to grasp the connection between Tolstoy's anarchism and Lenin's Marxism, the character of the Tsar and the disrespect for law and order, the alienation of the student and the influence of railway construction, the repression of the national claims of Poles and Finns and the character of revivalist sects, a demographic upsurge and great-power rivalry, bureaucratic corruption and Western influences.' Above all, this polarization was self-reinforcing, centrifugal; the tendency was repression and greater extremism, not compromise or reduction of conflict. There might be a startling plethora of different views as to what was wrong or what should be done to put it right, probably greater in range than the policy dissensus that to some extent exists in all societies, but on one thing almost all the critics were agreed: a sense of impending catastrophe. It runs through the literature of the three decades before 1917, of both fact and fiction, like an incessant roll of thunder.

Autocracy also involves centralization. For two hundred years and more the Russian system of government had developed a bureaucratic structure not unlike that of the great French monarchy at the turn of the seventeenth century. The parallel holds in the social sphere as well, for the growth and power of such a bureaucracy necessarily took place at the expense of the traditional aristocracy, who were faced with the choice of a decorative but insecure role at the court of the monarch, or a retirement to their estates and a life of often effete rural splendour. The competing themes of closed Russianness or opening towards Europe were thus matched by an alternative set of conflicting official emphases: state bureaucracy versus reliance on the 'loyal' class of aristocracy and higher clergy. An efficient and determined ruler would rely on his bureaucratic apparatus to enforce his decisions, especially where innovation was concerned. A weak ruler faced by social unrest necessarily came to depend increasingly on his social peers, the aristocracy. As in eighteenth-century France, the aristocracy proved an uncertain and brittle shield in extremity, broken by the very monarchy which finally sought its support. Long excluded from access to positions of trust, the aristocracy could block the power of reforming ministers like Witte and Stolypin, but not take their place; its younger members were sometimes found flirting with reform, or even revolutionary ideas and practices.

Perhaps one of the most significant features of the eighteenth century in Europe (outside England and the United States) was the enormous emphasis on international rather than internal symbols of modernization. Russia's strength under Catherine the Great had been its international status. The limited social group who had a voice in the affairs of the country were much more concerned with westward expansion than with internal change. This much neglected aspect of history helps partly to explain the great change brought about by the French Revolution. For the first time people concentrated on their domestic political and social situation, and sought domestic rather than international remedies. French and British prestige in the nineteenth century were due to each country's respective social institutions and domestic wealth. This change in outlook had not affected Russia, and an increasing gulf grew between Russia's international prestige and her domestic backwardness. It was not until 1861 that serfdom was abolished in Russia. Other administrative changes under Alexander II only served to open up vistas for the eventual social and economic development of the country rather than actually bringing it about. The erosion of the peasant commune and the hope of creating some mobility among the land-frozen peasantry were legally blocked in the 1880s when the peasant commune was once more officially regarded as the archetypal form of Russian society and the best hope of its 'salvation'. The change of policy at the end of the 1870s, when the Procurator of the Holy Synod, Pobedonostsev, became the Tsar's chief adviser, put a full stop to the slow and difficult process of change.

This lack of correspondence between Russia's international and domestic situation did force itself on the consciousness of literate and enquiring people at home, but the whole basis of comparison was itself already a foreign import. The second half of the nineteenth century witnessed a rapid increase of communications all over Europe. This was the great era of railway building in central and eastern Europe, with Russia coming into its own only in the decade 1890–1900. Postage and telegraph facilities developed and brought about a sizable reduction in costs. Cheap newspapers in large editions were making their impact; not even the overstaffed censorship could prevent foreign comment and subversive Russian literature from circulating at home. Travel slowly ceased to be the exclusive preserve of the very few, and became more widespread both within the country and abroad. Systems of communication work both ways; in the second half of the century there was a great revival of interest in Russia and things Russian by the literati of central and western Europe. Russian topics, particularly literature, became something of a fad among the bourgeoisie as a whole. But in many ways the most important aspect of this interpenetration was economic. The perennially capital-starved Russian state began to float loans in Paris and elsewhere. These were well subscribed. Foreign engineers, particularly British (or rather

13

Scots), came to Russia to build railways and factories. Foreign capital began to favour Russia as a market for profitable large-scale investment.

An important change in European diplomatic alignments towards the end of the century gave all these developments a great fillip. Russia had traditionally been on the side of her autocratic sister-monarchies Prussia (Germany since 1871) and Austria-Hungary. After 1870, however, Austria and Russia began to compete seriously in the Balkans. When Bismarck fell in 1890, the Germans soon abandoned the policy of reinsurance and came down more and more openly on the side of Vienna. Russia in turn looked elsewhere to redress the balance (balance was of course the magic formula of Europe before 1914). The result was a diplomatic rapprochement between the most autocratic of all monarchies and the most democratic of all republics, Russia and France. After 1900 Britain too began to hover on the periphery of the alliance to counteract the growing naval power and colonial ambitions of Germany.

4 'Back to the past' – in art as well as politics. This painting of the evangelists (1910–11) by Natalia Goncharova harks back to the early Russian tradition of ecclesiastical painting

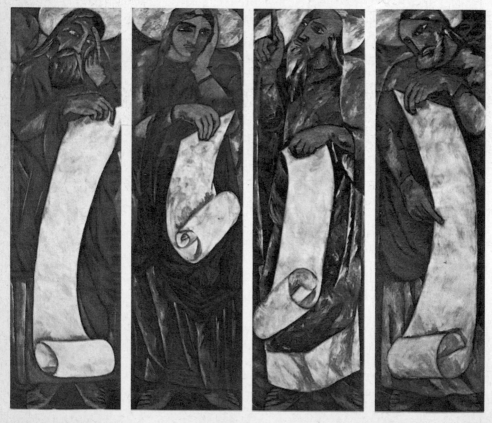

5 The influence of folk art. *Soldier in a Wood* (1908–9) by Mikhail Larionov

Diplomacy and intellectual attitudes went hand in hand. Russian patronage of the Slav successor states to the decaying Turkish empire in the Balkans was gradually transformed into support for Serbia against Austrian expansion into the Balkan vacuum. This was matched at home by the Slavophil revival of the '70s and '80s: an intellectual revolt against European influences, and a belief that the solution for Russia's problems must be found in her own history and peculiar institutions. This inward-looking tendency had a double aspect, both reactionary and revolutionary. On the one hand it emphasized the need for stability, the position of the monarchy and the church as the cornerstones of Russian society, and the more or less crude suppression of the nationalistic pretensions of various nations under Russian rule. Its revolutionary version glorified the peasants, overwhelmingly the largest social group, as the real foundation of Russian society, and in its more extreme form harked back to a distant pre-autocratic past, often absurdly romanticized, when Russia was a society of free and self-governing peasant communities. Without conceding anything to rationalist and revolutionary ideas emanating from Europe, one group of radicals among the Slavophils, who eventually came to be known as Narodniks or Populists, preached a specifically Russian doctrine of revolution aimed primarily at liberating the peasant. Both reactionary and revolutionary wings were agreed on one thing: less influence from Europe, and opposition to industrialization by private enterprise. The whole concept of European liberalism, based as it was on a bourgeoisie emerging from and controlling rapid and large-scale industrialization, was anathema; contrary to later Bolshevik assertions, however, many of them accepted the inevitability of industrialization, but realized that in Russia only the state could bring it about. Dostoevsky tells us that the idea of doing away with railways altogether was a serious subject of debate among certain members of the Russian intelligentsia, while others saw salvation in state enterprise on a growing scale. Populism, far from being a cohesive ideology, was a strident and conflicting chorus of opinion; the very term was a convenient and oversimplified political category later invented by its socialist opponents.

At the beginning of the twentieth century Russia was beginning to catch up in the European scramble for industrialization. In the decade 1890–1900 industrial output was doubled. A late starter, her rate of growth was, in the last few years before the First World War, approaching 10 per cent per annum. Moscow and St Petersburg were beginning to take on the appearance of essentially industrial cities, with conditions similar to those in the large industrial cities in the West – though the surrounding halo of overcrowded tenements was, if anything, even gloomier. The beginnings of an urban middle class and an industrial working class were discernible at least in a few of the major towns, the latter especially in the new industrial regions of eastern Poland, Ukraine, Georgia, and the Trans-Caucasian mines.

But where Russia differed from the West was in the extent to which this industrial growth was government-sponsored, if not directly government-controlled. No single minister in Europe (other than the marginal John Bright in England) had a clearer sense of industrial purpose than Count Witte, in power at the turn of the century. None was willing to assign such a predominant role in the process of economic development to government.

Where the rising industrial middle classes of England and France, and to some extent even Germany and Austria, had begun to view their interests as diverging from that of the government, and specific political organizations were being created to enable middle-class interests to be effectively represented, the Russian entrepreneurs knew well from the start to what extent they depended on the Tsarist government for support if not indeed survival and regarded themselves almost as a kind of industrial civil servant. The regulation of employer–worker relations was regarded not primarily as a means of enforcing a humanitarian minimum but peculiarly as a matter of direct state concern – understandably, for industrial unrest and revolution were first cousins in Russia. The substantial labour legislation from 1886 to 1897 was designed to avoid disturbance, nothing more. Strikes were illegal; so was any attempt to form or operate a trade union. From the end of the century unions did come into being with reluctant official permission – founded and managed by the police! The notorious Colonel Zubatov, head of the security police of Moscow, became a great initiator of unions whose over-enthusiastic working-class leaders were provoked into exposure, arrest and exile.

These factors are important because, as we shall see, the most significant difference in the social structure of Russia in 1917 compared to the rest of Europe was the almost complete absence of an independent and organized middle class. Far from having to make a difficult decision between an aristocratic government uninterested in liberal concerns of trade and industry, and the pressure of radical, often proletarian, socialism, the alignment of the Russian middle classes (such as they were) with the government forces was almost predetermined by their weakness, and correctly recognized as such by some of the revolutionaries. Even within the amorphous collectivity commonly called the middle class or bourgeoisie, civil servants and professionals far outweighed the liberal industrial group. All the descriptions of businessmen in the socially sensitive Russian literature of the period emphasized their identification with the state, and the desire to be received into the ruling circles. Mostly they were figures treated with profound contempt. A Russian John Bright or Richard Cobden was inconceivable.

We are therefore left with the Tsar's government, its large bureaucracy and dependents, a small but growing and highly concentrated industrial proletariat, and apart from these an ambivalent and ineffective aristocracy on one hand and a vast multitude of peasants on the other. Government policy veered between contradictory alternatives, reflecting the uncompromising polarity of the social structure: European or closed, reformist or reactionary, industrializing or shoring up the peasant against the worker.

6 Tsarist diplomacy, 1895. The 'lovable little father' of all the Russias wants to be friends with France as well as Germany; but offering a little to all satisfies none

The Witte policy of industrialization was mainly at the expense of the peasant; the halt to industrialization between 1901 and 1906 lightened the peasant's load. This was the scissors crisis which was to make its portentous reappearance after the revolution and lead ultimately to the Stalinist pattern of forced industrialization.

One final policy alternative needs mention, for it was inherent in Slavophilism and in the official policy of repression. It also suited the personal proclivities of Nicholas II and his intimate advisers. As in most overwhelmingly peasant societies, the periphery was mute – except for periodic outbursts of considerable violence, as in 1900–1. The atmosphere towards the end of the nineteenth century was strongly nationalist, especially in the provinces, and the government attempted to divert the substantial reserves of latent rural and urban unrest away from social into national channels. The Russian word *pogrom* has become a synonym for violence against foreign minorities, especially Jews. At this time the Russian empire consisted of a number of subject peoples at the western and southern periphery. The eastward expansion into the great plain of central and eastern Russia in the course of the

18

nineteenth century – a terrestrial or landbound equivalent of the maritime imperialism of Britain and France – had added a host of new undeveloped subject peoples. The Russians claimed cultural superiority for their deliberate policy of Russification, but in some cases – such as Poland, Finland and particularly the scattered Jewish minorities in the permitted settlement areas of the 'Pale' – these claims were resisted and justifiably resented. Nicholas II who simply equated Jews with subversion became a paying member of the anti-Semitic Union of the Russian People. The severe pogroms in Kishinev and Gomel in 1903 were directly encouraged by the authorities. When his ministers counselled moderation, the Tsar paraded his conscience; when he agreed to give the Polish language official status, the bureaucracy buried the proposal in inaction.

Resistance to the government accordingly moved on the same conflicting dimensions as official policy: national resentment on the part of suppressed and persecuted minorities, revolutionary leaders speaking for an as yet unorganized and mute peasantry, a small group of westernizing intellectuals determined to fashion Russia in a more democratic and liberal image, socialists voicing the demands of the new industrial proletariat, and finally a

7 No one loves the bourgeoisie. Costume sketches by Alexandre Benois for a stage production of Dostoevsky's *The Idiot* in 1924

tradition of violence which was the symmetrical complement of the autocratic and often repressive system of government. The oppositional and revolutionary movements were as disparate and conflicting among themselves as they were without influence on government. Who would draw these unrelated movements together? Similar problems were faced by other countries in Europe, if not to the same degree. It was enough to cause difficulties, to inhibit change – but not to result in complete breakdown. For that a severe outside blow to the stability of the system was needed. The preconditions for successful revolution in Russia were therefore two-fold: some form of co-operation, even if limited in time between the various disaffected sectors through which revolutionary energy could be channelled and concentrated, and a blow to the security and stability of the system of government and society.

8
The ubiquitous Russian Policeman, a drawing from the journal *Satirikon* in 1912

Russia had a long tradition of social and political revolt. From top to bottom, conspiracy and murder had been regular means of eliminating opponents and obstacles – whether an unpopular local official or a mad and ineffective Tsar. Societies which produce violent changes in the succession among their rulers rarely have stable, peaceful processes of change lower down. Throughout the nineteenth century there had been frequent plots of various sorts, some of which, like the Decembrists of 1825, actually broke out into open revolt. The normal Russian reaction to dissatisfaction was violence. Official response was equally violent. By the end of the nineteenth century the Tsarist secret police, the Okhrana, had become notorious as an all-prevailing instrument of penetration and repression. Government and conspirators were locked in a never-ending battle, which became an integral part of Russian political life. To understand the atmosphere at the turn of the last century we have to be quite clear about the total absence of open or legal debate about major issues in Russia. Sooner or later any determined and consistent reformer either capitulated, withdrew into metaphysics, or became a conspirator. There were few intellectuals in Russia who had not at one stage or another been on the fringe of subversion, had trouble with police or censorship, or at least been friendly with some of those who were directly involved.

From 1870 onwards four distinct strata of opposition had emerged. First the hesitant middle-class intellectuals oriented towards a Western model. These were typically the creation of the climate of Alexander II's period of reform. Once his successor clamped down they were faced with a choice of either joining more radical groups or withdrawing from politics. Many of them turned then to 'pure' literature or 'pure' commerce. Secondly the Populists, who aimed at the liberation of the Russian peasant by various means, ranging from education to revolutionary conspiracy and terrorist activity (the so-called *Narodnaya Volya*, 'The People's Will'). Next a small group of anarchists who provided the extreme left wing of the revolutionary movement. In many ways anarchism was a feature of excessive social imbalance, combining awareness of industrialization as a modern phenomenon with a refusal to accept its collective social implications. Finally, as last-comers, the emergent socialist groups, whose ideas were linked directly to Marx and whose social model was taken directly from western Europe with a view to adapting it as effectively as possible to the agricultural and autocratic Russian environment. These latter three groups were agreed on the need to overthrow and destroy Tsarist autocracy but on little else; they fought each other, often savagely.

9 The ubiquitous Russian terrorist; illustration from a St Petersburg journal in 1905

The genesis of social-democracy in Russia can probably be dated from 1879, when Plekhanov and a group of friends broke away from the *Zemlya i Volya* (Land and Liberty) organization of the Populists – in fact its first formal revolutionary party – and a few years later formed in Switzerland the *Group for the Liberation of Labour*, to propagate and study the ideas of Karl Marx. Within the next two decades a number of younger Marxists emerged from various revolutionary groups and circles in Russia. As police activity increased, the leaders were regularly arrested or forced into emigration. By 1900 both Martov and Lenin, who were to be the main protagonists of two opposed wings of social-democracy in Russia, had arrived in the West.

The next seventeen years were the history of a three-fold struggle: the battle for domination within the socialist party, the competition among revolutionary groups for the support and leadership of the broader social movement in Russia, and finally the see-saw fight for organization and, indeed, survival against the Russian authorities. By 1903 the socialists had made sufficient inroads on the loyalty of active conspirators in Russia as well as many industrial workers, and had developed an organization sufficiently impressive for the Minister of the Interior, Muravev, to report to the Tsar that the social-democrats were the state's most dangerous enemies. Such was the attraction of Marxism in its various forms that social-democracy drew into its orbit a great number of intellectuals, some of whom, like Struve, were later destined to provide Russian liberalism with leadership during its brief and unsuccessful flowering after 1905. Off the record the government could see the intellectual appeal as well as the organizational success of its opponents. In a strangely prophetic moment Prince Tolstoy, Minister of the Interior, confided in 1884 to Bülow, the future German Chancellor, that if Tsarism were ever overthrown, its place would be taken by 'the communism of Mr Marx of London who has just died and to whose theories I have given much attention and interest'. At that time Mr Marx had not yet broken through to an entry in the English *Dictionary of National Biography*.

The fact that most of the social-democratic leaders were in exile, that communications with their supporters at home were difficult, hazardous and above all expensive, and finally the strong tradition of individualism and diversity in the spectrum of revolutionary activity all made the creation of a formal and unified party exceedingly difficult. There was no party tradition in Russian political life. It was not until March 1898 that a founding congress of the Russian Social Democratic Workers' Party took place in secret at Minsk – and most of the delegates were arrested immediately afterwards. The Party depended heavily on the better developed and more experienced Jewish workers' organization, the so-called *Bund*. Right from the start there arose problems of autonomy and control; these were to continue for the next two decades. The émigré leadership was almost incessantly locked in disputes. To understand the Russian Party in this period, it is necessary to remember that this was a group of exceptionally able men, committed to a doctrine of class revolution and a determinist philosophy. Every one of them was independent-minded and not at all amenable to compromise, let alone discipline. Moreover, men like Plekhanov were more honoured as theoreticians in the international sphere than as prophets in their own country; their voices often carried more authority in Germany and France than at home.

The Second Congress of the Party met in Brussels in July 1903, moving to London when the Belgian authorities began to make life difficult for the motley collection of outlandish-looking foreigners. Questions of inter-party discipline and relations with other revolutionary organizations were much to the fore. The proceedings of the Congress, which witnessed the break between Lenin's majority Bolsheviks and the so-called Mensheviks, have become part of the folklore of communism.

The Bolshevik conception of the party formulated by Lenin embodied the strictest discipline. Party democracy consisted of the free election of delegates to congresses, followed by the election of a party central committee by each congress. In this way different views represented by individuals or groups would find expression; and at the congresses, as well as in the central committee, policy would be fully discussed and thrashed out before a vote was taken. Once decided, however, it could no longer be challenged. Everyone was bound to obey the decisions whether he had supported or opposed them at the time, or did so now. Since party work was illegal, the most rigid conspiratorial discipline had to be observed. The system thus combined, at least in theory, a democratic form of elections and decision-making with an authoritarian hierarchy of control and obedience. Lenin's organizational outline naturally coloured the conception of what sort of people could be party members and over this the Bolsheviks and Mensheviks parted company. The latter desired to create a mass party which any adherent to the programme could join, the former a disciplined and if necessary smaller party with a stiffer threshold of entry. From this, in turn, followed differing views about the relationship between party and working class. The Mensheviks envisaged a gradual shading-off among organized leaders, members and supporters in a mass movement whose sheer numbers would eventually overcome opposition: a very European conception based on an industrial proletariat of overwhelming numbers who would inevitably be drawn towards social-democracy. Lenin, on the contrary, believed in rigid organizational differentiation between party and working class. He placed less emphasis on the early likelihood of industrialization in Russia on the European scale and with European perspectives. Even when it came, the ideology of the industrial working class would not be sophisticated enough to add up to revolutionary class-consciousness but remain at the bread-and-butter level of trade unionism. Therefore the organization of the fully conscious and dedicated advance guard had to be kept distinct from the mass: the former leading, the latter led. Naturally socialist success could come only if the working class had confidence in and approved of 'its' party. But it would demonstrate this in action and not by formal processes of voting or organized collaboration.

Critics were not slow to point out that Lenin's concept of rigid organization approximated much more closely to that of the Socialist-Revolutionaries, who had emerged as successors to the now defunct *Narodnaya Volya*, than to the 'advanced' socialist parties of western Europe. Lenin was accused of distorting Marxism into an excessively Russian framework. He replied that Russian conditions demanded such concessions without in any way invalidating Marxism; indeed Marxism required such adjustment. This was central to his thinking. Later he added a most important variant to received wisdom in his characterization of the peasant problem in Russia. Far from ignoring the peasant and basing themselves on an ever-growing proletariat, Russian socialists should acknowledge the social preponderance of a potentially revolutionary peasantry and find a means of inducing the peasants to support the socialists at least as far as the crucial moment of revolution. In practice this came to mean a policy of land distribution to the peasants, the break-up of large estates and the creation of a land-holding peasantry. This too was anathema to the orthodox Mensheviks.

One other aspect of Lenin's ideas at the turn of the century proved to be pregnant with future importance; it, too, was an adaptation of a Marxist generalization to the particular strategy dictated by the Russian situation. Russia was a multi-national empire, and no revolutionary party could afford to neglect the problem of the subject nations, since their ambitions for self-determination provided a vital source of revolutionary energy. Most of the Social Democrats were pledged to national self-determination in one form or another. A substantial proportion of the Russian Party were Jews, and both Bolsheviks and Mensheviks were particularly strong among fringe nationalities like Georgians, Lithuanians, Letts and Estonians. Lenin insisted on making the right of national self-determination a major plank in the Party's platform. In this matter as in perhaps no other, tactical considerations combined with a profound and personal commitment on the part of Lenin Great Russian chauvinism (as Lenin called it) was always to be his particula *bête noire*. Lenin's subtle understanding of the distinctive features of Russian society, and the consequent tactical imperatives for any Marxist revolutionary party, was here matched by a real hatred for Russian cultural pretensions.

But Lenin distinguished clearly between a right of national self-determination for subject nations on the one hand, and a federated party on the other. He fought savagely against all those who interpreted the Party's programme for national self-determination as a reason for demanding a decentralized party structure, with each constituent national unit authorized to pursue a separate policy and adopting a different form of organization. From 1903 onwards Lenin opposed the continued existence of separate organizations like the *Bund* and the Poles within the Russian Party. Occasionally he had to make concessions, but the concept of a federal party organized on national lines was always repugnant to him. This of course produced a paradox in the vision of the revolutionary future; how could independent states continue to be combined with a centralized party after the revolution? The short answer was that the policy of national self-determination provided optional, not mandatory, independence; every nation had the right to secede or to remain within a revolutionary socialist Russia. And in the long run it was out of these apparently theoretical debates during the first fifteen years of the century that the eventual paradox of a Soviet federation bound together by a highly centralized party was born – an entirely new and unique concept of a multi-racial society.

At this time Lenin, like all his socialist contemporaries, was still committed to the notion that the revolution, when it came, would have largely bourgeois forms, enabling Russia to catch up with many of the social developments of western Europe which she had so far missed. We have to distinguish between Lenin's 'Russification' of revolutionary *means* and his pre-1917 commitment to European *results*. The inability, indeed unwillingness, to plan beyond the coming revolution was understandable among people who were in no sense utopian visionaries or mystics but highly practical revolutionaries concerned with programmes for the here and now, with the application of their historical science to contemporary reality. One of the greatest tributes to the genius of Vladimir Ilich Lenin is precisely the fact that his conceptions, related to a non-revolutionary present, could in fact be applied in such large measure in a revolutionary and even post-revolutionary situation. Even though the whole climate of revolutionary possibility was transformed after 1905 and again in 1917, and Lenin abandoned his originally bourgeois perspectives of revolution in Russia, his ideas on organization and nationality policy were only confirmed and strengthened when they came to be applied.

10, 11, 12 The year of revolution. Above, troops firing on the workers of St Petersburg on 22 January 1905. Far left, one of the many executions that followed the spontaneous uprising. Left, the forces of order: the 1905 government

The sectarianism of the Russian émigrés, their apparently pointless quarrels over purely theoretical problems – which had already begun to upset some of the leaders of the western mass parties in the International – were put to the test when, quite unexpectedly, revolution broke out in Russia early in 1905. No doubt the famine of 1900, the violence which found an officially directed outlet in the pogroms of the next few years, and the wave of mass strikes among the workers, all contributed to the atmosphere of social unrest. But what no one had foreseen was the crucial extent of demoralization in Russia after the surprising defeat of the formidable Russian army and navy in the war against Japan. A peaceful procession to the Winter Palace in St Petersburg on 22 January 1905 with the object of submitting a petition of grievances to the Tsar was dispersed by troops with a cynical brutality unusual even for Russia. But the resultant wave of strikes and demonstrations all over the empire was as unexpected for the authorities as for the revolutionaries. The spectacle of weakness and debility that now unrolled before the world was even more startling than the military defeats. The ironclad Russian government, unable to cope with the situation at home, made concession after concession over the next few months.

13 Striking workers in Kharkov, 1905

We have hitherto characterized the struggle between revolution and government in Russia as essentially a frontier action, in which the broad mass of the population, whether workers or peasants, took little direct part. The 1905 revolution was precisely the creation of social forces with whom no one had bothered – the masses: unsettled by a destabilizing decade of intense industrialization and the squeeze of accumulation, unorganized by the various revolutionary movements, uncomprehended by the authorities who were more concerned with penetrating and destroying the known revolutionary organizations. The very narrowness of the apex of power in Russia now proved a dangerous weakness, for in emergency everybody prepared to defend the régime looked upwards for instructions, and was paralysed when none came. It is easy to exaggerate the extent and co-ordination of revolutionary activities in Russia. The main centres were the big towns: Moscow, St Petersburg, Warsaw and a few others. Peasant activity was widespread if localized, and not related to events in the cities. The sense of impotence on the part of the authorities created an anarchic free-for-all which only in retrospect acquired the title of revolution. In the absence of government support or even instruction, individual factory owners gave way quickly to the immediate demands of strikers. In the countryside peasant activity was mostly aimed, as always, against the local gentry, the hated tax collectors and other organs of central authority. On the whole both peasants and workers wanted concessions, not revolution; a better, not a different, government. Until the late summer, when the organized revolutionaries abroad recovered from their surprise and took a hand in the proceedings, there was no formal or general programme of political action. By this time, moreover, the liberal constitutionalists and intellectuals of St Petersburg were already hesitating between further pressure for constitutional concessions from the reluctant Tsar, and the fear of further mass action and lawlessness from those groups who would not benefit substantially from even the most liberal constitutional reforms.

What the revolution demonstrated above all was the total lack of ideas at the top, the brittleness of the bureaucratic system of government, and the extent to which the will and power to act had been eroded. The Tsar himself, the centre of all power, was an amiable but limited and strongly prejudiced man, quite unable even to comprehend the nature of the demands being made upon him, much less to satisfy them. It was all the fault of unscrupulous agitators and modern horrors like the telegraph. The significance of the 1905 revolution for the historian lies in its demonstration of government weakness rather than the power and potential of organized revolution in Russia.

14 Nicholas II
seeks scientific advice
on how to deal
with the demands
for a constitution

Advised by Count Witte, the Tsar issued his October Manifesto, which in fact contained the first Russian constitution. Three days later, on 2 November, because of the insistent demands of the St Petersburg liberals, there followed a political armistice which, it was hoped, would finally rally support for the government. The constitution was a concession to Octobrists and Constitutionalists, in other words to the Liberals – the only reformers of whom the government had even the remotest understanding, even if it had no sympathy. Socialist ideas and demands, the socialists as a type, were well beyond the comprehension or interest of the government. In any case the Tsar regarded his amnesty as a tactical concession wrung from him in bad times, and withdrew many of its provisions a few weeks later, when martial law was declared. Reaction moved to the counter-attack. But the constitution had at least given birth to a new institution of popular representation, the Duma. It was based on a very unequal suffrage, and both its powers and representativeness were progressively eroded over the next five years. Yet the energy of many liberal intellectuals turned gratefully to this major constitutional event. Henceforward they were more concerned with making the most of what they had instead of pressing for more. The socialists and Socialist-Revolutionaries initially decided to boycott altogether the elections to the Duma, though they later came to regard them more favourably as a useful form of agitation.

Most of the Russiam émigrés did not reach Russia until after the armistice in November 1905. By this time the major wave of revolutionary effort was almost spent, and the authorities, with the backing of employers and landlords, were rallying strongly. Of the major socialist figures only Trotsky

29

had been in Russia since the beginning of the year and had participated in that new phenomenon of democratic self-government, the Council of Workers' Deputies, or Soviet. These were spontaneous organizations which helped to coordinate the strike movement, issued a great many manifestoes, integrated themselves within the revolutionary process and helped to organize it, and at various times acted as a rival to the government. The most famous 1905 Soviet was that of St Petersburg, formally constituted on 27 October. It numbered 550 delegates and represented a quarter of a million workers. Trotsky and his then friend Helphand tried to put a Social Democratic stamp on this very mixed organization. It was a specifically urban phenomenon and its range of action was entirely confined to the towns. By mid-December the Minister of the Interior acted, and leading Soviet members, including Trotsky, were arrested. In Moscow, where the Soviet was more directly controlled by Bolshevik supporters, an attempt was made to organize an armed insurrection towards the end of December, and the high point of the revolution was reached with street fighting and barricades. By the beginning of 1906, however, the government was able to re-impose control in the main towns. The year 1906 saw mainly economic strikes of diminishing vigour, and a good deal of rural disquiet.

By 1907 the government was back in full control of the situation. A wave of repression followed, with the usual sentences to Siberian exile, prison or death. When the second Duma was dissolved on the Tsar's instructions, the Social Democratic deputies were arrested and deported. Many revolutionaries succeeded in escaping; some, including Lenin, went to ground in backwaters like Finland. A new and sterner set of ministers came to power. Having dismissed Witte in July 1906 because his concern with industrialization and efficiency suddenly smacked dangerously of liberalism, the Tsar appointed Stolypin as Prime Minister. In no way liberal, Stolypin organized the armed dispersal of the second Duma and the nationwide destruction of the remaining revolutionaries and their organization.

But in one sense he too was a reformer. Well aware of the creaking inefficiency of the bureaucratic apparatus, he now attempted to make it more efficient. Above all his name will be remembered for land reforms, which enabled the peasants to acquire land legally and effectively. In this way the beginnings of a commercial system of agriculture were created. If there was sufficient prospect of land ownership the revolutionary fervour among the peasants might eventually be damped down. Hitherto peasants, though nominally free, were in practice unable to escape from complete economic and personal dependence on their landlord. Here at last was the introduction of capitalism on to the land which the Mensheviks saw as the essential

15 P. A. Stolypin,
appointed Prime Minister in 1906
to liquidate the revolutionaries –
and, if possible,
some of the causes
of the revolution

precursor of an effective and revolutionary socialist policy for Russia. Lenin viewed the Stolypin land reforms more accurately and – from his point of view – more gloomily. 'If this continues for long it may well force us to renounce any revolutionary agrarian programme altogether. . . . Agriculture will indeed become capitalistic and any revolutionary solution of the agrarian problem will become impossible under capitalism.' It was an echo of the fear the early socialists had expressed nearly ten years before, when the spate of official labour legislation seemed in danger of pre-empting the revolutionary fervour of the exploited industrial workers. We shall never know how effective this process would have been had it continued; in September 1911 Stolypin was murdered by one of those ubiquitous *agents provocateurs* who played both ends of the political spectrum against the middle. Stolypin's successor was a less far-sighted man. Though the process of land acquisition by peasants continued slowly all over Russia, it failed to receive the impetus and the time to develop into the conservative social factor which Lenin feared.

One thing had become quite clear to all the socialist leaders during the 1905 revolution; how irrelevant their factional divisions and polemics had proved when confronted by events in Russia. Lenin himself admitted that 'the former disputes of the period before the revolution were replaced by solidarity when it came to practical matters.' In 1906 a unity congress of both wings of Russian social-democracy took place in Stockholm. In spite of fundamental disagreements over how to interpret the revolution, collaboration and unity were the prime considerations – at least in public. By 1911, however, the two factions were at each other's throats once more.

The Mensheviks were determined to preserve party unity at all costs. They now regarded Russia as on the threshold of the European social experience, and called for a Russian party whose organization and outlook corresponded to those of the successful European mass parties. The Bolsheviks, and especially Lenin, soon came to regard the euphoria of forgive-and-forget as a mistaken concession to revolutionary pressure; unity could take place only on the basis of the acceptance of the Bolshevik programme. Determined to revive the organizational separation of his faction, Lenin pursued the most determined splitting tactics, which finally cut him off from his Menshevik colleagues, divided the Social Democratic representation in the fourth Duma from 1913 onwards and earned him the opprobrium of almost the entire Second International. By 1914 he had become a pariah in the European socialist movement.

Most of Lenin's opponents within and outside the Russian Party viewed Lenin's attitude as obstinate and sectarian, the consequence of being cut off from Russian reality once again – typically émigré behaviour! Between 1907 and 1914 even many Bolshevik adherents left his group. There were bitter polemics with Trotsky. But the lesson Lenin had drawn from the events of 1905 was that unity would be the product of victory and come about through the capitulation of opponents, not a wishy-washy form of compromise. Only the separate organization of the successful revolutionaries, unswervingly agreed on their programme, could provide the necessary lead. It was the 1903 thesis reinstated in full measure. The October Revolution as we know it could probably not have taken place if Lenin had not cut himself and his remaining colleagues off from the rest of the Party, and pursued his own line.

After 1905 Lenin began to realize that the revolution in Russia, when it finally came, would not bring about the model copy of a hundred years of bourgeois revolutions in the West. There now existed an industrial proletariat, an active Social Democratic Party. The élan of the 1905 revolution had been provided by workers and peasants. They must indelibly stamp their dominating presence on any forthcoming revolution. In fact Lenin had become converted to the idea that a mainly bourgeois revolution would be created and underpinned by socialists. In the longer term no doubt one revolution would be geared to the next. Once socialists had attained a share of power, they would quickly push through towards the next phase of the dialectic and attack the same middle classes they had succeeded in installing in power against the autocracy. Lenin did not go so far as Trotsky, for whom this was a single, continuous, though long-drawn-out process, with the bourgeois and socialist phases hardly distinguishable any longer. In this process the Russian revolution would set fire to more advanced countries in the West while these in turn reflected their sharpened revolutionary situation back into Russia. This was the doctrine of permanent revolution which Lenin attacked as utopian in 1908 and which was later to be denounced as a dangerous left-wing heresy by Stalin.

But even so Lenin and Trotsky were closer to each other than to the Menshevik conception. Their perhaps more orthodox, and certainly more classic, Marxism placed its faith in the Russian Liberals as a bourgeois revolutionary force against feudalism and autocracy. The logic of history assigned the honours of the coming battle to them. Lenin, more accurately, considered the Liberals and Constitutionalists as a spent force, either sulking in their tents when the Tsar ignored them, or actually supporting the government against the rising socialist tide of revolution. 'We were invited to assume office as long as it was thought that the Red forces were behind us. . . . But once it was noticed that we were a strictly constitutional party we were cast aside as useless by the Tsar', wrote Miliukov, one of the Liberal leaders. Not the bourgeoisie but the peasantry would be the temporary allies of the proletariat. The tactical consequence of the 1905 revolution was the famous slogan, 'the revolutionary democratic dictatorship of the proletariat and peasantry', which was to play so significant a role in 1917. From 1906 onwards Lenin insisted on the absolute need of peasant support for any revolutionary party in Russia which claimed pretensions to success.

16
1908 was
a bad year
for the
revolutionaries—
and chess,
according to Lenin,
helped concentrate
the mind.
Here he is shown
playing
with Bogdanov
at Gorky's villa
in Italy, 1908

The First World War, like the revolution of 1905, was something incessantly talked about and planned against for many years, but nobody was ready when it did break out. The symmetry of unpreparedness was complete on both sides of the social chasm, for European governments as much as socialists. The latter were helplessly adrift, with no chance to influence or control events. Of all the governments in Europe in August 1914, only the Germans had seriously made plans against the contingency of war. Yet once general mobilization had been ordered war was almost inevitable – though none of those searching for a last-minute solution realized it. Only in Russia were responsible voices raised to warn the government that it, and the social system it represented, might not survive a major conflict. The long period of successful reaction and quiet on the home front had already begun to crack in 1911. Between the shooting of the strikers in the Lena gold fields in Siberia in 1912 and the unprecedented incidence of strikes in the industrial areas during the spring and summer of 1914, a great new wave of social unrest was sweeping the empire.

But as elsewhere there was also the hope of a strong nationalist backlash. Obligations to allies had to be honoured and Germany was growing exceedingly arrogant. It was argued that a war would provide a rallying point for the loyalty which the Tsarist régime so badly needed. Russia was not alone, as she had been in 1904. Relations with France had never been better. The Autocrat of all the Russias had visited the proud successor of the Jacobin Republic and had been well received; the French President had returned the courtesy in St Petersburg; French capital was deeply involved in the renewed growth of Russian industry after 1907. The ties with England were looser, but once Belgium had been invaded, the Triple Entente came alive. And events seemed to justify the optimism of the war party. The strikes in Russia stopped in August 1914, cut off almost overnight. Some of the most rabid socialist opponents of Tsarist Russia and everything it stood for suddenly discovered the call of the motherland in danger. Even Plekhanov, who more than any man had helped to provide Russian social-democracy with its Marxist outlook, came out openly in support of the war. The Second International, which had emphasized international class solidarity against narrow patriotism, was killed stone dead.

Lenin and his group of Bolsheviks in Austrian Poland were by now on the fringe of official socialism. His immediate entourage consisted of Zinoviev, Radek and only a few others; he had quarrelled with nearly everyone else, on either organizational or intellectual grounds. It is not surprising, therefore, that Lenin's view of the war should differ radically from the majority: 'They would never do us the favour', he had written some time earlier when the

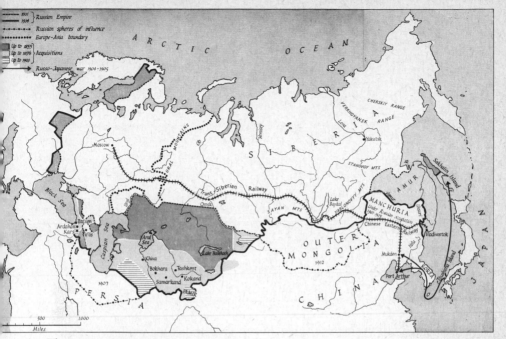

17 The Russian Empire at the outbreak of war in 1914

chances of a major European war had been discussed. He remembered the most immediate lesson of 1905 which so many had forgotten – that nothing had proved so destructive of the social fabric as an unsuccessful major war. In 1914 every socialist had an agonizing decision to make. All of them deplored war as a disaster to civilization – the many who supported their national government, the few who opposed it. Only Lenin and his small band of supporters felt no part of the universal sense of tragedy, and regarded the war as a positive opening for revolution. 'Turn the imperialistic war into civil war'; at the time the slogan appeared as unreal as it sounded callous.

But it would be foolish to suggest that a vision of the future – revolution, Soviet state and all – somehow unrolled before Lenin in those last months of 1914, as he and his friends settled down in Switzerland. His energy for the last few years had been devoted to inter-party struggles. In the fight against the so-called liquidators – Mensheviks whom Lenin accused of wanting to abandon illegal party work altogether – the contact with events in Russia had for a time almost taken second place. The seven years from 1907 had not been a fruitful period for socialist activity; the presence of police agents

18, 19 Lenin in Poland in 1914, and Karl Radek, brilliant writer and intellectual gadfly for the Bolsheviks in their campaign against the war

in the revolutionary ranks had put the socialist groups on the defensive and turned them even more against each other. In these circumstances the war became primarily a touchstone for socialist behaviour. It served to distinguish sharply between good and bad socialists, between those who supported their governments and those who put the class struggle first. What affected Lenin above all between 1914 and 1916 was the collapse of organized social-democracy in Europe: of those disciplined, self-assured mass parties like that of the Germans whom he had admired so long. In swimming against the stream during these years, Lenin was in effect cutting himself off from a socialist tradition which, for all his disagreements, had been the background of his life and work. Opposition to the war became primarily not so much a slogan for revolution in Russia, which was out of the question, but a means of building up among the émigrés in western Europe a group of supporters for whom opposition to existing society still had absolute priority, war or no war. The slogan of turning war into internal revolution has to be understood initially in this context. It had little practical consequence at least until 1916, when a hesitant caucus of left-wing oppositionists to official European socialism met first at Kienthal, then at Zimmerwald in Switzerland, and Lenin almost managed to create an even more radical and determined nucleus of revolutionary opposition within it, the so-called Zimmerwald Left. Far-sighted as he was, Lenin's position during the war was that of an oppositional socialist determined above all to break with the Second International – a logical extension of the old struggle for organizational and theoretical differentiation within the Russian Party.

This does not detract from the achievement. The insistence on a clear break with the pre-war socialist movement was to have the greatest possible consequences. It was on this question more than any other that communists came first to be distinguished from socialists, the Third International from the Second. If Russian Bolshevism dated from 1903, as Lenin claimed, then international communism was born on 4 August 1914.

Most of Lenin's work during the war was concerned with explaining the failure of the Second International. His theory of imperialism and its effect on workers' movements was elaborated at this time in the libraries of Zürich and Geneva. There were also the usual polemics over what now seemed to have become remote abstractions – economic and nationality problems. Not without reason could left-wing socialists in belligerent countries simply ignore the small group of about eight Russian scribblers whose involvement with the realities of the world war seemed so slight. And as the war went on the early optimism faded; Lenin himself was obliged to remit his view of effective revolution to the far distant future. In January 1917, six weeks before the first of the events in Russia which were to change the history of the world, he told a Swiss audience that 'We, the old, will probably not live to see the decisive battles of the coming revolution.' He was at that time forty-six years old.

20 Even in 1921, on the fourth anniversary of Red October, the revolution is still depicted as sweeping forward irresistibly

21, 22   A street demonstration in Petrograd against Kerensky's provisional government.
Below, *Bolshevik*, a painting by B. Kustodiev

The revolution that broke out in Russia in March 1917 looked at first like a re-enactment in detail of the events of 1905–6.* Once again a war had fatally but imperceptibly weakened the government. Once again the uprising was spontaneous. Government and revolutionaries were equally taken by surprise; the masses intervened yet again to take matters in their own hands. In 1917, as twelve years earlier, the revolutionary impetus came from the towns, with St Petersburg in the lead. The countryside was not specifically revolutionary in any active sense, but the breakdown of the government made itself felt there much more strongly than in 1905.

Yet there were substantial differences between 1905 and 1917. The Emperor at his GHQ was completely isolated; for the first time a Tsar had simply become irrelevant. The government was divided and stagnant, the police disorganized. But above all, one factor emerged with chilling certainty: the growing consensus among the Duma leaders, the society of the capital, and a good many ministers that nothing could be done with the obstinate and totally unperceptive autocrat. He would have to go, and maybe even the system. These *gens biens*, solid citizens all, were not of course completely revolutionaries but frustrated politicians, patriots who had become pessimists, enthusiasts who had become fatalists, often men of wealth and prestige whose patience and sense of propriety had turned to outrage.

And outside the capital, along the hundreds of miles of fighting front, as well as behind the lines, things were very bad. The war had effects on Russian society which made the defeat by the Japanese seem like the mere bite of a gnat. In 1905 the loss had mainly been prestige followed by a loss of confidence. Now Russia was fighting the strongest, best-armed European power – and in addition employing tactics which could not win. The advantages of the Russian environment – the vastness of the country, the harshness of its

* Since Western dating has been adopted in this book, even for the period when Russian dating differed by being thirteen days earlier, the two revolutions of 1917 will accordingly have to be dated respectively as March and November. In Russia the events took place in February and October respectively. The Julian calendar was officially changed to conform with the European (Gregorian) one on 1 February (Russian dating), 14 February (Western dating), 1918. Hence the contradiction of referring here to the February and October revolutions as the Russians still do, but dating actual events in March and November.

climate, and the stubborn resistance of its people, which have hitherto made Russia unconquerable – can only operate in a defensive war. Such had been the war against Napoleon and such would be the Second World War. But the 1914 war was fought offensively, on foreign territory. The Russian generals – most of them incompetent even by the shoddy standard of the time and certainly much less capable than their German opponents – hurled Russia's manpower against the iron defences of Germany and Austria. The strategy of the time measured defeat or victory not in terms of human loss, but in meaningless pieces of territory. According to such criteria the Russians were doing moderately well until 1917, even though the Germans and Austrians had broken through the Russian front at Gorlice in May 1915. The real difference between the eastern and western fronts was one of scale – spatial and quantitative; Russian losses in killed, wounded or captured ran to an estimated eight million in three years. No one took any notice of the feeling or morale of the troops. Even where a sense of dissatisfaction communicated itself, it was ignored or stamped out. By 1917 war weariness had set in all over Europe; mutinies broke out in France and Italy, and in Germany there appeared the first signs of political opposition and large-scale strikes. The Russian revolution of March 1917 expressed in an acute and perhaps uniquely Russian form an almost universal sense of frustration and hopelessness. It is only on such occasions that social cohesion or lack of it, a tradition of legitimate authority or of alienated subjection, make a crucial contribution to events.

At first no more was at issue than a mild version of constitutional change, which might finally bring Russia into line with France and Britain. Nicholas II was forced to abdicate, but for a time hopes prevailed that the monarchy as an institution might be preserved. Now, as previously, the Emperor understood nothing of what was happening around him. As late as the end of February he had waved away the warnings of his ministers as undignified and unnecessarily alarmist and had urged them to proceed, not to the agenda, but in to dinner. World opinion was pained rather than surprised at his abdication. The Western Allies were more concerned with ensuring Russia's vigorous prosecution of the war than with giving vent to the sort of outrage which had seized Europe's crowned heads in 1792 (though the assassination of the imperial family nearly eighteen months later produced a much stronger reaction). The government that took over with the title of 'provisional' was well within the acceptable minimum of social status. Its leaders, Prince Lvov and Miliukov, had been treated as politically irrelevant by the monarchy, but at least such men were socially acceptable, and they had no wish to overthrow the most basic institution of government, the monarchy. The forced abdication of the Tsar soon after the March events was reluctantly accepted as inevitable by the new government in view of the threatening demeanour of the Petrograd population, increasingly leavened and radicalized by disaffected soldiers from the front. Tsarskoe Selo, like Versailles, was almost within striking distance of the capital on foot.

But was Petrograd (patriotically renamed at the beginning of the war) the equivalent of Paris – the nerve centre of the country which could effectively establish revolutionary control? In spite of appearances, the answer was no. While revolution see-sawed in Petrograd, the country on the whole lapsed into anarchy. Over the next few months effective and centrally controlled government of any sort ceased to exist. The historian has to follow a binary set of events: the revolution in the capital and other large cities, and the country at large. It was to take nearly four years before the two opposite though complementary tendencies of revolution and anarchy were to be fused under Bolshevik leadership. And this was only possible because the Bolsheviks formally conceded what was already an accomplished fact in the countryside, and based their programme not only on the demands of urban workers, but on the probability of what would satisfy the country as a whole.

23 Patriotic hopes of Russian victory. In 1915 this cartoon by the émigré Léon Bakst foretold a Russian leap from the Carpathians to Berlin in the style of the Russian ballet

We shall see this policy in action under two main heads, 'land for the peasants; peace for all'.

The provisional government in Petrograd was behaving predictably. Its leaders were good Liberals growing elderly and perhaps a little tired from their over-long period of political exile. Having managed the abdication, they expressed their intention to call a constituent assembly in the autumn, whose task it would be to decide, democratically and without constraint, on the future form of government. The intention was never acted on. Meanwhile there was the problem of a rival to the provisional government's authority in the shape of the resurrected Petrograd Soviet, which had appeared as spontaneously as its 1905 predecessor, and was once more duplicated in Moscow and other large cities. The Soviet was officially recognized by the government, and efforts were made to divide respective spheres of authority. This was a sensible concession to reality since the government disposed of only the now shaky bureaucracy and an army of very uncertain loyalty, while the Soviet had the support of the urban crowds, particularly the factory workers and the radical and vociferous sailors of Kronstadt, the near-by naval base. This division of authority between two co-ordinate bodies was perhaps untenable in the long run since, as Lenin correctly diagnosed, power in such (or any) situation is indivisible. Moreover the government had no clear programme, and took its provisional status literally.

In any case the war would be pursued. In April 1917 Miliukov, the Foreign Minister, formally confirmed the new government's commitment to its wartime allies. Such a full-scale and definite *prise de position* aroused considerable opposition and he was forced to resign. In Prince Lvov's second government the socialists were more strongly represented, though there were no major changes of policy. The social or political role, into which so many former oppositionists had suddenly entered when they themselves came to form a government, often dominated their personal views. Kerensky, a former Socialist-Revolutionary; Tseretelli, Menshevik and former state prisoner; Chernov, one of the leaders of the Socialist-Revolutionaries; and Skobelev, who had been an assistant and pupil of Trotsky – all suddenly developed as ministers a passion for law and order. For them a substantial part of the revolution had already been achieved. What was now needed was consolidation – against left as well as right.

The revolutionaries had again been overtaken by events; their programmes and organization were in disarray. The Bolsheviks in Petrograd were represented by a very junior trio. All the more senior leaders were still in exile in Siberia or abroad. There was great pressure for collaboration with the Mensheviks installed in the Soviet and in the government after its reconstitution in April. The momentary sense of achievement in Petrograd was considerable; only a few weeks earlier the overthrow of Tsarism had appeared as the problematic end of a long road yet to be travelled. Revolution, particularly in big towns, always provides a heady atmosphere for those involved. There was a deluge of speeches and pamphlets from March to November, an elixir of words on which to get easily drunk. The Russians are by nature an open and outward-going people, to whom inter-personal communication is the sheet anchor of social life. Those whose experience of meeting Russians has been confined to the tight-lipped caution of Stalinist officials cannot easily assess the emotional efflux of 1917, the spontaneous outburst in which the thoughts, wishes, fears and hopes, bottled up for so long, were all released at once, as well as the idea – however naïve – that social problems could actually be solved through discussion. In this sense Lenin in Switzerland aptly characterized the situation when he said that Russia was now 'the freest country in the world'.

He and his companions arrived in Petrograd on 16 April 1917. By this time the amnesty had already brought back Stalin and other senior Bolsheviks from Siberia. The only way for the émigrés in Switzerland to return to Russia was with German permission and assistance – in the famous sealed train. This led to the convenient accusation that Lenin was a German agent. But there was never of course any bargain. It was in the German interest to support anyone remotely opposed to continued Russian participation in the war, and Lenin wanted to get home to revolutionary Russia. To ascribe the October revolution to German help (and their substantial efforts to finance subversive agitation in Russia) is like putting the French Revolution down to Marie-Antoinette's injunction to eat cake if no bread was available.

The next few months witnessed Lenin's efforts to hammer out a consistent and distinct policy for the Bolsheviks and to impose it on his supporters. We need not be too closely concerned with the detailed slogans, which changed continually with the situation and often contradicted their predecessors. The early emphasis on support for the Petrograd Soviet against the provisional government was transformed into more anti-Soviet positions as Lenin tried to differentiate as sharply as possible between Bolsheviks and Mensheviks. This process of brutal differentiation was his prime concern. In the general revolutionary euphoria, there was a danger that the carefully nurtured distinctiveness of Bolshevik attitudes and organization might once again dissolve in an amorphous group of socialists. It was a period of extreme (and perhaps typically Russian) individualism. Each socialist was his own little party, and every event revised the shifting arrangements and alignments among the many small groups. At the Bolshevik Party conference at the end of April, Lenin fiercely defended his April theses, written before he left Switzerland, which the Petrograd party committee had initially rejected. Here for the first time was not only the demand for the transfer of all power to the Soviet and the overthrow of the provisional government, but also a programmatic declaration of further intent – a republic of workers' and poor peasants' Soviets drawn from all over the country. To view this statement as a cool assessment of actual possibilities is a mistake. The April theses and Lenin's line until the summer made sense only in terms of a process of strict self-definition and differentiation from others.

This did not mean that Lenin turned his back on all those who did not formally belong to the Bolshevik Party. The emergence of a revolutionary situation once more undermined some of the factional extremism of émigré politics, as in 1905. But in comparison with the organizational and pro-grammatic concessions which the Bolsheviks had been prepared to make to their opponents eleven years earlier, the policy of conciliation was now more restricted. Former opponents would indeed be welcomed, collaboration with other organizations was certainly possible – provided that the Bolshevik *line* was fully accepted. One candidate for such collaboration was Martov, Lenin's contemporary in the migration of 1900, and his most skilful and determined opponent after the 1903 split between Bolsheviks and Men-sheviks. Martov had opted for the same uncompromising opposition to the war as Lenin – a capital question, as we know. But the effort to collaborate with Martov and the group of 'international Mensheviks' failed.

24 The brutal facts.
Mass surrender of Russian soldiers in 1917

25 *Wounded Soldier,*
drawing by Chagall,
1914

Lenin was more successful with Trotsky, another old thorn in his flesh. Trotsky had been neither Bolshevik nor Menshevik throughout the last ten years, and had never ceased to castigate Lenin for his splitting tactics before 1914. He too had not hesitated to denounce the war. He had returned to Russia later than Lenin, and headed a group known as *Mezhraiontsy*. On 23 May Lenin offered him collaboration. Trotsky demanded a formal concession to his internationalist perspective – he was always more aggressively European than Lenin, and wanted his thesis of the inter-relatedness of revolutions among different societies formally inscribed into the joint programme. On this occasion the attempt to collaborate failed. But little more than a month later it became clear to Trotsky that only the Bolsheviks were pursuing genuinely revolutionary tactics, and were prepared to act as well as to talk. In July Trotsky and his supporters formally joined the Bolsheviks, and henceforward Lenin and he worked closely together – Trotsky openly, with his rousing speeches in the street and at congresses, Lenin secretly and often in hiding, organizing, manipulating and planning. No formal conditions for collaboration were imposed, but in effect Trotsky now accepted the Bolshevik organizational discipline, and Lenin the international commitment.

On 1 July the provisional government, still under heavy pressure from its foreign allies, decided to sweep away the arguments about future participation in the war by ordering a large-scale offensive against the Germans on the south-western front. Kerensky later admitted that not only the urging of the Allies, but the hope of pulling the country together through a resounding military victory, prompted the decision. Even the army had begun to disintegrate since April; up to the last moment of the offensive 'the officers did not know whether the soldiers would follow them in the attack'. On the whole they did. Once more, and for the last time, thick-packed ranks of soldiers marched into the scythe of machine-gun and artillery fire. The casualties were enormous. When the offensive proved a total failure only ten days after its beginning, the heart went out of the front-line troops. Events at home had made their subterranean impact in spite of the officers' strenuous attempt to maintain discipline. From then on mass desertions began to take place and spontaneous soldiers' councils appeared both at the front and at home. Not only had a further offensive become impossible, but the long and only half-orderly retreat before the German and Austrian armies now began. Whether the government remained in the war or not, the effectiveness of Russian participation had almost ceased. Certainly the German High Command drew the right conclusions, and transferred growing numbers of troops to the western front throughout the autumn.

All through the hot summer Petrograd alternately simmered and boiled. In early June a conference of Petrograd factory workers gave the Bolsheviks their first official majority against the provisional government in any formal meeting. In mid-June came the All-Russian Congress of Soviets. The Bolsheviks had 105 delegates out of 822, the Mensheviks 248, the Socialist-Revolutionaries 285, with 195 delegates organized in minor groups or not at all. This approximately represented the party line-up in the major towns; it may be assumed that Bolshevik support in the countryside was infinitesimal. However much Lenin might cry for 'unity from below' against the official organizations – instead of an amorphous collaboration among the leaders – the policy of differentiation was proving an effective means of recruiting support only at the top. Tseretelli justified the legitimacy of provisional government by stressing anarchy as the only alternative: 'There is not a single political party which can say: "Give us the power, go away, we will take your place." There is no such party in Russia.' It was intended as a rhetorical demonstration of the obvious. But Lenin rose at the back of the hall. 'Yes there is – the Bolsheviks.' The record tells us that the majority of delegates roared with laughter.

Yet it was not merely a verbal challenge, for the Bolsheviks now began to call their supporters out on street demonstrations, which reached their peak after the failure of the July offensive. The Bolsheviks hammered at the majority in both the provisional government and the Petrograd Soviet, and derided the Mensheviks as indistinguishable from their Liberal-Constitu-

26 Delegates to the first All-Russian Congress of Soviets held in Petrograd in June 1917

tionalist (Cadet) allies. As in all processes of differentiation, there were efforts to make all opponents look more or less indistinguishable, so that the world consisted only of 'them' and 'us' – a style of simplified political demography which was to become deeply ingrained in Bolshevik thinking and took on more subtle contours only after Stalin's death. But this time the government at last responded sharply. Encouraged by the numerical weakness of Bolshevik representation at the Congress of Soviets, and by the election of a friendly Central Executive Committee, the government drafted loyal troops into the capital, suppressed the two Bolshevik newspapers and arrested all the Party's leaders on whom it could lay hands. Though the failure of the military offensive led to the final fall of Lvov and to the appointment of the apparently more left-wing Kerensky as Premier, the suppression of the Bolsheviks continued apace. The period of vacillation was over for the Liberals. Their efforts were now increasingly devoted to the elimination of the menace from the left.

During the period from July to October the Bolsheviks were transformed 'almost overnight from a persecuted, slandered, outlawed minority whose leader, like Marat in the great French Revolution, had to hide in cellars, into the absolute masters of the situation' – as one famous, if critical, admirer was to write. The process of social disintegration was accelerated by the last great military failure. The longing for peace, hitherto mute and inchoate, was

47

turned into active agitation by the growing number of soldiers and sailors 'available' for revolutionary purposes in and around Petrograd. There had not yet been any sign of reaction to the events in the capital from the supporters of the Tsar; it was almost as if they had been swept from the face of the earth. And when finally this reaction did come, in the form of the Commander-in-Chief, General Kornilov, who marched on the capital without or against (no one knows which) the orders of the government, and may have planned a Tsarist restoration, the attempt petered out in farce. The loyal troops melted away and Kornilov was left in the most derisory of roles, a leader without an army. But the danger from the extreme right had changed the balance of forces once again – this time decisively.

In the end the real and only beneficiaries of the Kornilov affair were the Bolsheviks, who for the first time secured majorities in the Soviets of Petrograd and Moscow. The Socialist-Revolutionaries, pre-eminently representatives of the peasantry, had no precise political programme for the immediate situation. The revolution was almost ready for its second stage. It was not to be a spontaneous outbreak, but took the form of a coup d'état carefully planned by the Bolshevik leaders and brilliantly executed on the night of 7 November (25 October in the old Russian calendar). The second All-Russian Congress of Soviets was meeting in Petrograd at the time and did duty as a convenient platform for legalizing and publicizing the Bolshevik victory. Beyond this it served no other purpose. After adopting two revolutionary decrees on the need for immediate peace and the distribution of land to the peasants it disappeared – leaving power in the new Council of Peoples Commissars which had displaced the provisional government.

The Bolshevik Central Committee's decision to try armed insurrection was not taken easily. Zinoviev and Kamenev resisted to the last; they considered the plan premature if not foolhardy, and took their opposition all the way into public print – a breach of security and discipline for which Lenin almost succeeded in having them expelled from the Central Committee. Only on the eve of the chosen date was the Central Committee once more unanimous. The dispute was obscured in the kaleidoscope of successful revolution. Not until Stalin came to undo the reputation of his former colleagues in the great purges twenty years later were these pre-revolutionary disagreements revived: Trotsky the latecomer, who had stood out for so long against Bolshevik discipline; Zinoviev and Kamenev, the vacillators who had opposed Lenin and endangered the Party – all of them were to be forced to redigest their long-forgotten sins.

The organization that supervised the insurrection was a military-revolutionary committee of the Petrograd Soviet, by this time under Bolshevik

27 Inside the Winter Palace in Petrograd, troops guard members of the provisional government on the eve of the Bolshevik October revolution

control. Within the Central Committee individual leaders were assigned immediate tasks of supervising the various branches of government and administration as they were wrested from the feeble hands of the provisional government. Thus informally and in the course of planning an efficient coup d'état the basic control structure of the future Soviet state suddenly emerged. State institutions and organizations would come and go, serving their often fleeting need before being unceremoniously consigned to the administrative scrap heap, while the basic continuity of control and decision-making remained firmly in the hands of the party and its leading members. In the words of E.H.Carr, 'the victory, though won under the slogan "All power to the Soviet", was a victory not only for the Soviet but for Lenin and the Bolsheviks'. The qualification was soon deleted in practice, leaving the Party to administer its victory alone.

Beneath the dizzy excitement and cataclysmic optimism of these days, some fundamental problems were temporarily pushed out of sight. Was the Bolshevik seizure of power the fulfilment of Marxist dialectical logic? Was it thus that capitalism would be overthrown and give way to socialism? If so, why should this happen in the most backward of Europe's capitalist countries, where a bourgeois revolution had haltingly begun to challenge an almost feudal society? The Bolshevik analysis of the revolutions of 1905 and 1917 claimed that organized socialism would inevitably play a very important part in the development and achievements of bourgeois revolution. More

49

specifically, Lenin had been considering the question of state power, and had come to the conclusion that far from any attempt to adapt existing institutions, these must be destroyed and overthrown. A bourgeois socialist revolution would only be imprisoned in any institutions which it tried to adapt from its predecessor. There was, in short, no blueprint to put into practice after the seizure of power, neither in Marx nor in Lenin, only a few immediate imperatives for physical survival. We can ignore the later explanations and justifications, according to which Lenin understood that history had telescoped its processes to such an extent that the bourgeois era was historically eliminated and that socialists must take full and exclusive control and forcibly create the social conditions to maintain themselves in power. Even more specious were the attempts of Kautsky in Germany and other anti-Bolshevik Marxists to measure the objective socialist possibilities of Russian society and, finding them wanting, to deny the justification for Bolshevism. Lenin realized very well that the maintenance of Bolshevik power depended in the short run not on any objective indices of overall societal 'readiness', but on the twin immediacies of peace and land. Though the peasants and the disillusioned soldiers were not remotely interested in any sophisticated programme of socialism, they would support any government that fulfilled these promises.

Here the Bolshevik conception of democracy is crucial. Far from any programmatic platform on which the Bolsheviks could go forth and solicit electoral support, and which the electorate could evaluate with reason or prejudices, the Bolshevik view of democracy postulated action first and foremost – action which anticipated the expressed or if necessary deduced needs of the population: a commitment not a mandate. Such a conception might be short on measurable criteria like majority votes, which bourgeois democracy valued so highly, but it was long on the unmeasurable but much more real links of action which bound leaders and mass. The successful maintenance of power postulates continued popular commitment and support; the equivalent of being voted out of office is successful counter-revolution. A fellow Marxist and sympathetic critic of the Bolshevik revolution summarized this difficult paradox between the two forms of democracy: 'The party of Lenin was the only one which grasped the mandate and duty of a truly revolutionary party . . . they ensured the continued move forward of the revolution. Thereby the Bolsheviks solved the enormous problem of "winning a majority of the people" which has always weighed on [those who support the idea of bourgeois elections] like a nightmare. . . . Only a party which knows how to lead, how to attain things, wins support in stormy times.'

Granted this, could the Bolsheviks survive? Even the few enthusiastic foreign supporters of the October revolution expressed grave doubts – not to speak of its universal enemies. The Bolshevik victory was confined to Petrograd, Moscow and one or two other large towns. We do not know the innermost thoughts of the leading Bolsheviks, though we may suppose that those who opposed or hesitated over the decision to stage a coup d'état were also pessimistic of the long-term chances. The fusion of the ideas of Lenin and Trotsky in the formulation of Bolshevik policy emphasized the likelihood that the seizure of power in Russia must very soon spark off sympathetic revolutions in neighbouring and more 'suitably' industrialized countries. Specifically the Russians placed their hope on Germany, equally war-weary and before 1914 the spearhead of organized mass socialism. Every effort was made to influence the German workers and soldiers with revolutionary propaganda. Some Bolsheviks, like Radek, believed in the immediate possibilities of a sympathetic revolutionary outbreak, but it may be doubted whether Lenin did. A dangerous contradiction now arose. If the Bolsheviks were to fulfil their promise of peace, would not the German government be strengthened rather than weakened and pursue the war to a quick victory in the West? This became acute when Trotsky began armistice discussions with the German High Command, and the harsh conditions for any possible peace began to be revealed. All Trotsky's skill could not cancel out the imbalance of power. The Germans demanded the cession of large parts of Russian territory. By the end of 1917 they began to take a hand in the troubled internal politics of the Ukraine by supporting an anti-Bolshevik nationalist government under Shkoropadsky. The Russian troops were in no position to offer effective resistance, nor could the Bolsheviks reasonably ask them to do so. Yet as negotiations proceeded in the winter of 1917–18 the leading Bolsheviks were severely split over the problem of signing a treaty. What the Germans demanded was no less than the dismemberment of Russia; at the very moment of revolutionary victory German imperialism was exacting its enormous price for peace. Could the precious revolution survive?

A majority of the Bolsheviks were determined to carry on the war out of sheer necessity – a revolutionary war in which the defence of socialism and the motherland provided novel though complete justification. Trotsky believed, like Lenin, that further war was a betrayal of the very basis on which the Bolsheviks had seized power. His solution was 'neither peace nor war'; further retreat if necessary but no formal acceptance of humiliation. Lenin on the other hand urged acceptance of the terms – on the iron grounds of necessity. In the end, after prolonged and heated debate his view prevailed. On 3 March Sokolnikov signed the Treaty of Brest Litovsk.

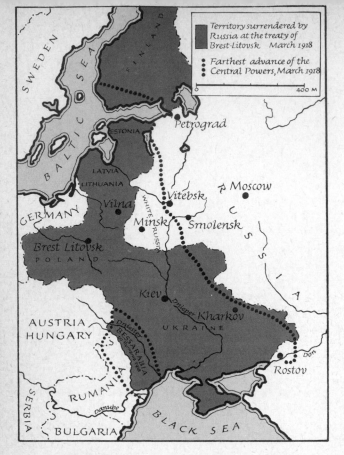

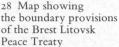

Territory surrendered by
Russia at the treaty of
Brest-Litovsk March 1918

Farthest advance of the
Central Powers, March 1918

28 Map showing
the boundary provisions
of the Brest Litovsk
Peace Treaty

Within a week or two the Germans seized most of the Ukraine, including Kiev; the Austrians were in Odessa and the Turks in Trebizond. Even the oldest and feeblest of Russia's enemies was benefiting from the revolution. The Germans swept away the nascent Soviet in the Ukraine and installed a thoroughly anti-Bolshevik government. But the Bolsheviks had kept their promise to their supporters, the masses who wanted peace above all. After further heart-searchings, an emergency Party congress followed by a congress of Soviets decided to ratify the Treaty. In the course of the negotiations Lenin had twice offered to resign, and Trotsky and his colleagues claimed that they had sacrificed their deepest convictions in the interests of Bolshevik unity. It was the first great test of unity for the leaders and the Party in the face of the agonizing realities of power.

Everyone regarded the gloomy situation as temporary. Lenin emphasized that in the existing state of the world any peace dictated by the imperialists could not be permanent. And six months after the signature of the Treaty of Brest Litovsk Lenin's policy seemed to receive the accolade of ultimate justification, for in October 1918 the Germans were suing for peace in the West, and hardly a month later the long-awaited revolution had actually broken out in Berlin. The centrepiece of Soviet revolutionary thinking had been obscured for many months, but it had not disappeared: for the next three years the policy of the young Soviet republic was based unswervingly on the expectation of revolutions abroad. The rapidity of institutional change at home, the tactical advances and retreats imposed by civil war and foreign intervention, the apparatus of the terror which was beginning to appear – all were excused on the assumption that these were temporary measures to await the victory of European revolution, which would save Soviet Russia and break its isolation.

But the peace of Brest Litovsk had set one crucial if unintended precedent which was to have the gravest consequences for the future. When a choice had had to be made between the immediate support of foreign comrades – the German extreme left who denounced the Brest negotiations as a shot in the arm for their own government – and the maintenance of Soviet power at home, the Bolsheviks, however reluctantly, had chosen the latter. This policy of revolutionary egoism could be justified, but it also introduced into Soviet thinking a structure of priorities which was to become permanent. The change from revolutionary egoism to the later 'socialism in one country' was one of degree rather than kind. And in the end the wheel was to turn full circle: almost fifty years after the October revolution a new communist China challenged this very policy and accused the Russians of betraying the international revolution with their self-sufficient and nationalistic pre-occupations. Stalin was the executant architect of Soviet self-regard, but its intellectual foundation dated from the choice made by the Bolsheviks at Brest Litovsk a few months after their first seizure of power.

At home, too, the period immediately following the seizure of power produced policies of exigency which had been neither foreseen nor planned but which were to become a fundamental part of Bolshevik orthodoxy in the future. Though the Bolsheviks had seized power on their own, and Lenin's preoccupation with the Party's distinctiveness and separate organization had been triumphantly justified, the problem of governing alone or with other like-minded groups had been neither posed nor resolved. In the fluid situation, organized outside forces were perfectly capable of making their wishes effective. The Menshevik-controlled Railwaymen's Union of Petrograd and the majority in several important city Soviets forced the new government to enter into negotiations with the Socialist-Revolutionaries and

Mensheviks for a coalition government. Lenin wanted to abandon these negotiations as quickly as possible, but was strongly opposed by his colleagues. The elections to the constituent assembly, however, which the Bolsheviks had, for tactical reasons, supported in the summer, decisively changed his mind once more. The Socialist-Revolutionaries, still the revolutionary peasant party *par excellence*, obtained 410 out of 707 seats, the Bolsheviks a mere 175 – less than a quarter. Both Liberals and Mensheviks had been reduced to tiny fractions. It was clear that the confrontation was no longer between two rival versions of Marxism but between revolutionary countryside and revolutionary cities. Every other party or tendency had, in Trotsky's contemptuous words, become irrelevant. 'You have played out your role. Go where you belong, to the dust heap of history.' But the Socialist-Revolutionaries had themselves split into two factions, with the radical and majoritarian left closest to the Bolsheviks. A coalition was now arranged between them and the Bolsheviks on what Lenin insisted was a socialist platform. In this way Bolshevik defeat at the constituent assembly elections was turned into an apparent victory for the new coalition.

During the next few months the coalition broke up mainly over the question of Brest Litovsk and the continuous infiltration of Bolsheviks into the most important organs of state power. Already at the beginning of 1918 the Cadets and other parties now in opposition were being accused of supporting the counter-revolutionary forces assembling in southern and central Russia for a fundamental reckoning. Shortly afterwards these parties were officially proscribed. The Left Socialist-Revolutionaries, once they had officially retired from the coalition in the late spring of 1918, resorted to their traditional tactics of assassination. On 6 July two Left Socialist-Revolutionaries killed the German ambassador in order to undermine the precarious peace with Germany. On 30 August they decided on their own version of an armed uprising. Uritsky, a senior Bolshevik, was assassinated in Petrograd, and in Moscow a Socialist-Revolutionary called Kaplan managed to wound Lenin seriously. Henceforward the Socialist-Revolutionaries were also proscribed. In the countryside the Soviet policy of requisitioning grain and forming committees of poor peasants, whose opposition to their richer fellows was designed to help extract surpluses, put the Socialist-Revolutionaries in sharp political opposition to the Bolsheviks.

All this gave rise to the Red Terror of the autumn of 1918, for which the murder of the Tsar's family in the night of 16–17 July served as the opening signal. Most of the victims were those whose former position justified their being placed in the category of counter-revolutionaries, as well as the supporters of peasant uprisings, of which a serious instance took place at Penza

29, 30 New power and old. F. Dzerzhinsky, head of the Cheka (special police); and the deposed Tsar at Tsarskoe Selo towards the end of 1917

in August 1918. The Socialist-Revolutionaries were linked specifically and ideologically with peasant unrest, and the hand of the Cheka or special police fell heavily upon them. This instrument of revolutionary vigilance grew rapidly in importance and activity at this time. Its chief, Dzerzhinsky, described it as follows: 'The Cheka is most important. The Cheka is the defence of the revolution just as the Red Army is. The Cheka must defend the revolution and conquer the enemy even if its sword falls occasionally on the heads of the innocent.' The machinery of counter-terror and repression grew piecemeal but rapidly from each challenge to Bolshevik authority.

The constituent assembly had been dispersed early in the morning of 19 January 1918 soon after it had begun its sessions; a Bolshevik resolution had just been defeated. Its legislative functions were formally placed in the lap of the All-Russian Congress of Soviets which met four days later. But from now on it was the Bolshevik Party that made the policy; the Soviet organs discussed and ratified it officially. By mid-1918 the Bolsheviks were not only governing alone, but treating all their former opponents and allies as potentially hostile. The concept of exclusive power to one party thus sprang not primarily from doctrinal predisposition, but from a revolutionary situation in which neutrality or indifference was meaningless. Those who were not with the Bolsheviks were against them. The notion that power might be shared outside the Party was buried for ever.

But this did not mean the exercise of repression and terror against all non-Bolsheviks. Soviet terror was at that stage primarily defensive, designed to protect the sensitive areas of the new and very insecure Bolshevik power structure. There was no general politically motivated retaliation; the Red Terror was haphazard in application and selective in its victims. Makhno, the Ukrainian anarchist, whose forces were causing, and would cause, the Bolsheviks much trouble in the Ukraine, came to Moscow in August 1918 and met Lenin and Sverdlov. The Mensheviks still continued to exist as a separate party, pledging support to the Soviet defence of the republic against its enemies but continuing to protest against the arbitrary and dictatorial nature of Bolshevik rule. Many so-called 'former people' who possessed special qualifications were permitted to work in their field, especially during the civil war, provided they declared their loyalty to the new state. The case of the former engineers and officers whom Trotsky integrated into the new Red Army and most of whom served loyally to make careers in the future in industry and the armed forces is well known. Lenin and Trotsky had to defend them several times against their more dogmatic colleagues. From former Mensheviks, anarchists and other opponents of Tsarism the Bolsheviks welcomed individual adherence to Party or Soviet state service, provided discipline and policy were accepted. The Mensheviks, intellectually still the firmest of their opponents, had to choose. Plekhanov and Martov remained unregenerate opponents of what they described as a Jacobin conspiracy instead of an application of Marxist socialism. Most of their supporters left Russia quite freely for the next few years. Plekhanov died in Russia in 1918 and was given a shamefaced official funeral for his past intellectual contribution, but Party members were discouraged from attending. (When Kropotkin, the distinguished old anarchist, died in 1921 the official funeral was attended by many thousands.) Martov went back into exile a disappointed man; it is said that in spite of their unbridgeable differences Lenin was saddened by the news of Martov's death shortly before his own. But many others now joined the Bolsheviks, and as long as Lenin was alive this buried past differences. Some former Mensheviks were to achieve prominence in the Soviet Union. Chicherin, the first Foreign Minister, and Vyshinsky, later the prosecutor at the great trials and Foreign Minister after the Second World War, were both former Mensheviks. The Planning Commission was almost 'a nest of former Mensheviks', as Stalin was to claim when its past was frighteningly dug up again fifteen years later. And even many of those who refused to convert were left in withdrawn isolation provided that they did not engage in active politics. The great round-up and imprisonment of former Mensheviks did not begin until the late 1920s. The intolerance of which Lenin has so often been accused was real enough, but it was confined to organizational problems and to personal differences over policy, not to an endless and unforgiving memory of the past. Lenin was essentially concerned with present and future. It was Stalin who invoked the past in order to justify and rearrange the present.

This is one of the moments when the temptation to regard the fifty years' existence of the Soviet Union as an overtly logical structure of events organized by the iron law of history becomes overwhelming. The determination of Soviet historiography to create such a logical structure induces a powerful efflux of sentiment. Either one accepts the view that things could not have been otherwise, or one rejects it and sinks forthwith into a den of demons and everlasting accident. The middle path is a razor's edge of discomfort. Certainly a kind of logic begins to creep into events in the Soviet Union after the October revolution. The very fact that such a logic was incessantly postulated by the leaders to explain and justify their actions, is partial evidence that they were managing to create a sense of logic where none existed otherwise. There are also moments when genuine choices were available, when things happened in a particular way because of conscious preferences and even mistakes. The October revolution itself was one such event, Stalin's switch to industrialization eleven years later another. Both can be explained – but not as inevitable.

Was a Bolshevik seizure of power historically necessary? Was it only the Bolsheviks who could have taken over in November 1917? When we bear in mind the way in which the Bolsheviks seized power, the answer must be no. A similar coup d'état could have been undertaken by the other revolutionary parties, particularly the Socialist-Revolutionaries – if their leadership had been more determined. Lenin was under no delusion about this. He and Trotsky alone realized at this stage how true was Marx's dictum that the 'real history of real men' depends not only on large social forces but on the will and power of small groups of individuals. Whatever else Lenin may have contributed, his decision to act transformed a group of active intellectuals into a ruling party. But if the other parties might have seized power, it is clearly unlikely that they would have held it. None appeared capable of developing the severe measures required to steer the new state through its stormy infancy; none would have rejected so completely the various possibilities of compromise with the old régime. The right if brief answer probably is that the determination of Lenin and Trotsky to seize power was something of an historical accident. The Bolshevik survival has deeper social significance.

What about the policy choices after the Bolshevik seizure of power? We have seen how much faith was placed in the necessity of a supporting international revolution. But once it was clear that foreign revolution might be delayed, and worse still might fail instead of succeeding, the maintenance of the Soviet régime at home became an imperative for the very existence of communism in the future. If the Soviet republic were extinguished all future revolutions must find their task infinitely harder. This was the state of mind from the beginning of 1919 – a determination to keep both options open, to adjust emphasis according to what was happening abroad. We are still a long way from the period of Soviet self-sufficiency and 'socialism in one country'.

It was quite obvious to most of the Bolshevik leaders that the social measures taken in the early months of 1918 would not in themselves help to create socialism, let alone communism. Such attainments were viewed as long-term prospects. Lenin characterized the difference between communism and socialism with one of his brutally simple aphorisms: 'Soviets plus electrification equals communism.' This emphasized the importance of economic development in its starkest form. Yet far from advancing, the Soviet economy was in the grip of a major crisis. Whereas production had been increasing substantially until the end of 1916, it fell back disastrously from 1917 to 1921.

31 Lenin and Trotsk[y] plotting the world revolution. A poster issued in Rostov by the anti-Bolshevik armies, c. 1920

32 Incomprehensible
and despicable;
the Bolshevik leaders
in Red Square,
according to a
caricature of *c*. 1919

In the first four years of communist rule, industrial production dropped to something like a fifth of its level in 1916, and agricultural production to less than half. Far from the Party's being able to launch any immediate offensive for the construction of socialism, circumstances forced the full attention and energy of the rulers into the barest struggle for survival. Determined after July 1918 to go it alone, the Bolsheviks had to struggle on every front at once.

For Lenin the first requisite of self-preservation was the undiluted integrity and autonomy of the Party. His original intention on the morrow of victory in 1917 had been not to join the government as such, but to leave this to others while he himself concentrated on Party work. The long-term intention was not to rely on the governmental structure to overcome the main hurdles of large-scale social change but to develop the Party and keep it organizationally and ideologically distinct from the routine business of governing, to prepare it for the long socio-cultural haul to socialism. In the broadest sense Lenin's emphasis on Party gave expression to the need to distinguish between the present and the future, to differentiate between survival and advance, between leadership and administration. This relationship between Party and society as a whole provides the key to the period from the October revolution to the 1930s, and explains Lenin's willingness to undertake such violent changes of course without any sense of compromise in his long-term aims.

59

From the very start the new Soviet republic was marked by a striking dichotomy : strict Party discipline for Bolsheviks, relative freedom in non-political spheres outside the Party. Emphasis on the purely political history of the early Soviet Union tends to show a continual and unrelieved erosion of freedom. Yet the same period witnessed an unprecedented effervescence of experiments in a number of fields which were just as important as politics. Education, literature, painting, music, all seemed to burst out of the constraint of a tired, autocratically inhibited society, which had weighed heavily on the creative atmosphere in Russia since the turn of the century. The early Soviet period shook the very foundations of the family, the anchor of all integrated civilizations. For a brief period free love was officially in vogue among the political intelligentsia of the main cities, who felt committed to demonstrate their own liberation and the hope of ushering in the new millennium. On the whole the Bolshevik Party did not encourage such extreme experiments, and most of the leaders were 'square' about such problems or simply disinterested in them, but the anarchic aspects of the revolution cannot be ignored. Effervescence is a more normal part of social revolution than Stalinist conformity and cultural quiescence; the People's Democracies of eastern Europe, where the literature and the arts have in a sense been in the vanguard of the new post-Stalin communism, show this clearly enough. Only the Soviet Union has undergone a full-scale imposition of intellectual and cultural Stalinism – and China may be undergoing it now.

33, 34, 35 The new Soviet art in the early 1920s. Right, a page designed by the Constructivist artist, Lissitzky, in 1923. Opposite, a wash-drawing by Larionov for A. A. Blok's 1918 poem *Dvenadstat*; and a photomontage by Aleksander Rodchenko, illustrating Mayakovsky's poem *Pro Eto*, 1923

In that sense the arts in the rest of the socialist bloc have remained relatively free – to set, at least in part, their own autonomous standards. The simultaneous combination of political orthodoxy with relative cultural freedom, which has distinguished contemporary eastern Europe from the Soviet Union in the last ten years, is thus not new, but corresponds more closely to Lenin's (and especially Trotsky's) conception of revolution than to that of his successors in the Soviet Union.

The Party had deliberately dropped the disgraced title of Social Democrat in March 1918. It was self-consciously and determinedly a workers' party, whose historical role was to be the vanguard of the working class – which theoretically embraced both urban and rural proletariat. At the same time the Communist Party was not a party of workers. The proportion of genuine workers had been larger among the Bolsheviks than the Mensheviks, but even among the Bolsheviks almost all the leading positions were held by people who can best be described as intellectuals. Their role had been specifically expounded by Lenin in his 1903 pamphlet 'What Is To Be Done'. The potential contradiction of a workers' party run largely by intellectuals was accordingly resolved in advance. If these people had no very clear view of the type of society they wanted to create, they did agree on what constituted the proper attitude and morality of a revolutionary. Revolution was a liberating experience, not only for an oppressed class but in furthering the personal emancipation of the individual.

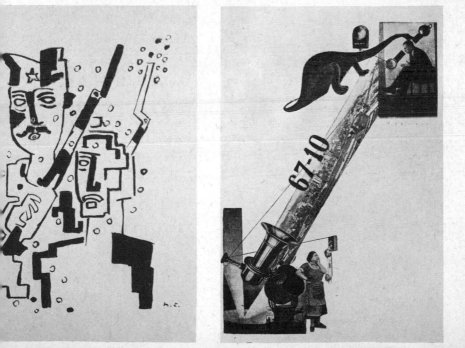

The fact that Lenin was a man of action and an excellent conspirator, who disliked cloudy theorizing and always attempted to relate the wider aspect of theory to action, did not limit this vision of human emancipation but enhanced it by submitting every action to its wider context of revolutionary morality. When doubtful means had to be used, like the armed raids against government banks in 1909, or the techniques of subversion borrowed from less ideological forms of conspiracy, Lenin did not hesitate in the knowledge that these were lowly means to an end; and he had little time for moral debates on such issues. They were necessary acts – but not spontaneous or pragmatic lines of action. A number of leading Bolsheviks certainly considered the moral aspect of action to be secondary; they were manipulators whose fund of moral indignation was a vacuum to be filled by slogans. Zinoviev was one of these, and Stalin unexpectedly proved to be another. But they were in a minority among the Bolsheviks at the time. With everyone seeming to speak the same language, who can tell the difference between a deep sense of moral discrimination and a mere verbal commitment to accepted norms – except in retrospect?

Yet at the same time it was this personal commitment to action rather than speculation on the part of the Bolsheviks that made possible the eventual transition from Leninism to Stalinism. The temporary phenomena of repression, designed to maintain the Party in power during hard times, turned into familiar objects of necessary revolutionary experience. There was a sense of pride in their hardness, in the practical willingness to take the consequences of any situation. The plea of necessity to justify the terror did not really suit those who for the last twenty years had justified their claim to be different from everyone else on the grounds that they, and only they, were willing to act ruthlessly, and not merely talk revolution. Thus terror was to be described proudly as the armed sword of the revolution. The slaughter of the Tsar and his family at Ekaterinburg, and the other numerous acts of repression against opponents, were proclaimed as a demonstration that revolutionaries could be tougher, more determined than any of their rivals. The belief that indecision and weakness were symptomatic of the left, that the only acts of terror of which they were capable were cloak-and-dagger assassinations – these were widespread attitudes which the Bolsheviks were determined to prove wrong once and for all. Here too was an unresolved paradox.

Only the emergence of Stalin and the increasing isolation of the Soviet Union eventually tilted the scales in favour of retaining terror as a permanent institution of Soviet society, reducing the idea of revolutionary morality to mere verbiage, and equating terror with morality *tout court* – like Robespierre

36 The struggle against racial prejudice. A poster of 1929 proclaims: 'Anti-semitism is counter-revolutionary, anti-semitism is our class enemy'

and St Just. This possibility was contained in the situation which followed the revolution itself, but not necessarily predetermined.

As people the Bolsheviks were quite different from anything that had ever been seen in positions of leadership in Europe. The combination of ideological commitment to an all-embracing philosophy of absolute certainty, with a propensity for strong action; of sensitive morality and extreme toughness; of a wide intellectual horizon and opposition to all forms of professionalization with an absolute devotion to technology – all these produced a type of man who stood out from the social and cultural environment of Russia and Europe as a whole. The Bolshevik claimed the right to rule not from any divine or inherited legitimacy, but by the force of his achievement. Moreover, he claimed to combine within himself the two complementary but conflicting moieties of intellectual analysis and practical action. He discarded, indeed turned upside-down, the subtle distinctions of dress and manner which are signs of a high status category in all societies – until the informality of behaviour and shapelessness of dress themselves turned into a new status ritual of their own. 'Comrade' epitomized both the revolt against the old and the eventual formalism of the new. Above all the Bolshevik had put a substantial area of human self-determination decisively in pawn – at least until full communism eventually brought about the ultimate liberation by resolving all contradiction between self and collectivity, self and environment. For the moment the largest dimension of his life was

63

not available for inspection or assessment since it belonged to the Party. A Bolshevik was thus anti-social in the normal sense of the word. He did not communicate readily, he did not seek friends, he did not attempt to make himself agreeable, he had no time for sociability or relaxation as such. Since he believed in a philosophy which was totally incomprehensible to non-Marxists, it was often difficult even to talk to him. Most of the few Western diplomats who were in Russia during the period of the revolution again and again expressed surprise that they were able to make any contact with the new men, that they turned out to be human beings after all.

The Bolshevik despised and rejected the basic ideology of Russianness. The Russians were sociable and gregarious, given to demonstrations of emotion and to indiscretion (classical Russian literature is one long series of indiscretions, their consequences and ramifications); social life was based on the willingness of each person to pawn a part of himself to his fellow men and privacy was the worst form of mental exile. The Bolshevik was silent, reserved and secretive. The impenetrability of the Russian character, on which so many observers have commented, was preserved by a smokescreen of words. The Bolsheviks hid themselves in silence, and reduced their language to a code of complex symbols.

The dichotomy between Party and society in the early days was thus reinforced by a clash of cultures and of language. The old antithesis of Russianness versus European influences seemed to have merged into a new and quite different antagonism, with the Bolsheviks representing a new version of Europe. To their fellow Russians, the new rulers – many of them members of national minorities and Jews – were incomprehensibly foreign; to their fellow socialists in Europe they appeared incurably Russian. In fact they were neither. The cultural basis of society, by which men could be distinguished and classified according to ethnic origin and language, was seriously put in question with the arrival in power of men to whom nationality seemed irrelevant, who welcomed Poles, Finns and Jews indiscriminately to positions of power in Russia, and seemed to have more in common with them than with their 'proper' fellow countrymen. Moreover these new men introduced criteria of judgment and differentiation which were utterly unfamiliar : ideological categories based on class instead of the more familiar cultural, ethnic and religious means of self-definition. Beneath the social and economic revolution created by the events of November 1917 there loomed an even more important cultural conflict. The early years of the Soviet republic witnessed its initiation, the taking up of positions; it was to be resolved only in the degeneration of conformity imposed under Stalin more than a decade later.

From its very beginning the new Russian Soviet Republic was to be beset by problems which challenged its very existence as well as the authority of the new communist rulers. Two things saved it – and them. The first was the fact that when faced with the practical alternatives at the time, the new régime found enough support to enable it to deal with its enemies. We have already looked at the theory of Bolshevik democracy; between 1917 and 1921 it was to be put to the acid test. In the elected bodies, both Soviets and Constituent Assembly, at the end of 1917, the Bolsheviks had been in a minority, which gradually turned into majorities over the next few months, but these elected bodies could not adequately test the latent support for the Bolsheviks in a time of crisis. This test came when Allied troops landed in Murmansk and Archangel in the north, Odessa in the south and Vladivostok in the Far East; when White commanders rallied opposition to the new republic and advanced on Moscow from north, south and east; when the food supply of the cities was threatened by anarchy and destruction in the countryside. If the Allies and White Guards had been welcomed by the majority of the population, or even passively supported, the Soviet republic could not have survived. This did not mean that the majority of people enthusiastically supported the Bolsheviks once peace with Germany had been made. But faced with a choice between a White Tsarist restoration or the maintenance of Soviet power – and these were the alternatives during the civil war – they opted for the Reds. Nothing so clearly demonstrates the futility of any middle or reformist solution in pre-revolutionary Russia, and undermines Kerensky's later claim that only an accident of history prevented him from establishing a legitimate government of moderation, as the way in which the latent polarity of Russian society came out inexorably into the open during these years.

The other factor was a chronological accident. Instead of having to face its enemies simultaneously, the Soviet republic was able to deal with them piecemeal. At the end of 1917 and the beginning of 1918 the primary menace was the Germans and their puppets in the Ukraine and the Baltic states; by the time the war ended at the beginning of November 1918 this problem was solved. The rise of internal reaction to the Soviet government, the formation of White armies and their gradual move towards the heart of the country, took place only from the second half of 1918 onwards. Even there, on military and strategic grounds, the Red Army was able to deal with its enemies singly – the White commanders were never able to co-ordinate their strategy – and from interior lines of communication astride the outward-radiating net of railways centred on Moscow. The new Red Army, literally stamped into existence by Trotsky out of nothing in the summer of 1918, first

37 The foreign and internal enemies of the revolution join forces, and are driven to their ruin. General Wrangel and Poland are drawing the cart which bears the bourgeoisie, the Social Democrat, the landowner and the Tsar. Other White leaders, Denikin, Kolchak and Yudenich, have already been defeated at right

contained and defeated Kolchak and the insurgent Czechoslovak legion on the upper Volga. By the beginning of October this area was clear; the White forces had been thrown back into Siberia. Next it was the turn of Denikin and Krasnov on the southern front. The White forces overran the Ukraine, including Kiev, and were thrown back only in the late summer of 1919. Yudenich laid siege to Petrograd in the autumn. Kolchak, too, made another attempt in the spring of 1919 to advance towards the Volga. In the summer of 1919 the Soviet republic was at the height of its peril. It was only at the beginning of 1920 that the White forces were reduced to individual marauding bands, which were picked off one by one in the course of the next twelve months.

The Allied intervention, moreover, had been more diplomatic and symbolic than military. Having landed at their designated ports, the troops sat and waited for a few months. The French garrison at Odessa revolted; having been the first to call for intervention, the French were also the first to withdraw. The whole Allied operation achieved little except to provide the Soviet communists with a bitter memory of imperialism's intervention, and to broach the idea of a rapprochement with the less dangerous and itself recently defeated Germany, which was to come to fruition at Rapallo in November 1922.

The period of civil war had an important effect on the relations of the Bolsheviks with their internal rivals. For the time being the offensive against the Mensheviks and the Socialist-Revolutionaries calmed down after the end of 1918. Faced with the brutal choice of White restoration or Red rule, Mensheviks, anarchists and Socialist-Revolutionaries opted for the latter, and the Soviet government in its dire need accepted all the help available. Once the wave of terror at the end of 1918 was over, both Socialist-Revolutionaries and Mensheviks continued to lead a shadow existence and to elect delegates to the various city Soviets as late as 1920. Formally none of this organized activity was possible; in practice it continued apace. It was only in December 1920 that the Mensheviks as a separate organization made their final appearance at an All-Russian Congress of Soviets; afterwards they would no longer be tolerated. As a result of Martov's departure at the beginning of 1920, the effective Menshevik leadership in Russia collapsed. The remaining rank and file of the party now retired or joined the Bolsheviks. Once the civil war was over, the Bolsheviks ceased to suffer the existence of any organized opposition, even a momentarily loyal one well outside the effective centre of power. By 1922 the legal clamps were firmly screwed down, and a whole group of imprisoned Socialist-Revolutionaries was formally put on trial.

38 A street poster by Lissitzky, 1919–20.
'Beat the Whites with the Red wedge'

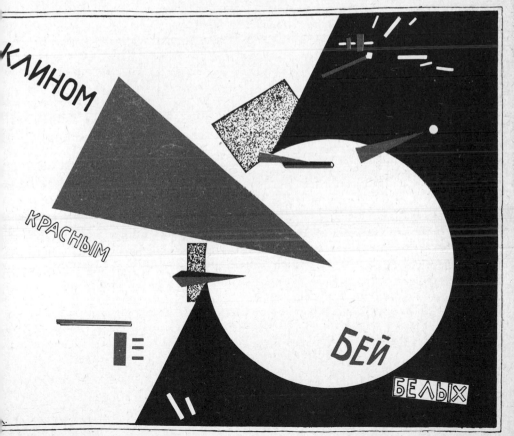

As all formal opposition in Soviet Russia was finally dispersed and destroyed, dissensions within the Party itself began to take on an increasingly serious aspect. However much the Bolshevik leadership appeared to its enemies as a cohesive élite, there had always been disagreements on policy questions, sometimes serious and protracted. The permitted debate prior to a decision had at times, as already noted, continued in the shape of opposition to decisions already taken. Even during the civil war these dissensions continued among the top leadership, though every effort was made to prevent them from becoming public knowledge. Trotsky's effective but high-handed methods of promotion and demotion, his increasing reliance on former officers who pledged their loyalty to the new republic, above all the jealousy between different section commanders and Party leaders at the front which caused the first open clash between Trotsky and Stalin, resulted in much backbiting and appeals to Lenin for final decision. The creation of organs of repression like the Cheka and their rapid increase in power during the civil war produced resentment and disappointment among senior Party members for whom, with all due allowance for the emergency, the Soviet régime began to look less like the democratic and self-liberating experience they had expected. By 1920 the external situation seemed safe enough for the dissenters to voice their views openly within the Party, and to solicit support from possible sympathizers.

Ever since the debate over the Treaty of Brest Litovsk and the problem of revolutionary war, a faction of Left communists had developed within the Party. For a time they even published their own paper, *Kommunist*. Having lost the argument over the peace, they transferred their criticisms primarily to economic matters, especially the failure to move quickly forward to full state ownership in industry and the land. By the end of the civil war another opposition within the Party emerged, the so-called 'workers' opposition', with whom the names of Shlyapnikov and Kollontai were associated. Unlike the Left communists, some of whose supporters were to reappear in various groups and platforms of the opposition for the next ten years, the workers' opposition had no clear programme, but at the same time it was a more cohesive and self-conscious group or faction. Its origin was due mainly to dissatisfaction with the increasing hierarchy of control within the Party, which eroded all possibility of influence by the organized workers in union or factory. As efficiency perspectives became more important to solve the economic crisis, management of factories was increasingly placed in the hands of individual and fully responsible managers. The trade unions were reduced in power and ceased to have much say in major problems of production; in the more directly political arena Party tradition had anyhow never allowed trade unions any independence or institutional influence. These were the factors on which the opposition concentrated its fire, demanding greater worker-participation in industry, and in general a more liberal atmosphere within the Party. A more widespread body of opinion sought to buttress internal democracy within the Party organizations. The old Bolshevik slogan of democratic centralism was taken up; it should be made effective by being formally institutionalized instead of serving merely as a justificatory concept.

These criticisms and demands gave rise to lengthy and fundamental discussions among the Party leaders, culminating in the debates at the Tenth Party Congress in March 1921. The raising of substantive problems was at the best of times inhibited by the Party's commitment to discipline and the antipathy towards organized faction. The Tenth Congress met in an atmosphere of crisis and a substantial majority voted against the various opposition platforms in turn. Strong resolutions on Party unity and against all manifestations of syndicalism (a blow at the workers' opposition) were passed. In a secret, unpublished addition to the resolutions on Party unity, expulsion by the Central Committee for factional activity (any attempt to organize behind a platform) was authorized. In the end the Party shrank from the use of such extreme measures at the time, and in any case the threat sufficed. But as so often, temporary measures to deal with a particular problem gave rise to the creation of a body which was to have unexpected durability and significance in the future. The Congress created a Party Control Commission, parallel to the Central Committee, with the task of examining all complaints against Party members and dealing with matters of Party discipline. Henceforward no one could get a hearing at Party Congresses or meetings once the accusation of 'organizing' had been raised against him.

The most serious crisis had arisen in March 1921 when the sailors of Kronstadt, the torchbearers of revolutionary loyalty and Trotsky's most reliable shock troops during the civil war, suddenly rebelled against the Soviet government. This was not a plot organized by opponents of government or Party, nor connected with any theoretical disagreement about policy within the Party itself. Instead it was a spontaneous but violent reaction among previously loyal supporters of the Bolsheviks against the increasingly authoritarian and heavy-handed methods of the leadership. Strikes had broken out in a number of Petrograd factories; the peasants were resentful and co-operating only minimally with the government which raided them incessantly for supposedly hoarded grain surpluses. The air was everywhere full of discontent. Rumours of severe repressive measures in the offing spread like wildfire in this atmosphere. At meetings in Kronstadt slogans like 'freedom of elections to the Soviets' and indeed a call for a third revolution were beginning to be heard. The reverberations of the demand 'Down with political tyranny' echoed across the ice of the Gulf of Petrograd.

The Soviet government took alarm. The makeshift and regretful air with which early repressive measures had been applied was already giving way to a more determined assertion of revolutionary violence as a fundamental part of Bolshevik rule. Trotsky particularly, in the debate with the workers' opposition, stressed the role of the Party as pre-eminent, historically necessary and therefore justified even in its most authoritarian aspects. Lenin had hitherto supported the organization of individual platforms within the Party. 'To form ourselves into different groups (especially before a congress) is of course permissible (and so is canvassing for votes). But it must be done within the limits of communism (and not syndicalism) and in such a way as not to create ridicule.' But he too had become disturbed by the 'fever' which seemed to be shaking the Party to the foundation of its unity and cohesion. In a situation of precarious rule in a country devastated by famine and civil war, the limits of these rights would have to be scrupulously observed. The Kronstadt revolt came at a peculiarly sensitive moment, and seemed to echo Lenin's and Trotsky's worst fears. It was decided to suppress the Kronstadt rising by force. The task of issuing an ultimatum and if necessary storming the fortress across the ice a few days before the spring thaw fell ironically to Trotsky himself.

While the fortress was being captured and the leaders of the revolt shot, the Tenth Party Congress was already sitting in Moscow. The statements of the Bolshevik leaders reflected the agonized schizophrenia induced by the situation. They were no longer fully able to distinguish belief from propaganda, and propaganda from reality. All enemies of the Soviet régime had become lumped together as counter-revolutionaries and White Guards, and the official explanation of the Kronstadt rising was simply that a group of counter-revolutionary mutineers were led by White officers. Yet at the same time the Bolshevik leaders spoke of Kronstadt as an event to be regretted rather than condemned, of the participants as 'misled sailor comrades' rather than outright enemies of the state. It was a hopeless rebellion, since in any event the Kronstadt sailors had many demands but no organized support in the Party. If they can be categorized at all they were anarchist revolutionaries mainly of peasant origin who had recently been drafted into this historic stronghold of Bolshevism and had taken Bolshevik hopes and promises literally.

The suppression of the mutiny was in any case to have serious consequences. For those who had eyes to see, this was merely one manifestation of the widespread unrest. In its fight for survival the revolution was becoming, or had become, distorted. In their determination to stay in power, the Bolsheviks had let all other priorities lapse. What gave the Kronstadt revolt a particularly sour taste for the Bolsheviks was the previous unquestioned loyalty of the sailors. Outside observers, including foreign communists visiting Russia, shared and voiced the quandary : the absolute need to enforce discipline coupled with strong sympathy for these particular rebels. A complete change of policy was in fact around the corner, for a week after the opening of the Tenth Congress the broad outlines of the New Economic Policy (NEP) were to be announced by Lenin. The feeling, the knowledge, that things could not continue as before had already seized hold of some of the Bolshevik leaders. But the Party now had the chance of admitting its own errors, at least of attempting to explain more fully the processes and actions which had caused so much dissatisfaction. Instead it chose, albeit reluctantly, to lump Kronstadt with the generalized notion of the counter-revolution as a whole, and thus justify itself in advance and by definition rather than reason.

The idea that the Party as such could not, equally by definition, ever be wrong, that mistakes might be rectified but never admitted as mistakes, really dates from this time. Thirty-five years later a Soviet government was again to refuse to recognize an uprising for what it was, and write it off as a counter-revolutionary plot. The Hungarian revolt of 1956 was the direct and linear descendant of Kronstadt. On both occasions foreign communists, while admitting the historical need and justification for ruthless counter-measures, were severely to question themselves and their faith in a Soviet Union smothering a genuinely proletarian revolt.

39 Poster of 1919
honouring
the Red Fleet

40, 41 The peasants get their land. Above, a peasant in the Ferghana region, Uzbekistan, is given a certificate of land and livestock. Below, propaganda of about 1920 illustrating the advantages of joining a collective farm

III CONSOLIDATION: 1921–1928

(The civil war and foreign intervention followed so soon after the October revolution that Bolshevik economic policy in these first few years could do little but cope with one long emergency) Accordingly any judgment on its long-term implications or intentions is hard to make. The decrees breaking up the landlord estates and the distribution of land in the form of small-holdings to the peasants were little more than confirmation of an existing and irreversible process (Lenin and the Bolsheviks had a clearer sense of the nature and importance of the peasant problem and its relationship with their own survival than probably any other socialists in Europe) (and this in turn was no more than a recognition of the primacy of the peasants in Russia). But even so, Bolshevik analysis of economic conditions on the land lacked the subtlety with which industrial problems were being analysed – even if not yet solved. (The Bolsheviks divided the peasantry into three groups – the *kulaks*, who owned land and equipment (to be dispossessed as counter-revolutionaries); the poor peasant, who as often as not was a landless labourer and on whom the Bolsheviks pinned their revolutionary hopes in the country-side; and in between, the third and ambiguous category of the middle peasant) The Bolshevik attitude to this last group hovered uncertainly between support and enmity. When viewed as inimical, the middle peasant moved up conceptually to become a *kulak*, or capitalist exploiter; when supported, the borderline between poor and middle peasant tended to disappear, and the latter was merely an efficient poor peasant who had benefited from the distribution of land – a belated Stolypin product. The three categories were thus as much political as economic.

In any case there was little chance to embody this rural class analysis in the exigencies of agricultural policy in the first years after the revolution. The civil war and the threat of famine forced the Soviet government to take away with one hand much of what it had given with the other, and the polite nomenclature merely served to cloak these inevitable actions in Marxist respectability – though gradually they tended to obscure the clarity with which the Party was able to assess the realities of the situation. One of the illusions of the civil war period was that the middle peasants had large reserves of grain; if only these could be extracted by requisitioning, the food shortage

would quickly be solved. In the majority of cases this proved false. But in the meantime the Bolsheviks created an instrument of coercion by forming committees of poor peasants whose class antagonism to their richer fellows was intended to produce the necessary results. Their efforts were supplemented by more direct measures; in 1919 city Soviets sent out dozens of detachments numbering thousands of people to enforce the collection of foodstuffs, grain, meat, fats, sugar and potatoes. This system of official raids had been one of the major causes of the final break with the Left Socialist-Revolutionaries. It too eventually proved futile, because the peasants were simply unable to supply the requirements of the government. Moreover, they concealed what little stocks they had and kept their sowing to the minimum required to feed themselves and their families. The peasant, by the nature of things, can always respond to pressure by more effective passive resistance than any other economic producer.

Apart from any deliberate return to subsistence, agricultural production for obvious reasons dropped disastrously between 1917 and 1920. The Soviet government tried various expedients to raise the amount of available grain, but most of these failed. After the end of the civil war, the problem of satisfying the peasants became urgent if food production was to increase. The New Economic Policy was thus concerned with alleviating peasant unrest, but even more with an attempt to find a longer-term solution to the imbalance in the relationship between agricultural and industrial production.

42, 43 The peasants defend their land. A meeting votes in favour of resistance to the invaders, 1918. Right, anti-Bolshevik propaganda of about 1919 makes the most of government requisitioning of food

The communist leaders were in the last resort prepared to alienate the peasant if food deliveries could be assured. What they could not do for any length of time at that stage was to live with both a political problem of resentment and an economic one of chronic shortages in the countryside. In one sense NEP solved this problem within three years, by abolishing the requisition of grain and replacing it with a tax in kind which left the peasant a surplus to trade on the open market, but it eventually created what the Soviet leaders came to regard as a peasant stranglehold on industry. The severity of collectivization after 1928 was to a large extent a measure of the success of NEP in the previous five years. The entire history of Soviet agricultural policy for fifty years can ultimately be reduced to the variable play on the alternatives of more extraction or more overall production, the former a repressive policy emphasizing force, the latter a more liberal policy of incentives. The either–or quality of agricultural policy was already foreshadowed in the debates which preceded NEP, and continued to be voiced throughout its seven years' existence.

In industry the basic intention of simply expropriating all middle-class owners had also been mitigated by expediency after 1918. Many of the former owners still found themselves willy-nilly running their own factories. As in the army, sheer technical need reduced the crucial test from membership of a social class to ability and a willingness to co-operate. Here, too, the period of civil war obscured the overall policy direction of the Bolsheviks,

and forced it to resort to devices with strictly short-term aims. It was not until November 1920, the month in which Wrangel, the last White Russian commander, was defeated in the north, that full-scale nationalization of all enterprises employing more than five workers and possessing some form of mechanical power, or ten workers without any mechanical power, was put into effect. Even then a period of transition was envisaged during which former owners continued as managers until new arrangements were made.

At least as important as legal ownership was the problem of organizing the administration of industry at the top. Already at this early date certain basic trends in Soviet industry had become evident, particularly the top-heavy concentration of trusts and ministries in Moscow. The system was not uniformly effective, and from the beginning of January 1919 Bolshevik leaders were protesting against maladministration and inefficiency in industry. Their remedy, however, was always still more centralization and stress on a national outlook which would place the need of the whole of society before that of individual enterprises. Getting rid of profit as the central motivation of economic activity was one thing, but this did not solve the self-regarding concerns of individual managers with the welfare of their particular enterprises at the expense of the national economy as a whole.

(Industry suffered even more severely than agriculture. By 1920 production was one-fifth of the 1913 level. In both industry and agriculture the breakdown of production and distribution resulted in informal mechanisms of exchange which bypassed the money economy altogether, and ruined all attempts to plan and allocate production) The process of 'bagging' (the barter of all kinds of produce particularly for food) and informal exchange between producers developed to such an extent that the formal organs of government lost control of much of the economy. The currency had become completely devalued, and the presses were producing paper money of uncertain value. In this sense, too, NEP provided not so much a basic departure from the past as a means of coping with a situation that existed already.

For all its faults and shortcomings, and even though it represented a series of *ad hoc* measures to combat emergency situations, the crisis period known as War Communism from 1917 to 1921 was not without its theoretical defenders. There were Bolsheviks, especially economists like Larin and

44, 45 More anti-revolution-
ary propaganda, *c.* 1919. Consumer goods are in desperately
short supply (above) and
money has lost its value (right)

СЧАСТЛИВЫЙ
РАБОЧІЙ ВЪ
СОВДЕПІИ

Kritsman, for whom the physical exchange of production between units, both agricultural and industrial, under the planned or at least rigidly controlled supervision of central authority spelt the implementation of socialism. These people believed that money was itself a phenomenon of the bourgeois market; its very existence as a medium of exchange necessarily led to its being regarded as an object worth possessing and thus diverted interest and energy from pure production to problems of exchange. The Soviet emphasis on production at the expense of distribution and exchange was fundamental, and has been shared by all communists since the October revolution. One of the inevitable 'vulgarizations' of Soviet Marxism, which viewed the Bolshevik régime as 'making up for' the absence of a previous bourgeois revolution in Russia, was precisely this primacy of accumulation. But War Communism had carried this logic farther than Lenin and most senior leaders were prepared to go. By the end of 1920 the time had come to distinguish the haphazardness and shortcomings of War Communism from the ideas behind it. For many, the failure of War Communism was not so much that it was a mistaken policy, but that the policy was not effectively carried out.

ПОМОГИ

ПОМНИ о ГОЛОДАЮЩИХ!

The influence of this attitude can be measured by the reluctance and heart-searching with which Lenin's NEP was debated and continued each year after 1921. It was always considered a retreat from an ideal – to some the total abandonment of socialist perspectives in the economy, to others a temporary relaxation which gave the necessary priority to economic growth. From 1925 onwards the discussion of the effects of NEP on socialism and class relations in the Soviet Union was to provide the main battleground for programmatic and personal leadership in the Party.

It is also necessary to bear in mind that the tendency towards centralization and concentration of industry into large units, which flourished during the period of War Communism, was not new but a continuation of established Tsarist tradition and processes of government. Just as the French Revolution reverted, albeit in the name of Liberty, Equality and Fraternity, to the centrally controlled administrative perspectives of the old régime, and reversed the anarchic tendency for local autonomy of the years 1789–91, so the Bolsheviks, with all their desire for basic change, took up the centralizing tradition of imperial Russia under the banner of the new democracy. The period of War Communism must therefore be understood as a basic contra-diction between centralization of control and decentralized anarchy in practice. NEP, on the other hand, relaxed much of the economic centraliza-tion. By legalizing and institutionalizing the individual motivation in small-scale production and exchange, allowing private entrepreneurs not only to own small industrial enterprises but to conduct most of the retail trade, it re-incorporated these practices within a wider area of social control while formally abandoning the attempt to supplant them with direct politico-economic decisions from the top. One of the major problems during the NEP period was how to assess accurately what was happening and would happen in the economy. As production increased in industry and agriculture, the Bolshevik leadership became uncomfortably aware that the increase was in large measure outside its control. This conflict, too, was to have repercussions in the political arena after Lenin's death.

But such economic generalizations, however essential, cannot do justice to the feeling of the times – and this formative period of Bolshevik rule has become part of the mythology of the modern Soviet Union. Every disaster that could happen to a country did happen – invasion, civil war, famine, economic disruption. Millions of people died. If individual hardships and tragedies could be computed into meaningful units of measurement, then the statistical shortages of the economy of War Communism would be matched by a high level of human unhappiness. In the last resort NEP meant the lightening of an almost intolerable burden on society – not political pressure which might generate social change, but physical and human misery which weighed on society like an incubus. Whatever the arguments about the theoretical merits of NEP Lenin, its determined proponent, knew that the change had become imperative, and that this froze all arguments in a vacuum of sheer irrelevance. Lenin has often been described as a superb tactician, and his enemies have accused him of being willing to sacrifice his frequently articulated principles to practical advantage whenever necessary. This is to confuse realism with pragmatism. By 1921, as we have seen, the maintenance of Soviet power had become the main preoccupation of the Bolsheviks, and Lenin certainly felt that the régime was in danger unless a period of consolidation and construction took place. He knew better than others to what extent this implied a retreat, and he always referred to NEP as such.

The full extent of the necessity for NEP can be understood only if we relate the foreign situation to the domestic state of the new Soviet republic. War Communism at home had reflected the confused but hopeful prospects of revolution abroad. In November 1918 the great moment seemed to have struck. In spite of the failure of the rising in Berlin in January 1919, sympathetic Soviet republics sprang up in Hamburg and Munich, in Hungary, the Baltic states and Finland in the course of the same year. In almost all Western countries separate Communist Parties were being founded, drawing their main inspiration from the Bolshevik revolution even if there was no feeling whatever of intellectual or disciplinary subordination to the Bolsheviks. Already during the war Lenin had spoken of the need to create a new and separate Third International on the ruins of the 'stinking corpse' of the Second. At the end of 1918 the time had come to make this a practical reality. The Constituent Congress in March 1919 was composed of few actual delegates and rather more odd foreign sympathizers who happened to be in Moscow at the time. Only considerable sleight of hand and Bolshevik determination converted the preliminary conference that had been announced into a Constituent Congress. None the less the Bolsheviks felt certain that their act of faith would soon take on concrete reality and grow into a powerful international movement. Their hopes were above all pinned on the German Party, even though its outstanding leaders, Luxemburg and Liebknecht, had been murdered two months earlier.

The revolutionary year 1919 in Europe coincided with the height of the civil war in Russia. Despite the establishment of one or two bureaux of the International and the despatch of a few emissaries (of whom Karl Radek became the archetype), the Soviet republic was able to exercise little influence on events in Europe. To start with, these emissaries more or less made their own policy, since there was no apparatus of control or even communication from Moscow and certainly no desire to impose detailed rules of conduct. The western view of Bolshevism as an international conspiracy had at least one justification in that the activities of Comintern agents were necessarily conspiratorial. Legal communist mass movements were in an early stage of creation, and the very hazards of coming to and going from Moscow gave the whole operation a cloak-and-dagger appearance, the importance of which was much overrated.

The revolutionary fermentation in western Europe continued to a greater or lesser extent in various countries until 1921. The Soviet leaders regarded each setback – the destruction of the few Soviet republics in 1919, the ban-

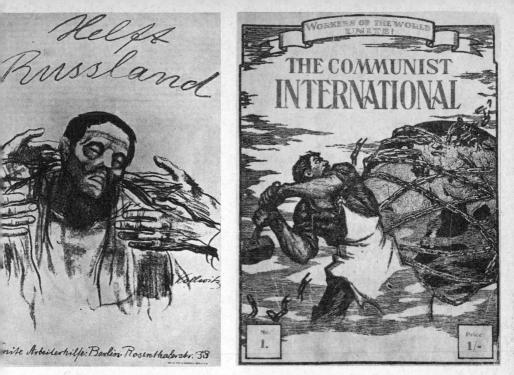

49, 50 Foreign communists appeal for help for the struggling Soviet republic. Left, 'Help Russia', a poster by Käthe Kollwitz; and the first issue of the English-language *Communist International*

ning of the German Communist Party in the same year, the unexpected tranquillity of labour in England and France – as a temporary ebb. By now they were becoming imprisoned in the historical chronology of their own revolutions, and foreign analogies with the period from March to November 1917 were frequent. The Kapp putsch in March 1920 in Germany, when two former generals attempted a coup d'état against the German Social Democratic government in Berlin, was hailed as an obvious parallel with the Kornilov affair – though the impotence and vacillation of the German Communist Party compared unfavourably with the resolute action with which the Bolsheviks responded to this event. The analogy of the Soviet October was applied to events a year later, when there was a communist-inspired rising of workers, especially coal-miners, in central Germany. The complete failure of this attempt caused the first serious acknowledgment in Moscow that the revolutionary fire in western Europe might really be dying out. If Western capitalism could achieve a measure of stability, and the economic upheaval of the war begin to be repaired, the Soviet republic would have to recognize that it was unique and learn to fend for itself for more than just the immediate future. The measures of revolutionary exigency might thus develop into something more permanent: *rien ne dure comme le provisoire*!

Apart from this general change in the revolutionary rhythm, the Bolsheviks were also forced to reassess their own role within it. The conception of a revolutionary war had survived the peace of Brest Litovsk, but with Russia in the grip of foreign intervention and White counter-revolution, little direct support could be given to communist risings abroad. By 1920, however, when only a belated remnant of Denikin's army under the command of Wrangel remained to be dealt with, the use of the new battle-tried Red Army to aid foreign revolutions became at least a possibility; and the Polish invasion of Russia in April 1920 provided the opportunity. By June the Polish forces, who had occupied Kiev and most of the western Ukraine in early May, were in full retreat; the Red Army stood on the Polish border. The Allied conference at Spa in Belgium, still in search of stable post-war frontiers in Europe, was thrown into a panic at the prospect of a revolutionary offensive from the East. The Bolshevik leaders were divided as to the prospects of a revolution carried on the point of bayonets – Lenin sceptical, others enthusiastic. Enthusiasm prevailed, but the effort proved a failure, for the national loyalties of the Poles overrode any class sympathies, and it was the workers of Warsaw who helped the Polish army under its French advisers to organize the capital's defences. By mid-August the Poles were counter-attacking and now it was the turn of the Red Army to retreat. In October an armistice was signed along the line occupied by the two armies, and the Treaty of Riga on 18 March 1921 confirmed these temporary frontiers. The adventure had cost Russia a vital piece of territory in the north-east, occupied largely by White Russians. Worse still, it had been a heavy blow to revolutionary prestige, especially in contrast to the hopes of a few months earlier. In future the bayonets of revolution would have to be provided by the indigenous workers of the country concerned. Thus by 1921 both revolutionary war and internally generated revolution abroad seemed to offer little prospect of success. The Bolsheviks changed their tactics. In future the organization would come from Moscow, but the effort would have to be local. There were as yet neither means nor wish to enforce detailed Bolshevik control on foreign parties, but the blocking of the other two alternative ways to revolution made such developments possible.

The first effects of the new tactic had nothing to do with the export of Bolshevism, and little with the October revolution. Rather they were based on a much earlier event: Lenin's analysis of the causes of the Second International's collapse while he was in Switzerland at the beginning of the war. Now that the Third International had been founded, a rigorous and uniform set of conditions was evolved for those seeking to join – and they were by no means all self-styled Communist Parties. In one or two cases, two competing parties from one country both joined the Third International – at least for a while. War and the Russian revolution had radicalized the European left. Small but independent Communist Parties had sprung up all over Europe since 1918. Another group of socialist parties with a much larger mass following than the communists were teetering uncertainly between the final organizational break with social-democracy and the fear of the full radical leap to communism. These were the left's floating voters, radical in times of revolutionary flow, more cautious and hence conservative within their labour cosmos when the tide was ebbing. Such parties were welcome to join the new International provided they accepted its discipline, broke openly with social-democracy and declared their commitment to social revolution. The Second Congress of the International in July 1920, attended by over 200 delegates from thirty-five countries, was already much more representative and impressive than its predecessor the year before. It worked out twenty-one precise conditions for remaining in, or joining, the Comintern.

Over the course of the next twelve months, three of Europe's largest socialist parties, the German, French and Italian (the last already a member of the International) discussed these conditions. No doubt their choice looks clearer today than it did then, for we know that the French leaders, Cachin and Froissard, who brought the twenty-one conditions back from Moscow and presented them to the socialist party congress at Tours in December 1920, were not too clear about what they were being asked to do – or even how many actual conditions there were! As before, the Russians were especially anxious about the Germans, who would surely set the pattern for the others. The USPD or Independent Socialist Party, founded in 1917 as a middle way between socialist support for the war and extreme left-wing denunciation of it, was being pulled towards right as well as left. The decision of the extraordinary congress at Halle in October 1920 would be the acid test for floating revolutionaries. In the event, and with much Russian persuasion behind as well as before the scenes, the USPD decided to adhere to the Comintern, to accept the twenty-one conditions, and to negotiate with the German communists for a new United Communist Party – even though Martov, freshly emigrated from Soviet Russia, pleaded with them not to do so. For the first time a Communist Party in western Europe had acquired a genuine mass following. The French socialists followed two months later, shedding their name and a right-wing minority to go with it.

Only the Italians reacted differently. Their congress met at Leghorn in January 1921. The Italian Socialist Party also wanted to join the Comintern, but was not prepared to evict its right wing. The twenty-first condition could thus not be fulfilled. Here it was the communists who proved to be the dissident minority. The Italians departed from the Third International, leaving behind a small group of communists under the leadership of Bordiga. By this time, too, the enlarged German Communist Party had been in the throes of its first major leadership crisis. The first contingent of ex-communists was beginning to form, abused by the Bolsheviks as traitors and replying publicly in kind about interference from Moscow. For the first time the newspaper-reading public was given insight into the processes of these outlandish political activists.

But for all the abuse on both sides, the distinction between breaches of Party discipline and the right to dissent from policy in private was carefully observed as long as Lenin was alive. This vital difference was only extinguished after his death, when, under the leadership of Zinoviev, an insensitive ruffian, the Comintern was more and more directly subordinated to Russian control and direction, while foreign dissent from its directives and policies got even shorter shrift than opposition at home. Whereas the foreign parties had originally been only too conscious of their inferiority, mainly because of the magnitude of the Bolshevik achievement ('What am I,' Serrati had explained in 1920, 'compared with Comrade Lenin? He is leader of the Russian revolution. I represent a tiny party'), they were now openly reminded by the Russians themselves of their inferiority and dependence. Comintern headquarters could not under existing circumstances be anywhere but in Moscow, although the possibility of locating it in the West had originally been discussed. Growing Bolshevik domination of the International was at first a product of circumstances rather than any deliberate Russian wish to turn the international revolutionary movement into the foreign army of the Russian Communist Party. None the less, especially after Lenin's death, the Russians did complete the process until the Comintern and the whole international movement was under their control.

The Bolshevik success with the Third International of communist or at least sympathetic parties sponsored further attempts to project Bolshevik international influence in two other fields. The Profintern was founded under the chairmanship of Lozovsky, with the intention of creating a communist-influenced international trade union movement, and to assist communist penetration of reformist trade unions in the West. Though it continued formally to exist for quite a long period, its success was marginal. This was partly because the Bolsheviks' uncompromising attitude towards the relation-

51 Caricature of G. Y. Zinoviev, chairman of the Comintern, who was executed in 1936, during the Stalin régime

ship between Party and trade unions downgraded the status of the latter in the Soviet Union to a mere appendage of the Party in the political sphere, leaving them to perform more or less welfare and disciplinary functions – and partly because the organized trade union movements in the West resisted attempts to draw them into its orbit. A similar, and even less successful organization was Krestintern, an international for peasants. This was founded in autumn 1923 and was intended to exert influence on peasant movements, particularly in eastern and south-eastern Europe. But here again the difficulties of the Party leadership with the peasants in the Soviet Union, and above all the miscalculation as to the nature of peasant parties in south-eastern Europe, led eventually to severe setbacks. After the Croatian Republican People's Party had disowned Krestintern, and the disastrous fiasco of the Bulgarian Communist Party and its relations with Stambolisky's Peasant Union in Bulgaria, the bankruptcy of this policy became evident, and the Soviet leaders, particularly Bukharin, head of the Comintern, lost interest in the whole exercise. In future the few attempts to influence agrarian policies in south-eastern Europe were handled more or less effectively through local Communist Parties alone.

Though international communism was the Bolsheviks' main foreign preoccupation during these early years, the alternative dimension of contact with foreign governments had also to be considered. Any hopes of dispensing with this dimension altogether immediately after the revolution, by concentrating efforts exclusively on foreign soldiers and workers through revolutionary appeals and subversion, were short-lived. The Western Allies had attempted at least to maintain some sort of contact with the new government from November 1917 until the period of intervention, although they were careful not to accord it any recognition. Contact was minimal, especially during 1919 when Soviet Russia was diplomatically isolated and more or less effectively blockaded. The initial attempts of the Soviet government to open up trade channels were discouraged, especially since their offer to pay in gold was met by the refusal of foreign banks to accept what they considered to be stolen gold which might one day be reclaimed by the original owners. But a country of Russia's size could not long be ignored. From 1920 onwards informal Soviet delegations were appearing in many Western capitals, mostly under the leadership of the indefatigable Krasin, director of Bolshevik procurement raids on banks before the war, now engineer in charge of the roving Soviet delegation for foreign trade (which meant procurement of essential imports). Some tentative American efforts to help relieve the famine of 1920–1 provided additional contact. But these were exceptions, whose importance the Soviet leaders tended to exaggerate. Lenin was at this time heavily dependent on a motley collection of foreign sympathizers residing in Moscow for advice on Soviet policy towards foreign governments. Though he himself was quite prepared to extend diplomatic contacts and use diplomacy to further the advantage of the Soviet Union, foreign governments viewed the Bolsheviks as unreliable diplomatic partners – both as revolutionaries and because they had published the secret treaties of their predecessors. Perhaps Soviet isolation in 1919–20 was partly responsible for the relative lack of discrimination which the Bolshevik leadership showed towards foreign left-wing sympathizers on the periphery of communism proper. Lenin, for instance, urged the British communists not to be too severe in their conditions for co-operation with sympathetic groups. It was to be another year at least before the Comintern worked out its stiff conditions for adherence, and the respective diplomatic and revolutionary channels of communication became increasingly distinct and separated.

Between 1917 and 1921 Soviet diplomacy was a makeshift affair. Radek, sent to help and advise the German communists, sat in a Berlin prison and received not only comrades of the left but emissaries of the German army. A policy of rapprochement with Germany was gradually emerging from 1921 onwards – not from any ideological sympathy but because both countries saw an immediate short-term interest. Both were diplomatically isolated – losers in the European power game. For Russia particularly the rapprochement with Germany represented a breach in the diplomatic quarantine. All that had previously been achieved was a trade agreement with Britain concluded in March 1921, and three treaties with Russia's immediate neighbours Persia, Afghanistan and Turkey, concerned mainly with frontier problems. Attempts had been made to approach France and other European countries, but apart from Britain only Germany responded with a provisional trade agreement in May 1921. The Russo-Polish conflict of 1920 for the first time confronted the Soviet republic with the European powers as self-appointed arbiters of European peace. For Soviet Russia the Genoa Conference of April 1922 on general European questions was thus a major breakthrough, even though nothing of consequence was agreed – no recognition for the Soviet government, no foreign investments and no conclusion of the financial claims against it. From Genoa to Rapallo is a few hours' drive, and the Russians proceeded straight from one to the other. The Germans too had reason for dissatisfaction with the Western powers. The concrete results which the Russians had failed to obtain at Genoa were more than compensated for by the Rapallo Treaty signed on 16 April 1922. To some extent the Soviet government had even succeeded in getting the best of both sides, for it had played one off against the other. From now on the chancelleries of Europe could no longer ignore the Red republic.

Henceforward Soviet diplomacy began to take on a life of its own. Organizationally separated from the immediate concerns of the international revolution, it induced in Moscow as well as abroad a permanent situation of double-dealing: support of revolutionary movements against governments with whom the Soviet Union would be negotiating or trying to negotiate. This paradox operated on several levels. At the executive level it produced a separation of effort which tended to isolate the two components; the structure of the Comintern and of Soviet diplomacy became personally and organizationally distinct. There were no more Radeks after 1923. Only at the top, in the Politburo and the Council of Peoples Commissars, could the threads be drawn together. Here the organizational and instrumental separation was resolved by laying down explicit or implicit priorities: *either* the international revolution, *or* the interests of the Soviet Union as a state, expressed through its diplomatic activities. Frequently the two marched hand in hand. But often they did not, and it was on these occasions that the priorities were invoked. The distinction became particularly relevant once a negative decision had been reached about immediate prospects of foreign revolution. By 1921, when the revolutionary wave was definitely perceived to be ebbing, the demands of Soviet diplomacy began to take priority over foreign revolution. Soviet diplomats were more directly controllable than foreign communists: the former servants, the latter allies, however unequal, of the Soviet state. Accordingly the latter had to be organized through the Comintern until they too became reliable instruments and ambassadors of Soviet policy. Only then could the necessary priorities be controlled and put into efficient operation.

The most important single act of consolidation which marked the end of the period of War Communism was the formal constitution of the Union of Soviet Socialist Republics, the USSR, at the end of 1922. The system of alliances among the republics remaining in the Soviet orbit after four years of flux was replaced by a federation. Each constituent republic was nominally separate and independent. In view of the huge geographical, demographic and industrial preponderance of one of its members, the Russian Federal Republic (RSFSR), and the sharp differences in the levels of education and cultural attainments, the constitutional arrangements did not entirely cover the reality of the situation (even the Russian word *soyuz* means both alliance and union without distinguishing clearly between them). This imparted an air of *maquillage* to the constitutional arrangements now and in the future, and western commentators have readily scoffed at the discrepancy between Soviet constitutional fiction and political reality. This criticism has the same justification as any exposure of legal fictions; what is important in any constitution is not the letter but the spirit in which it is worked in practice. The proclamation of the USSR on 30 December 1922, followed by the elaboration of the relevant constitutional document in the following year, at least formalized the existence of the new state, and seemed to give expression to the freely expressed demands of all the peoples committed to the new form of Soviet rule.

To appreciate the extent to which the Soviet Union represented a genuine federation rather than a Russian imposition of unity in federal form it is necessary to glance back briefly at the events leading to its formation. The constitutional arrangements which followed the Bolshevik seizure of power in November 1917 had applied exclusively to the Russian Soviet Republic. A glance at a map will show what territory this involved; right from the start the RSFSR not only provided the prototype for the development of Party and Soviet rule, but also constituted by far the largest and most important territory of what was to become in 1922 the Soviet Union. At that stage it contained over 90 per cent of the area, 70 per cent of the population and much the greatest part of industry. After the defeat of Germany and the withdrawal of German troops, Bolshevik governments were installed first in White Russia, with its capital at Minsk, and then in the Ukraine at Kiev. Soviet rule there was several times endangered and upset;

only at the end of 1920 was a Bolshevik government firmly installed with Rakovsky, an old Bolshevik, in command. In the north the attempt to institute Soviet régimes in the Baltic republics and Finland failed. These countries effectively passed out of the Soviet orbit, as did Poland and Bessarabia which had been seized by Rumania. In the Caucasus and the Far East, as well as in central Asia, nominally independent republics under Bolshevik leadership had been established by 1922, though not without many vicissitudes.

There was no area of political thought in which the Bolsheviks differed more sharply or self-consciously from their predecessors and from Russian tradition in general than over the treatment of nationalities. Lenin, whose nationality policy evolved at a time when revolution was in the distant future and all policy was primarily concerned to bring it nearer, firmly believed that self-determination should be accorded after the seizure of power; and in the immediate post-revolutionary period the right to secede from Russia was available to all who claimed it. It was naturally assumed that in the border territories the seizure of power by Bolshevik sympathizers would cause them to opt for a close form of alliance, if not federation, with the RSFSR. Bolshevik policy did not specify independence, but merely the right to claim it if desired. The fact that the secession of the Baltic republics and Finland was accompanied by suppression of nascent revolutionary régimes quickly soured many Bolsheviks' liberality towards the former subject-nations of the Russian empire; the exercise of the right to secede proved to be based on counter-revolutionary policies and was being claimed by counter-revolutionary régimes.

In any case the problem of secession had been settled within eighteen months of the October revolution. What remained was the far more difficult and intractable relationship between the Russian Soviet Republic and those neighbouring territories with sympathetic régimes, seeking close alliance and possibly federation. Once again even the elaborate discussion of nationality problems by Lenin and others before 1917 could not possibly encompass every eventuality, and there were large gaps which had to be filled more or less *ad hoc* – by decisions which in the event altered the substance of the policy considerably. It is much easier for us today to trace this change or corrosion of intentions, a process which continued until ideology and practice no longer corresponded. The commitment to fight mercilessly against Great Russian chauvinism remained in the forefront of Bolshevik thinking. The Twelfth Party Congress in April 1923, at which the constitutional provisions of the new USSR were hammered out, pronounced uncompromisingly on this subject. 'The Union of Republics is regarded by a considerable number of Soviet officials, central as well as local, not so much as a union of equal states pledged to guarantee the free development of national republics, but as a step towards the liquidation of the republics and the beginning of the so-called "one and indivisible" republic. . . . Such attitudes are anti-proletarian and reactionary.' This seemed to contradict the Party programme, which stated that any such federal union was only 'one of the transitional forms towards complete unity'. This contrast was of course deliberate, not accidental – a dialectical unity. It reflects Lenin's emphasis on the unity of *national independence* with *Party centralization*, together with his justification of this policy. In 1923 the objections to the form of the proposed federation, in which a Supreme Soviet, consisting of a Council of Nationalities co-equal with a Council of the Union based on more or less equal constituencies, was created, came mostly from the delegates of the Russian republic – and were easily refuted with the accusation of Russian chauvinism. There is no reason to believe that those who thought about, and helped to formulate, the structure of the new union were motivated by anything other than the desire to shore up national rights and wishes against the Russification tradition of the Tsarist past. Hence the creation of constitutionally sovereign federal republics with considerable areas of independence, and for the smaller nationalities the status of autonomous republics within the Union – a federal arrangement which formally remained untouched and still exists today. Eventually, in fact, a great measure of centralization was achieved in practice through Party control and the taut structure of the economy, and the conflict between decentralized administration and centralized economy was resolved at the expense of the former.

The man in charge of the Commissariat for Nationalities, into whose lap these problems fell in practice, was Joseph Vissaryonovich Stalin, and it was in this context that he made his first major contribution to the history of the Soviet Union. Just before the war he had been Bolshevik spokesman and Lenin's research expert on nationality questions; since Lenin himself was extremely interested in this problem, Stalin's main role had been the exposition of Lenin's ideas. Now Lenin had other things to do, and the task of stabilizing and systematizing the relationship between the republics fell increasingly to Stalin. Whatever he was to become, at this time he was above all a good Party man, for whom, perhaps even more than for Lenin, the problem of internal Party cohesion had absolute primacy. Though he subscribed sincerely to Lenin's nationality policy, he viewed any conflict between Party and national perspectives almost exclusively from a Party point of view and acted accordingly. The narrow-minded and ruthless pursuit of his policy in the Georgian Soviet Republic, where Stalin was on his own home ground (he was born on 21 December 1879 in Gori), created a

52 'Soviets plus electrification equals communism.' The first electric bulb in a village in Bryansk Province, 1928

major scandal. Mainly at Stalin's instigation the Menshevik government of Georgia, opposed to the Bolsheviks in party matters but anxious for close republic-to-republic relations with the RSFSR, had been forcibly overthrown in February 1921 by an invading force, the political adviser to which was a henchman of Stalin. Although a Bolshevik government was now installed, it too resisted the dispositions of Moscow regarding the future arrangements of the area, in particular the proposal for a Transcaucasian regional republic in which Georgia would be submerged for the sake of administrative tidiness. Stalin organized a purge of the Party to remove the recalcitrant leaders whom he publicly labelled as bourgeois nationalist deviationists.

The Commissariat of Nationalities had been instrumental in founding autonomous republics within the RSFSR from 1918 onwards, promoting cultural autonomy, institutionalizing the separate languages of less advanced peoples and yet at the same time bringing to these semi-independent nationalities in the south and east of the Russian republic the first benefits of modernity without the more obvious overtones of Russian domination. Within the Party the reputation of the department was high. Lenin at any rate had no hesitation in accepting Stalin's version of the Georgia incident, even though Trotsky was already protesting at the end of 1921 against the high-handedness of Stalin's Commissariat.

Stalin's action proved unexpectedly significant. For the first time – but not for the last – enforcement of Party discipline had formally overruled official Bolshevik policy towards non-Russian nationalities. Though the Party leadership was always to be sensitive towards the maintenance of cultural autonomy, and the republics were always to have their own elaborate government and Party structure, henceforward all this took on something of the quality of ideological window-dressing. Effective centralized control was always available through *Party* channels, even though the federal nature of the *Soviet* structure was scrupulously observed. The boundaries within which all assertions of independence and separateness could take place were narrowly circumscribed. Local nationalism became one of the most serious (as well as one of the earliest) political crimes for which opponents were to be condemned without benefit of argument or appeal. The Soviet Union had hardly been created before cleansing campaigns against manifestations of nationalism were to take their toll of local Bolsheviks who were too much concerned with their own particular areas and too little with the general state of the union. Sultan-Galiyev, Prime Minister of the Tatar ASSR, who advocated the formation of a special Moslem Communist Party in 1923, was the first National Republic head to be arrested, and the Ukrainian Bolshevik leadership was repeatedly purged in the 1930s and 1940s for adulterating the pure wine of Marxism-Leninism with bourgeois nationalism – paying undue *political* attention to peculiar Ukrainian needs. The same problem in more directly economic guise persisted as late as the 1960s in the shape of regionalism in the Regional Economic Councils (*sovnarkhozy*).

The Georgian incident put Stalin, the individual, in the limelight for the first time, and brought him into an open conflict with Lenin. After thirty-five years of unremitting work, and the enormous and many-sided responsibilities of government since 1917, Lenin suffered a stroke at the end of May 1922. Almost speechless, he was sent away to the countryside by his doctors. He did not recover until August and returned to work only in October of that year. Having supported Stalin's action in Georgia all through the spring of 1922, Lenin on his return suddenly and sharply turned against him. He cabled the Georgian Bolsheviks a pledge of support for their position at the coming Party Congress due in April 1923. Then in the middle of December he had a second stroke. He was not to come to Moscow again. Between mid-December and 9 March 1923, when he had the third stroke which put him out of action completely, his participation in the affairs of the Party and nation was confined to a few dictated notes and letters from outside.

On looking more closely at the Georgian problem, Lenin had suddenly changed his mind with the brusqueness typical of the man. He was the first to throw the book at Bolsheviks who offended against fundamental principles – far more readily than many of his colleagues who in the last few years had begun to complain about the erosion of free expression in the Party. Lenin now concluded that Stalin's handling of his Bolshevik opponents was a flagrant instance of the high-handedness of the dominant central culture towards smaller nations against which Lenin had fought all his life. This sudden insight crystallized other dissatisfactions which Lenin had expressed at various times over the last twelve months, most frequently the sense of bureaucratization in Party work. Though Lenin himself had supported many of the actual decisions which led to this bureaucratization, like the defeat of the workers' opposition and the suppression of opposition platforms at the Tenth Congress, there is no real contradiction here. For the issue was no longer tactics or policy but basic values, the Bolshevik state of mind. One of Lenin's biographers has suggested that this sudden sensitivity to fundamentals at the end of his life, which made him apparently change his mind on a number of issues and express for the first and last time a general sense of malaise, 'of shame before the workers of Russia', as he put it, was due to an instinctive awareness of his own impending death. Perhaps his inability to participate in the major and minor questions of every day, so firmly part of Lenin's political life, contributed to a sudden propensity for introspection. In any case his decision to stage a fight with Stalin over the treatment of smaller nationalities now combined with a determination to attack frontally the current bureaucratic spirit of the Party. Pre-eminently responsible for it was the Party Secretariat – the locus of bureaucracy *par excellence*. Here a different set of threads led once again to Stalin, General Secretary of the Central Committee since 3 April 1922.

The Central Committee of the Party was the official ruling body for which the Politburo, consisting of its most eminent leaders, acted as an inner Party cabinet. The Secretaries of the Central Committee were intended as a means to make the decisions of Politburo and Central Committee effective, and to act as an executive staff. There was also an organization bureau (Orgburo) which dealt with problems of staffing, not only at the centre but in the republics and at still lower levels of the Party hierarchy. Since putting the right man in the right place was vital in a party which always placed great emphasis on correct organization, these top secretarial posts were given to senior and experienced Bolsheviks. But it was only in April 1922 that a single General Secretary was set above his colleagues. The position went to Stalin because nobody else wanted the job; his colleagues' almost unanimous agreement on his own eminent suitability was a backhanded compliment. It was detailed, back-breaking and routine work which gave little or no opportunity for cerebration, much less for speaking; most of the senior Bolsheviks, already over-burdened with tasks in Party, state and Comintern, considered this as a necessary but unrewarding chore. Stalin had always shown himself sound and efficient, if intellectually undistinguished. Above all he appeared to be personally unambitious.

In his contacts and correspondence with Stalin in the last few months of 1922 Lenin, once he had become aware of Stalin's high-handedness, now showed himself sensitive to Stalin's shortcomings as a whole. 'People dilate at great length and very flippantly on the notion of "proletarian" culture. We would be more than satisfied with real bourgeois culture for a start, and would be glad if we could dispense with the cruder types of pre-bourgeois culture, such as bureaucratic or serf-culture' – this was Lenin's reply to attempts to persuade him that the operations of the Party bureaucracy reflected a new proletarian culture of the future. He discovered, in addition, how unpleasant Stalin could be in personal dealings when crossed. Stalin appeared at Lenin's house in the country and abused his wife, Krupskaya, when she prevented him from seeing the stricken leader. Lenin dictated suggestions to Trotsky on how the problem might be dealt with, and also a sharp note to Stalin, in which he broke off all personal relations. In the first week of March Lenin was set for a major campaign from his sick-bed against Stalin. When this proved beyond him, he made his views plain in a testament with a special postscript. But on 9 March all this was guillotined by his third stroke. Though he lingered on precariously until 21 January 1924, he was totally incapacitated during these last ten months.

Stalin was well aware of these feelings and moves. His tactics at the Twelfth Congress in April were simple and effective. In order to stifle the impending attacks against him, which most of the other members of the Politburo knew about in general, he was prepared to concede everything immediately at issue. His speech on the nationality question was mild in the extreme, his praise of Lenin fulsome. He also attempted to build a bridge to Trotsky. He was prepared to condemn wholeheartedly, though in general terms, those who interfered in the affairs of the federal republic. Indeed, the resolution of the Congress condemning unitary perspectives in the Party, which has been cited above, was drafted by him. So he obtained his two major desires; neither Lenin's notes and proposals on the national question, nor his personal strictures on Stalin, were published. Lenin's illness was thus doubly useful to him. It removed the unquestionably authoritative attack on Stalin personally, and provided a reason for shelving the substantive questions at the very moment when the paralysis of the great leader enjoined the greatest possible demonstration of unanimity among the leading Bolsheviks.

The same argument applied even more strongly after Lenin's death. In the testament dictated almost a year earlier he had attempted to appraise his immediate colleagues. All had faults as well as virtues. The postscript amended Lenin's provisional characterization of Stalin to sharp and unrelieved condemnation: 'Stalin is too rude and such a shortcoming is unsupportable in the office of General Secretary. Hence I propose to our comrades that a way be found to remove Stalin from that position and appoint another man . . . more patient, more loyal, politer and more attentive to other comrades, less capricious and so on. This is not a trifle – or at least it is one that may acquire decisive significance.' Lenin did not designate a successor, nor did he feel that it was up to him to do so, but he did hope that his evaluation would be taken into account when the time came. In the event the very significance that Lenin had stressed was the best possible reason for shelving the testament; with Lenin dead how must such criticisms of his closest colleagues appear to the Soviet people as a whole? Putting Lenin's testament into temporary cold storage proved equivalent to putting it on ice almost for good, for Stalin was not going to resuscitate this damning document. Though made public by Trotsky in his memoirs after his expulsion from the Soviet Union, and known to most of Stalin's colleagues and many of his later victims, it was formally published only in the 1960s, more than ten years after Stalin's death. Those who agreed that the public interest demanded withholding publication at the time were never able to undo this fatal decision, for any attempt to publish later was bound to look like opportunist spite or ambition.

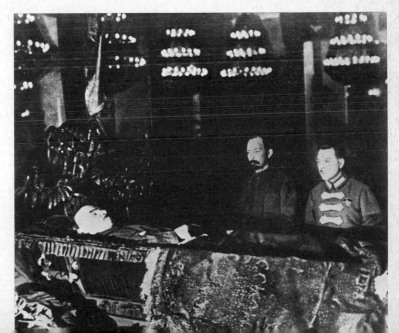

53 The end of an era. Dzerzhinsky and Voroshilov at Lenin's coffin, Moscow, 1924

Coincidences are normally a poor way of explaining events, and historians are rightly chary of relying on them for their interpretations. But if any single coincidence may be said to be significant in the history of the Soviet Union, it is the date of Lenin's death. If Lenin had lived, Stalin could not have survived the attack on him, nor would he have been in any position to adopt the later complex and shifting system of alliances which enabled him to out-manœuvre all his colleagues in the next six years. Stalin's method of survival, which later and quite imperceptibly changed into domination, consisted initially of making sure that he was never alone, always in the centre and hence able to play both ends against the middle. He was helped in this by the Leninist tradition of dramatic tactical changes, a dialectic which related these swings of course to consistent goals firmly rooted in Marxism. Stalin was to make a speciality of what soon came to be called 'Leninism' (a term of which Lenin would never have approved). This enabled him to clutch the intellectual and policy mantle of Lenin and wrap himself in it. Leninism came to be a set of ideas interpreted exclusively by Stalin, and quite unadorned by Lenin's rules of behaviour – the personal humility and simplicity, the readiness to admit mistakes, and above all the total freedom from personal ambition which had always been associated with the revered name. In practice, moreover, this body of ideas came to represent the dialectical combination of the immediately improbable with the long-term inevitable, expressed in sharp and sometimes grotesque paradoxes where peace meant war and black meant white and some were more equal than others – the formulations which George Orwell's later caricature made famous. The point was that its association with Lenin gave it a surface continuity and respect-ability, the value of which cannot be overestimated. Only in this way could the virtue of Lenin's *necessity*, which had produced paradoxes between tactics and ideology, turn into the virtue of Stalinist *orthodoxy*, which made them an intrinsic part of Bolshevik life.

The first line-up of the leaders in 1923 was more or less Trotsky against the rest. In the course of 1924 Stalin, Zinoviev and Kamenev hacked away at Trotsky's basis of support and isolated him within the leadership. Perhaps the widespread determination among senior Bolsheviks to ensure that Trotsky should not accede to the position of pre-eminence after Lenin's death was also a coincidence favourable to Stalin, for it gave the suppression of Lenin's views on Stalin a twist of tactical necessity. Having steered a grave and successful path through the potentially turbulent waters of the Twelfth Congress, Stalin was saved, mainly by Zinoviev's direct support, at an equally fateful meeting of the Central Committee in May 1924. Behind every substantive issue at the time loomed the question of succession. Whatever

54, 55, 56 NEP and the battle for the leadership after Lenin's death. Above left, Trotsky in 1924, the alchemist with all the answers. Above right, Bukharin and Preobrazhensky fight a duel of 'resolutions' over strategy; their reluctant seconds are Zinoviev and Piatakov, representing right and left policies. Below, militiaman Kamenev bars the way to the NEP sledge their public declarations about solidarity, collective leadership and the self-generating wisdom of the Party, the Bolshevik leaders quickly realized only too well how dependent they had been on Lenin, not so much as leader but as arbiter and guide. (Emerging from a Central Committee meeting in the summer of 1923, one senior communist slapped two of his colleagues on the back and exclaimed with delighted surprise: 'It's remarkable, we can manage thus far without the old man after all.') As far as personality was concerned, Trotsky clearly rose high above the rest – in the multiplicity of his talents, his oratorical gifts, his sharp mind and his ruthless determination. Yet it was precisely these qualities which made him suspect to his colleagues – in addition to the professional resentment of men who had been loyal Bolsheviks since the first decade of the century rather than a long-standing opponent who joined the Bolsheviks as an equal colleague only just before the great days of the October revolution. If the danger of a predominant personality existed in anyone's mind at that moment, it was Lev Trotsky. He was personally unpopular in the middle levels of the Party, especially among the intellectuals and the Party officials. The closing of ranks against him seemed natural as well as correct to a majority in the Party.

Already there was an ominous difference between the clashes during Lenin's life and the present confrontation between Trotsky and the Stalin-Zinoviev-Kamenev *troika*. This was no longer a leadership quarrel in the former sense. The campaign against Trotsky in 1924 was the first of the great ideological mobilizations, in which thousands of agitators at hundreds of specially convened meetings mouthed mechanical phrases accusing Trotsky of all kinds of heinous deviations before passive and often uncomprehending audiences, who voted more out of sympathy with the strong feelings demonstrated from on high than from any real conviction. Stalin's position as General Secretary was crucial here, since the selection of officials, their placing in strategic positions, and the connection between their appointment and their vote in Party struggles all became ominously related.

So Trotsky was defeated. He made no real attempt to bid for the leadership, disdained counter-manœuvres and merely defended his policy and the position of his supporters – though with a surprising lack of toughness and determination. Such support as he obtained came from genuine conviction rather than factional organization. In the Comintern only the Poles raised the problem of procedure; apart from the substantive issue as to who was right or wrong, was such a campaign of denunciation the proper way to handle differences between senior Party comrades? Stalin was never to forgive the Polish leadership for raising the matter. There were, of course, major problems of debate at the time round which the leadership struggles

57 Trotsky
as Commissar for War,
1923–4

structured themselves more or less tightly. The most important of these was concerned with NEP, its status, assessment and future. Trotsky began to oppose some of the consequences of the new course, particularly the tilting of the economic scales against heavy in favour of light industry and especially agriculture. This developed into a more basic argument for or against 'socialism in one country'. Here Trotsky was joined by a number of supporters. But these were policy alignments which he was not prepared at this stage to turn into an opposition platform, nor to organize into a disciplined voting bloc. He had been among the strongest supporters of the resolutions at the Tenth Congress in 1921 banning factions.

In the course of 1925 a right wing led by Bukharin emerged within the Party in support of the continuation of NEP, and also for Stalin's concept of 'socialism in one country'. Zinoviev and Kamenev now swung into opposition and attempted to use Stalin's own tactics against him. They hoped that a tactical alliance with Trotsky would redress the balance – not to restore Trotsky to his former lustre, but to at least even out what they now perceived as the benefits of victory for Stalin and Bukharin, who since Lenin's death had emerged as the Party's most able theoretician. But it was too late for any such restoration of balance. At the Fourteenth Congress the two old Bolsheviks, Zinoviev and Kamenev, were met by howls of disapproval while Stalin received thunderous applause. Zinoviev's attempt to rally the Leningrad delegation, who were his power base, produced a geographical demarcation which was regarded with disapproval. Zinoviev's supporters were publicly reminded of his opposition to the coup d'état of November 1917. Lenin had stated in his testament that this should not be held against them, but they could not cite this vital document! In desperation Zinoviev and Kamenev now turned towards Trotsky for help, but to no avail. 'Discipline, discipline' was the cry that drowned their efforts, and Trotsky, perhaps not entirely aware of what he was up against, submitted with almost deliberate self-immolation to its demands ('No man can be right against the Party'). Thus he cut himself off once again from his potential allies. And all the time Stalin's apparatus was advancing in size and cohesion.

In October 1925 most of the senior members of the opposition signed a statement in which they admitted their offence against the statutes of the Party: the attempt to organize a faction. But the intensity of the conflict and the consequences of defeat were both becoming greater all the time. Trotsky and Zinoviev were expelled from the Politburo, from the Central Committee and finally, in early November 1927, from the Party. The Fifteenth Congress in December of that year expelled seventy-five leading members of the opposition. Trotsky was deported to remote Alma Ata, capital of the Kirgiz Republic. In spite of his immense intellect and stature he had become a Bolshevik without a party, an acute observer and critic rather than a maker of history. Soon he was to be expelled from the Soviet Union altogether and except for his writings and the loyalty of a small sect of devoted followers fall into historical oblivion. On 20 August 1940 he was murdered in Mexico by an agent of Stalin.

Zinoviev and Kamenev capitulated and were re-admitted to the Party. They withdrew all criticism and were able to lead a precarious Party existence for a few more years, but ended in prison and were finally executed in 1936. Stalin and the so-called 'right' remained in power. NEP and 'socialism in one country' continued, for the moment without further criticism. But it was still not the end of factionalism, as many Bolsheviks who supported the severe disciplinary measures had hoped. Within eighteen months NEP was thrown overboard with the same brutal abruptness with which it had begun. The right-wing platform was jerked from under the feet of Bukharin and his friends; Stalin now turned his steamroller against them. By 1930 they too had been denounced. Stalin was left with a disciplined and completely loyal Politburo, a larger Central Committee whose importance was secondary, and a highly centralized Party, which he managed and controlled, and which acclaimed him with monolithic and indeed monotonous enthusiasm at every Congress. The General Secretary who represented the impersonal collective wisdom of the Party moved on to elaborate the greatest personality cult of modern times, rivalled only by that of Hitler in Germany.

In assessing Stalin's rise to supreme power we have to bear in mind not only his crucial control over the Party machinery but the fact that behind the arguments over policy there existed a fundamental pair of alternatives which surpassed the Marxist framework within which the debate was conducted. The new Soviet republic had been born in crisis and civil war. NEP promised a respite from social crisis, a return to normality. From the 'Platform of the forty-six' in 1923 (see p. 109) to Trotsky's final cry of alarm in 1927, the host of dissenting critics had emphasized the existence of crisis, the need for an end to the relaxation of NEP and 'socialism in one country', and a new period of *Sturm und Drang*. Was Bolshevism to be not so much permanent revolution as perpetual crisis? And could the Party handle it in the present state of affairs at home and abroad? Faced with these underlying fears of Congress delegates Stalin was soothing and calm, responding to all appeals for action with the assurance that there was no crisis – except that which the opposition was trying to manufacture. The issue was thus a conflict between two creeds – one of achievement and consolidation, the other of crisis and self-sacrifice. It is a common enough conflict in history and Stalin's victory was made possible because he personified just that sense of achievement, of 'calm after the storm', that delegates wanted to see. And Stalin's own achievement may well be his correct ordering of priorities. He was not responsible for the Party's withdrawal into autonomy and self-regard during this period; that had been Lenin's policy. But he defended this autonomy against those who wanted, perhaps prematurely, to do battle on the frontiers of society once more. His policy was first to gain complete command of the political system before launching out to control the environment, that is, to transform Bolshevik *consensus*, with its fireworks and argument and occasional threats of disciplinary action, into Bolshevik *conformity*, with only the top leadership in a position to express opinion and dissent. We shall never know how the opposition policy would have fared in the mid-Twenties; all we know is that Stalin succeeded in the Thirties.

These upheavals in the old Bolshevik leadership of Party and state during NEP were matched by important transformations at lower levels. Members of the Communist Party were not able to assess the full nature and issues of the leadership struggle. Manipulated and manœuvred as they were bound to be for lack of detailed information, they yet played a decisive part in making the changes possible. There was almost a virtue in the savagery with which the Party now dealt with even its most distinguished members – for had not Lenin always talked of the need for Bolshevik ruthlessness and steel-like hardness? Was not Stalin carrying out these intentions to the letter? The fact that Lenin had meant something very different and restricted the need for ruthlessness to the fight against counter-revolution, while preserving a much larger measure of toleration for his colleagues, was perhaps too subtle to be fully appreciated, especially as Stalin was determined to obliterate the difference. The new hardness of dealing with opposition in the Party at every level thus appeared as the inevitable consequence of everything that had happened hitherto, not the dangerous and reprehensible new tendency it really was. The surprising thing about the touching scene of Trotsky's secret departure for Alma Ata at a Moscow station in December 1927 was not the tears of the few people who had come to watch him go, but the fact that there was no crowd to see off the greatest surviving architect of Bolshevik victory. Sentiment was not a recognized medium of political exchange in Bolshevik Russia.

The change in attitude, which accompanied and made possible Stalin's rise to supreme power, was also matched by changes in the membership of the Party. The first big and deliberately organized purge had taken place in 1922, under Stalin's direction and with Lenin's approval. The number of Party and candidate members fell from 730,000 in March 1921 to 485,000 in January 1923 (the number of Party members at the beginning of 1918 is generally given as about 120,000). Its composition changed in the first few years of the 1920s, as efforts were made to stress the industrial proletarian base through special facilities for candidates of worker origin. The intellectual element in the Party accordingly declined; though sporadic efforts were made to recruit suitable candidates in the countryside, the requirements and qualifications for entry made this almost hopeless. Of course a substantial proportion of members were soldiers (mainly officers) serving in the Red Army at the time. The official figures published early in 1923 state that 45 per cent of the Party were workers, 26 per cent peasants and 29 per cent others. As a ruling party, it was obliged to protect itself against those who merely wanted to climb on a bandwagon of status or privilege, who abused the possession of power without the compensatory self-sacrifice and work. Except in the top posts of administration and industry, membership of the Party was not directly linked to employment in state or profession. It was a purely political choice and demanded a variety of political activities over and above one's job. Only much later under Stalin were politics and status or employment to become fused.

At the same time there was an enormous extension of the Party's activities during this period. Special attention was paid to the lower echelons, the Party cells and their relationship with the population at large. The apparatus of agitation, which ultimately turned into Stalin's great pedagogical and mobilization instrument after 1929, was built up in these years. For the vast majority of people in Russia, whether Party members or not, the goings-on in the Kremlin were still of secondary importance in the 1920s. The gap between centre and periphery was vast, in terms of both social and geographical distance. Concentration on the leadership struggle gives the mistaken impression that it took place before a fascinated audience of millions of informed participants.

Abroad, too, the disengagement from immediate possibilities of revolution turned the Communist Parties back in on themselves. The leadership which emerged in the course of 1924 in Germany, Italy, France and Poland was committed to a platform of Bolshevization – not in terms of programmatic content, but with regard to much more fundamental questions of attitude and organization. The Party of the new type was no longer to be organized, like the Social Democrats, on the basis of electoral constituencies but of cells in street, factory or institution, a radical departure from the accepted social unit of political organization. The leadership struggle in Russia was, of course, reflected in rifts and factions within Communist Parties everywhere. Just as the Communist Party of the Soviet Union evicted or demoted some of its most talented members and most famous intellectual adherents, foreign Parties also lost some of their most interesting personalities during this period. Unrelieved by the excitement and glamour of political power, the drive for conformity in foreign Parties appeared much more self-destructive and irrational than in the Soviet Union, the resultant monolithic conformity sectarian and uninspiring. Yet the Soviet debate over 'socialism in one country' in many ways had even greater relevance for foreign Parties, for Stalin's policy now dumped them in a desert of stable capitalism, on which the Soviet Union itself had turned its back.

How, then, to maintain loyalty of the membership? The answer was that the cause of world revolution now had to be viewed only through the health and strength of the Soviet Union, and communist policy abroad was wholly shaped to this end. Anti-communist writers have often pointed out the enormous fraud Stalin perpetrated on the revolutionary energy and hopes of foreign communists in this way, but the fact remains that Communist Parties were able to adapt to such perspectives and to survive, in many cases to prosper. Certainly world communism, from 1926 onwards, can only be understood if this almost total identification with the concrete entity of the Soviet Union is appreciated – not by outside imposition, but as a result of self-conscious conviction on the part of leaders and militants. It was their conviction that world revolution and the power of the Soviet Union were identical that induced a number of communists to deploy their energies in straightforward espionage on behalf of the USSR; this too could be recognized as a direct contribution to the advent of socialism at home. In practice, of course, this change of perspective coincided with the tightening of control. Those who objected to one or other were pushed unceremoniously out of the Party, into opposition or limbo.

The objective possibilities for manœuvre were becoming severely limited on all sides. Communist policy in capitalist countries was in future destined to alternate between collaboration with other left-wing parties, especially the Social Democrats, against the right, and an almost indiscriminate denigration of social-democracy as the 'labour' representative of bourgeois society. After 1923 the whole concept of class war began to lose its wider social context, and as often as not became a means of communist self-definition vis-à-vis other left-wing parties. Too often class war appeared to consist of an exclusive struggle against social-democracy and little else.

At the same time the gap between the Comintern and the official diplomatic channels of Soviet foreign policy became wider. At the beginning of February 1924 the British government followed up commercial relations with diplomatic recognition of the USSR. The British beat the Italians by a short week. France followed a year later; only the United States still remained adamant in its refusal to recognize the Soviet Union – a capacity for ignoring realities which the United States was to demonstrate again after the Second World War with regard to mainland China. At the same time relations with Germany were hardly impaired by the attempted uprising in Saxony of October 1923, even though this failure brought about a complete shake-up of the German communist leadership. In addition, NEP postulated closer economic relations with the capitalist West – both for the import of scarce machinery, such as tractors, and for the export of grain surpluses. The extension of Soviet diplomacy was thus accompanied by a reduction of the revolutionary activities of the Comintern.

If the demands of international communism and Soviet diplomacy resulted in alternatives in the West, they appeared to coincide much more closely in the Far East, where communist room for manœuvre was much greater. Lenin had emphasized the revolutionary possibilities which might result from an alliance between Communist Parties and the rising nationalist sentiment against colonial rule, which was making its first impact in Asia. Though communists must remain organizationally and intellectually distinct and not merge with bourgeois nationalist movements, an alliance or collaboration was certainly desirable – just as the Bolsheviks had collaborated with the Socialist-Revolutionaries for a limited time and purpose. In China the Comintern, under the rising influence of Stalin, urged the Chinese Communist Party to co-operate with the Kuomintang, in fact to join it. The

Communist Party was to form one part of the bloc of the four progressive classes and in return the Kuomintang was encouraged to seek representation in the executive of the Comintern. Russian military advisers were sent to help Chiang Kai-shek. This was the practical application of 'socialism in one country' to the Comintern; already we can see the beginnings of Stalin's basic isolationism – an orientation which was to prove such a dominating factor before and after the Second World War.

In the event, Stalin's China policy failed disastrously. The Kuomintang leadership rounded on the communists in the summer of 1927, expelled them from the bloc and arrested all the Party officials on whom it could lay hands. More in self-defence than with any hope of success Moscow now encouraged insurrection. The first attempt in September 1927 failed lamentably. A further attempt, this time under the direct guidance of two Comintern emissaries, took place in Canton in December 1927, and the Kuomintang retorted with wholesale slaughter. The organized remnants of the Chinese Communist Party were forced into a long period of retreat and reconstruction. Li Li-san and the Chinese Party leadership quietly drew some important conclusions from the recent failure; communist policy shifted from its concentration on revolution in the towns to greater interest in the countryside.

There was, of course, no open breach between China and Moscow; lip service was always paid to the new left line of the Comintern. Only in 1930 did the Comintern, after the removal of Bukharin from the chairmanship, attempt to bring the Chinese into line. Pavel Mif and twenty-eight of the brighter graduates of the Soviet Sun-Yat-Sen Academy – the so-called 'returned students' – were sent to remove Li Li-san and his friends from power. The Chinese Party fought more obdurately than most for its leaders and its line, but by 1931 Comintern direction, in spite of the failure of its policies, had been re-established. It was not until the Great March of 1934-5 to the inner Chinese fastness, and the final emergence of Mao Tse-tung as leading spirit in the Party at the Tsun-yi conference in January 1935, that effective Comintern control was eliminated. The towns were now more or less abandoned as an area of communist influence in favour of a People's War, firmly based on the countryside. Although the Chinese leadership continued to make outward obeisance to international discipline, Mao was speaking nothing but the truth when he celebrated the formal dissolution of the Comintern in 1943 with an article entitled 'The Comintern Has Long Ceased to Meddle in Our Affairs'. But the chief interest of these later manifestations of independence in the Chinese Party is their very uniqueness in the communist movement as a whole, especially when compared with the rigid discipline in the West.

Between 1923 and 1929 opposition to Stalin in the Soviet Union crystallized round both foreign policy and internal problems. The concept of 'socialism in one country' had originally appeared in December 1924 as a specific counterpoise to Trotsky's theory of permanent revolution. It covered both 'halves' of NEP: the internal self-reliance of the Soviet Union and the acceptance of a temporary end to the revolutionary period abroad. Trotsky criticized both aspects. Internally, the policy of relying on the peasant to produce the necessary surpluses for motives of gain was characterized as an abandonment of the industrial priorities of socialism. Abroad, the failure of the German rising of 1923 and later the Chinese débâcle of 1927 were attacked as the result of the leadership's failure to guide the international movement, which had confused the revolutionary proletariat abroad. By 1927 Trotsky was openly posing the basic problem of how the Soviet Union could conceivably survive on its own against the strengthened and newly aggressive capitalist countries which surrounded it.

There was by this time a general sense of dissatisfaction with the situation at home and abroad. The successes of Soviet diplomacy three years earlier had been frittered away; diplomatic relations with the British government were in danger, and Soviet collaboration with British trade unions had come up against the sternest opposition from the General Council. At home the *kulaks* seemed to be having things entirely their own way. Many Bolsheviks feared that the Soviet Union was degenerating into a capitalist society. But only Trotsky integrated all these individual laments into a general attack on the policy of the leadership, and he did so on his own behalf, not that of an opposition or alternative leadership. The Leninist sensitivity to dissatisfaction had disappeared; Zinoviev – in many ways the typical man of 1923–4 – did not notice it, and in the following period Stalin did not have to. Collectivization and industrialization, the twin hammers of change which were to knock so hard against the recently attained stability, now pre-empted the foreign and domestic criticisms of the NEP period, by providing a new impetus at a moment when that stabilization seemed to have run its course.

The best way to understand the NEP period in the Soviet Union is to regard it as one of substantial autonomy in different sectors of society, leading eventually to fears of a challenge to the political order and consequently to the massive response of Stalinism from 1928 onwards. Only in this way can the paradox between apparent consolidation and conciliation on the one hand, and increasingly sharp conflict on the other, be meaningfully resolved. We have seen how the leadership struggle in the Party developed; how the erosion of open discussion and disagreement gave way to subterranean manœuvring under the banner of unity, how the middle and lower ranks of the Party were used and aligned to support the General Secretary and his allies, how both the Soviet Party and the Comintern were organized into a disciplined, unitary force which totally identified the Soviet leadership with the strategy and tactics of 'socialism in one country'. We need not assume that it was all done by force and fraud; the real driving force of acceptance and commitment was the conviction among the growing stratum of Party officials that the emergence of a consensus from above was both desirable and historically necessary, and that Stalin was the right man for the job.

In short, NEP witnessed a sort of withdrawal of the political sub-system, the Party, into itself. Preoccupied with its internal affairs, it relaxed its hold over other sectors of society. By creating a situation of relative autonomy for itself, the Party was able to keep the influence of society and economy at bay, and reorganize itself in relative isolation, uninfluenced by outside considerations. That is why the leadership struggles of the 1920s appear so 'personal', so apparently unrelated to the needs and problems of the social sector. Thus while society as a whole, and especially the economy, was benefiting from a period of respite and consolidation, the Party as an autonomous political sub-system was undergoing sharp internal conflicts and reorganization. What emerged by 1930 was a very different Communist Party from that which had inaugurated NEP in 1921.

Let us look at the rest of society by way of contrast. At the beginning of the period a sustained attempt had been made to revive the structure of Soviets as organs of democratic government. During the civil war these organs of local government had for all intents and purposes lapsed; the Party was not only acting as dynamo and supervisor but literally administering the country. In order to make them effective as well as responsible, the Soviets – originally over-large committees of local government – now evolved a structure of committees and secretaries similar to that of the Party itself. Responsibilities and power were increasingly placed in the hands of individuals and small groups within the larger units. Every attempt was made, however, to keep Soviet democracy alive by insisting on regular meetings of Soviets from villages up to large administrative areas, and on maximum participation at these meetings. This made, and indeed was intended to make, Soviet democracy a mirror of the relations between existing social strata. NEP produced a crop of small entrepreneurs in the towns, 'the Nepmen', and middle or large peasants in the countryside. The persistent fear of the Party leaders, that economic liberalization was bound to result in the greater social and political influence of Nepmen, in the long run counteracted and inhibited the development of the Soviets; they inevitably conflicted with the social perspectives and class basis of the Party itself. With the coming of industrialization, and the great increase in Party manipulation of society, the development of the Soviet system of government in any sense independent of Party control rapidly withered away, and was not heard of again until the 1960s.

Within the Soviet economy NEP brilliantly attained its overall objectives: relaxation of intolerable pressures and dislocations, and growth of production in industry as well as agriculture. But there were serious problems too – especially for a régime committed to the fundamental manipulability of the economy, and against the free operation of 'bourgeois' market forces. For one thing, the liberalization of the economy exposed what the command economy of the civil war period and the large number of men under arms had effectively disguised – substantial unemployment in industry, and masked unemployment in the countryside. Increases in productivity could now be measured directly in terms of unemployment. Secondly, the 'scissors' crisis of 1923 had presented the Soviet leaders with the basic problem which remained with them throughout NEP. At first agricultural prices were disastrously low (about half the level of 1913), while industrial prices were maintained at almost twice the 1913 level by the determination of the newly established trusts to hoard their products rather than sell – carrying their rapidly accumulating stocks with cheap credit from the state banks. This dilemma could be resolved only by pressure on industry to sell its products, and by increasing the purchasing power of the peasants. It was as much a failure of distribution as of production – a typically capitalist phenomenon. Hence still further measures of liberalization were taken during 1923 and 1924. By 1924 the scissors had closed and in fact now went the other way, so that for the rest of the NEP period agricultural prices tended to be high while industrial prices sagged. The chief sufferer under NEP was heavy industry, where production growth was generally lagging, while agriculture and light industry flourished – helped by a number of good harvests. This imbalance too could, in the view of the leadership, be settled only by more doses of liberalization, stimulating agricultural production by incentives of profit, availability of machinery and desirable consumer goods on which profits might be expended. Small-scale private industry was accordingly encouraged to produce consumer goods which might attract the peasant. All the problems of a classical market economy jumped up in the face of a leadership ideologically committed to a very different type of economy, and ill-equipped to deal with this one. Monetary reform ensured a return towards a sounder currency, in which the peasants could have confidence, but this in turn reduced the credit available for industry. In the search for means to stimulate agricultural production, some of Russia's hard-earned foreign reserves from the export of grain were utilized to purchase tractors.

The leadership, and especially the 'left' opposition, were preoccupied from 1923 onwards with the social and political consequences of NEP. The nationalized sector of agriculture, the so-called *sovkhozy* or state farms, represented only a minute proportion of the whole. The immediate beneficiaries of NEP were those peasants who had, or could acquire, sufficient resources to accumulate more land. Would NEP produce a class of richer peasants or *kulaks* whose interests must irrevocably be opposed to the longer-term prospects of socialism, and possibly even to Bolshevik rule? It is in this context that the worries of the leadership and the more specific criticisms of what was loosely (and wrongly) called *the* Opposition must be understood. As early as 15 October 1923, forty-six otherwise unorganized members of the Party's Central Committee presented statements of reservations about the 'State of the Nation', most of which criticized the lack of firm control by the leadership – then (ironically) Stalin, Zinoviev and Kamenev. If the height of the government's pro-*kulak* policy could be dated to about the end of 1925, from then onwards more frequent anti-*kulak* statements could be heard from within the leading echelons of the Party. No detailed definition of what constituted a *kulak* was officially attempted; the preoccupation remained general rather than particular. Nevertheless from 1925 to 1928 there was a growing sense of malaise over the wider socio-political implications of NEP. At the end of 1928, when NEP was brusquely reversed, the timing may have provided surprise and even shock, but intellectually the frontal attack on the *kulak* had long been prepared. Hatred of the *kulak* was a widespread and accepted phenomenon in the whole of the Communist Party. The problem was to focus it and bring it into acceptable action.

So much then for the economy. The rest of social life was far freer still from direct Party control or manipulation. In a wider social sense, NEP was a period of great and free experiment. Many of the experiments went beyond the immediate competence and fund of ideas of the Party leaders. Once the civil war was over, many old, long-buried anarchic desires and ideas burst to the surface and found concrete expression in education, literature, the arts, and in the morality of personal relationships. The Bolsheviks themselves constituted almost a conservative force regarding the latter. Madame Kollontai, a leading communist and a member of the workers' opposition, had been a staunch advocate of free love; in 1919 she had stated that under socialism 'the family is no longer necessary'. Lenin and the official Party institutions disagreed with this completely. Yet in 1926 a law was passed making divorce even easier than its predecessor of December 1917. Jurisdiction over the validity or annulment of marriages was taken from the courts to the office of the registrar. The state in any case took over most of the responsibility for the children of broken marriages. In 1925 the Commissar for Health felt it incumbent on him to state officially that 'if you want to solve the sexual problem, be a public worker, a party member, not a stallion or a brood mare'. But in spite of official efforts, it was a period of considerable licence.

In the field of religion NEP also witnessed a great number of experiments. Good Bolsheviks were rigid atheists, and could not approve of any form of religious practice. But the full machinery of the state was only to be used against the church in 1929, after industrialization had begun; for the moment the assault against an outmoded idolatry was left to Party persuasion rather than state action. A so-called 'living church' broke away from the Russian Orthodox Church in an attempt to find a viable compromise between religion and the new system, but split into discordant sects almost from the day of its inception. Nothing shows the fever of experimentation so clearly as the curious history of that very curious institution *Orgkomsekt*, set up early in 1921 and surviving till 1927, whose task was to be the imposition of acceptably communist forms of settlement on a number of Russian communal religious sects like the Molokane, and which would have perpetuated this strongly religious phenomenon.

The period also produced an enormous crop of creative literature, little of it Bolshevik or even directly Bolshevik-inspired. Instead, the revolutionary perspective of the writers was anarchist. October 1917 was regarded not as a class struggle but as a form of individual liberation without any need for a class revolution but as a form of individual liberation without any need for the superstructure of socialism within which the political leaders insisted on confining it. Many of the writers of the period, like Pilnyak, had distinct Slavophil tendencies, and saw in the October revolution a renewal of the basic Russia to which they were still committed. Apart from Maxim Gorky only Mayakovsky became the exponent of anything resembling a specifically Bolshevik revolutionary literature. These were to be the best days of Soviet literature and the creative arts – writers like Babel, Pasternak, Zamyatin, Belyi, Vsevolod Ivanov, experimental film producers like Eisenstein and Pudovkin, the great theatre of Meyerhold. One need only read *Novy Mir* in 1967 to see the nostalgia and respect with which these artists and writers are now regarded.

The big debate of the period revolved round the notion of proletarian culture. Should the Party encourage this phenomenon – whatever it might be – or should bourgeois concepts of culture be accepted and propagated as Lenin insisted, until a totally transformed society would eventually produce its own new culture form, the content of which nobody could yet foresee? Here the Bolsheviks were as divided as the writers themselves, with Lunacharsky and Bogdanov firmly upholding the notion and proponents of *Proletkult* against Lenin and the more orthodox leaders, who were supported on the literary front by the so-called 'fellow travellers'. It was not a problem that agitated everybody, since there was so many other things to do. Perhaps Lenin saw more clearly here than his opponents, for the postulate of a proletarian culture and attempts to structure behaviour in accordance with it could not but be artificial in a society whose base still remained largely untouched by the surface political changes of the October revolution. Above all a proletarian culture could all too easily destroy what socialism in fact intended to build up; its accent was on freedom of expression rather than cohesiveness and discipline, self-sacrifice and work. And indeed behind the intellectual proponents of *Proletkult* there lurked the control organization of RAPP (the writers' association) and institutional bullies like Leopold Averbakh, the executor of Stalin's later purge of literature and forerunner of Zhdanov. Such luxuries as the claim to a special culture were possible in developed countries but hardly in a Russia of whose backwardness Lenin was always painfully conscious. For Lenin, culture was not something which intellectuals tossed at each other but a process in which everyone in society was involved. When Stalin later tried to integrate his own version of proletarian culture with the social changes of the Bolshevik industrial revolution, he extended and reshaped Lenin's version of cultural diffusion by laying down the precise pedagogical lines that writers and artists had to follow. Culture ceased to be social self-expression and became an enormous process of brutally simplified learning. Such a culture could not in any conceivable sense be called brilliant; rather it reflected bourgeois culture in its most vulgar and primitive aspects.

But perhaps the most exciting experiments were introduced in the educational field. In the city schools particularly (none of these changes had much effect on the countryside) there was a drastic revision of curricula. An attempt was made to integrate children's work round one large theme, known as the complex method, instead of dividing it into separate and distinct subjects. Group work among students was encouraged. Above all the traditional and disciplinarian relationship between teachers and pupils tended to give way to new forms of collaboration; 'the teacher must be an organizer, an assistant, an instructor and above all an older comrade, but not a superior officer'. Indeed in some cases pupils were invited to demonstrate and report any attempt to impose excessive discipline. Pupil self-government in the schools was encouraged. These experiments naturally had disorganizing results as well, particularly in a period of great shortages of buildings, teachers and books. There were complaints in the Party that nothing of any use was taught in the experimental schools, that the whole system of education had become a hotbed of anarchists. The Party now had its own youth organization, Komsomol, which had been 'captured' by the Party as its exclusive recruiting ground some time after the Komsomol's foundation as a relatively free or unattached institution for revolutionary youth. In fact the ordinary schools were not politically organized until the late 1920s or even later; official arguments were concerned with quality and type of education as a broad social rather than narrowly political process. In this context the Party viewed schools as one form of education, on a par with practical participation in various forms of work, both in industry and on the land. Visiting factories, museums, theatres and other places of public entertainment became an essential part of the school curriculum and remained so even after the re-imposition of orthodoxy after 1929. So did the emphasis on racial and sexual equality, even though the brief period of formal co-education was later broken up again under Stalin into separate schools for boys and girls.

58 Model of an experimental stage set by
Vladimir Tatlin, 1923

59, 60 The sustained Soviet campaign against illiteracy. Below, a 1920 poster, 'Knowledge breaks the chains of slavery'. Right, training peasants to read in the village of Algeshi, Chuvash SSR, 1928

61, 62 Two designs by El Lissitzky: a cover design for a book by Mayakovsky, 1929 (left), and a cover of an arts magazine edited by Lissitzky and Ilya Ehrenburg in Berlin in 1922 (above)

113

These examples show the way in which contrary trends revolved round each other during NEP. If we separate the areas of politics and economy from the rest of society we find considerable autonomy in each area and widely ranging norms within them. The area of politics became increasingly concerned with internal discipline and control; the economy was only partially controlled, though viewed with growing misgivings by the political leaders. Finally the rest of society was left free from direct political control, thus producing an explosion of experiment and creative energy. After 1929 this period of experimental self-expression in society was over for good. Such experiments as would now take place were controlled from above, and limited to the field of industry, technology and organization. The remainder of social life was committed to adapt itself to these priorities. The pattern was to be one in which experiment and conformity were closely structured, with precise allocation of suitable areas for each. Hence the enormous cultural conservatism of Soviet man as we have come to know him today, and the slowness and difficulty in re-defining new and acceptable areas for experiment and conformity in the post-Stalin era of full industrialization.

The Bolsheviks' second, industrial revolution began in 1928. It was this which ultimately gave the Soviet Union its modern character, the basic image and the various associations implied by the term Soviet Communism. In one sense this second revolution completed the work of Lenin and the old Bolsheviks. Where they had superimposed a new philosophy, a new instrument of rule and a new group of leaders on an ancient predominantly peasant society, Stalin and his new Bolsheviks reached right down into every cranny of conservatism with their plans of steel and concrete and their foreshortened but irresistible Marxist pedagogy. By the time Stalin died the Soviet Union had been completely transformed – not only as an international entity but as a society.

Yet the industrial revolution also involved a sharp break with Bolshevik tradition. Hitherto there had always been a clear contrast between the Party and the rest of society, between the Soviet Union and the capitalist world. 'We' and 'they' had been marked off from each other by discontinuities and conflicts which Marxists had learnt to recognize as instinctively as they told night from day. Indeed, they had been taught to maintain the distinction as sacred. Now these frontiers were to shift and to dissolve; people became capitalists or representatives of capitalist interests by edict, because Stalin and the leadership said so. The doctrine of objective treachery came to mean that you could spend a lifetime in the cause of communism, and yet be objectively bourgeois – a traitor. This applied not only to individuals, but also to classes. The *kulaks* were transformed almost overnight from a tolerated necessity to a hostile class which must be destroyed at once. Writers who criticized or merely abstained from praising Bolshevik achievements; workers who grumbled openly; Party members who dissented or merely confused yesterday's truth with today's heresy; finally leaders who disagreed (or had disagreed) with Stalin openly or potentially – all were cast into the same fatal mould of class enemies and bourgeois traitors. Bolsheviks had always conducted their polemics in hard language, following a tradition dating back long beyond Marx to 1793. But when Stalin, in one of his homely phrases, referred to 'dogs returning to their own dung' it was not only an earthy epithet but a reduction to subhumanity – and could well be a mandate for liquidation.

63 The Stalin era. The first Five Year Plan achieved in four years by kindly, disingenuous Stalin against whom international church capital and Social Democrats rage in vain

It all started so gradually, almost by accident. The government of the Soviet Union, the leadership of Party and Comintern – for all important purposes one and the same body of men – seemed, at the beginning of 1928, to be as firmly wedded to the economic and social guidelines of NEP as ever: state control of the commanding heights of the economy, small capitalist accumulation everywhere else.

The opposition in the party to NEP and 'socialism in one country' had either been expelled or had capitulated – and now humbly sought re-admission at the bottom like discards in a game of poker. The strongest advocates of the continuation of NEP, Bukharin and Rykov, were firmly in the saddle. Some people believed that these men would at last be able to rid themselves of their uncomfortable ally Stalin, the General Secretary, acclaimed at Party Congresses for always representing the majority – hence correct – line, but surely no match for so many experienced and clever men. Everything seemed set for at least a few more years of peace and quiet inside the Party, at home as well as abroad. Yet by the summer of 1928 a full-scale campaign against the *kulaks* was getting under way, and Stalin was moving against his right-wing allies in the Politburo. The towns were short of food once more. According to Stalin, the government purchases of grain fell two million tons below what was needed. Emergency measures were called for and these, as always, were legitimized by a simple slogan summing up the political line: 'The *kulaks* are disrupting Soviet economic policy.' So they had to be squeezed.

The campaign began in May, at first in the context of improving grain deliveries, if necessary by pressure. 'It would be folly,' said Stalin, 'to think of expropriating the *kulaks*.' But by the end of the year collectivization was already in full swing. All over the Soviet Union, Party workers from the big cities, flushed from their desks and with only the most rudimentary instructions, found themselves in the countryside, first pleading with, then bullying and finally forcing the peasants willy-nilly into the new collectives. It was like the raids on the farms in 1919 and 1920, but this time under the banner of Leninism and not merely as a means of alleviating an overwhelming food crisis in the midst of civil war. The hope that the operation could be converted into a self-generating class struggle in the country, by raising the poor and landless peasants against their richer neighbours, turned out to be illusory. In general, village solidarity proved too strong and the temporary Commissars had to rely on volunteers from the towns, policemen and above all the military, to enforce collectivization and the demanded supply of grain. 'We must smash the *kulaks*, eliminate them as a class. . . . We must strike at the *kulaks* so hard that they will never rise to their feet again,' Stalin thundered encouragingly from the Kremlin.

64 The wish dream of collectivization. Peasants in Belorussia queueing to join collective farms, 1931

Seen from that austere bastion, collectivization might perhaps appear as a process of revolutionary fervour. Certainly it was a statistical transformation. Within two years over half of all Soviet agricultural production had been turned from private farming to co-operative and state farming. But seen from below by those involved it was primarily a heartbreaking story of futile peasant resistance, of large-scale slaughter of animals and, in many cases, desperate starvation. A few peasants were willing to give the new collectives a try; the majority joined because they had to·or starve. A statistical revolution had certainly been achieved, but the problem of agricultural production was not solved. It was to be a running sore on the glossy surface of Soviet economic growth, mutinously erupting to trouble Stalin and his successors.

Why was it done? Those historians who like to think of Stalin as a demigod brooding over a totally subservient society have pictured him ruminating in the Kremlin as early as 1927 on what steps should be taken to bring about the Great Society. Others, more strictly chronological in their approach, see a very close connection between the destruction of Stalin's right-wing allies and the adoption of left-wing measures. According to this canon, collectivization in the Soviet Union was a handy means of getting rid of unwanted colleagues at the top, every colleague being a potential rival for power. Contemporary Russian historians, especially those who write official history, generally tend to describe collectivization and the industrialization drive of the first Five Year Plan as a necessary and logical step in the development of the Soviet Union, its timing governed by the termination of the historical usefulness of NEP. Finally, unrepentant opponents of Bolshevism and the Soviet Union emphasize not only the human tragedy and the brutal bureaucratic dictatorship which caused it, but its pointlessness; the NEP growth rate in industry and agriculture could, with some foreign help and investment, have reached the required levels without force or a Five Year Plan. Probably each of these explanations has some measure of truth. Those who like their history spiced with irony find a sort of monstrous satisfaction in Stalin's adoption of what was essentially the policy advocated by Trotsky, Preobrazhensky and Sokolnikov immediately after he had removed them from positions of power. The relationship between the adoption of a new policy and the destruction of those who first advocated it appears indeed to be one of the features of Soviet history. Certainly their earlier advocacy of forced industrialization did the left no good, for Stalin hit out at left and right from 1929 onwards with equal vigour and finished up a few years later by circling the triangle: left and right were pronounced to be indistinguishable, identical, a matter of personal idiosyncrasy of phrase. And certainly there was a real connection between the new policy in the countryside and the elimination of suspected opponents in the Party. At least such a connection was pointed up by Stalin when an extensive purge of Party members took place in the spring of 1928. Abroad, the failures of Soviet diplomacy in Europe and communist activity in the Far East cried out for a successful diversion at home. Seldom had Soviet foreign policy been at such a low ebb as at the end of 1927, with the virtual destruction of the Chinese communists by their former allies, the Kuomintang, Great Britain's rupture of diplomatic relations in May 1928, finally the assassination of the Soviet Ambassador to Warsaw on 7 June – the first attack on a Soviet diplomat abroad for some years. World revolution was not only at a standstill but in full retreat. Socialism needed some glamour in its one home country to compensate for its tarnished image abroad.

All these factors played a part. But the most important one has not yet been listed. The year 1928 also witnessed the first of the Five Year Plans, the instrument by which the Soviet Union was to become a predominantly industrial power. To achieve the required growth of industry, four basic conditions had to be met. First, the availability of natural resources. Here the Soviet Union was most abundantly supplied, at least potentially. Secondly, a population structure producing a relative surplus in the crucial category between twenty and forty-five years was required. This existed in the USSR; neither famine nor the war period of 1914–21 had seriously altered the basic demographic trend of very high fertility and rather high mortality (though the peak in births took place during the NEP period, providing the maximum reservoir of youth for the Second World War and the subsequent reconstruction). Hence the Soviet Union in the 1930s had a relatively lower burden of old people to carry than probably any other country in Europe. At the same time the ideological pressure to equate men and women in work load and professional opportunities also had a sound demographic basis, for between the ages twenty to forty-five the estimated ratio of men to women was abnormally low – 90:100.

The other two conditions were more directly controllable. Extra food would have to be available to support the growing population in the industrial towns, largely made up of peasants moving from the land to form the new labour force. And the final condition was the formation of extra capital for investment. Every second-year student of economics – and every politician in developing countries – knows that without surplus agricultural supplies and capital for investment, no major efforts at industrialization can succeed. Such surpluses exist in the form of money savings, and/or an agricultural surplus currently being exported or capable of creation through more intensive exploitation of under-utilized resources. Alternatively, surpluses have to be created artificially by squeezing consumption. In the

Soviet Union there were no obvious surpluses or spare capacity on any large scale. In calling for an intense drive against the *kulaks*, Stalin spoke of immense hoards of food, but these soon proved either laughable or illusory, just as they had in the lean years of War Communism. None the less, with the vast majority of the population living on the land, a food surplus could conceivably be squeezed out by force – providing that the same peasant, viewed as a consumer, could be forced to make do with far less. Henceforward the propaganda pictures of well-fed peasants sitting on tractors in the midst of glowing ears of corn emanated from one or two show collectives in so far as they were not studio portraits. In the vast majority of *kolkhozy* those who produced the food often did not have enough to eat, especially when the harvest was average or less.

There was also little surplus of capital available for investment in industry; this, too, the agricultural sector had to provide. The major part of the industrialization drive was thus financed, directly or indirectly, by the difference between the food prices charged to the urban consumer and the return to the peasant. The only way to maintain this disequilibrium was by rigid control of production and distribution – and by force, or at least the threat of it. As the purges of the 1930s got under way, an enormous reserve army of forced labour was created, which also played its part in the process of accumulation by working for almost nothing.

The collectivization drive and the first Five Year Plan coincided more or less in time. We do not know whether one led directly to the other, and if so which. The main political interest from 1928 to the beginning of 1930 was focused on collectivization, with the result that the percentage of collectives to total farm holdings rose from 4 per cent in the middle of 1929 to 58 per cent by the end of March 1930, when they contained 60 per cent of the rural population of the Soviet Union. From the end of 1929 onwards industrialization and the first Five Year Plan began to take first place in the preoccupations of the rulers of the Soviet Union. In fact the government became worried by the reports of the destruction of livestock and the general disorganization in the countryside. It called a halt to collectivization. On 2 March 1930 Stalin claimed that the campaign had caused people to become dizzy with success; now they must sober up. All along he had insisted on regarding collectivization in public as a voluntary process – with just a little push here and there. The excesses to which he now admitted were caused by 'stupid and reactionary' elements who wrongly wished to produce collectivization by force. But within six months the percentage of collective farms had dropped substantially as the peasants left the collectives almost as quickly as they had been made to enter them. So the drive was renewed with quieter determination, and collectivization went ahead from then on until by 1934 almost three-quarters of all farms had been collectivized. Nature took a hand and compounded the man-made tragedy; the depletion of livestock by deliberate slaughter and the destruction of grain and seed through disorganization and neglect contributed substantially to the appalling famine of 1932. Even the best agricultural areas of the Ukraine suffered; in the marginal areas the peasants starved, fled and died in tens of thousands. Famines in Russia are like hurricanes in the Caribbean, a recurrent disaster built into the life-cycle and consciousness of the population. But the famine of 1932 became a Soviet legend of horror, just as the simultaneous industrial depression in the West is still the cautionary basis of our industrial folklore. Nonetheless the squeeze and the Five Year Plan based on it were not relaxed. Agricultural production fell substantially in the early period of collectivization, but the quota of compulsory food deliveries to the state were maintained almost intact – 'the first commandment', as Stalin called it. The difference was made up in the kitchens and hearths of the collective households.

Little of this was allowed to penetrate into the official cognizance of the town-dweller, himself now preoccupied with the long assault on the new industrial heights of the *piatiletka*, the Five Year Plan – unless he chose to listen to the groundswell of rumour, the lamentations of country friends or relations. Many of the first generation of urban dwellers were socially still embedded in the village from which they had come, a common phenomenon of early urbanization. The new industrial towns in the Ukraine, on the Volga and in Siberia, especially the areas of forced resettlement, were at first populated by uprooted peasants barely leavened with urban Party volunteers – the beginning of the great move East which characterized the Stalin period. Here resentment was strong if inchoate, and the Party kept the strictest vigil. In the big cities of western Russia the process of finally divorcing towns from country, implicit in the sharp Bolshevik class differentiation between workers and peasants, was carried to its final stage by the twin policies of collectivization and the Five Year Plans. The Communist Party had been and continued to be an urban party, the efforts to broaden it feeble and spasmodic; the country was left to sink into an oblivion fitfully illuminated by an occasional flurry of statistics. Without some support in the towns, peasant discontent could find no focus of opposition. The press sang only the praises of the enormous upswing in industrial production, and kept mute about the agricultural failures. Officially, at any rate, collectivization followed the pattern which Stalin had tried to lay down: a sharpened class struggle in the countryside, guided by the Party, in the course of which the smaller peasants and landless labourers successfully asserted themselves

ПОМЕЩИК СМОТРИТ ЗЛЫМ БАРБОСОМ,
КУЛАК СОПИТ БУГРИСТЫМ НОСОМ,
ПЬЯНЧУГА С ГОРЯ ПЬЕТ ЗАПОЕМ,
ПОП ОГОЯТЕЛЫМ ВОЕТ ВОЕМ, ●

ШИПИТ ПРОДАННЫЙ ЖУРНАЛИСТ,
ОСТРИТ КЛЫКИ КАПИТАЛИСТ,
МЕНЬШЕВИЧОК ВО-ВСЮ ЯРИТСЯ,
ВОЯКА БЕЛЫЙ МАТЕРИТСЯ, —

ПСЫ, НЕ ПОСАЖЕННЫЕ В КЛЕТКУ,
ВСЕ, КТО СТОИТ ЗА СТАРИНУ,
ЗЛО ПРОКЛИНАЮТ ПЯТИЛЕТКУ
И ОБЪЯВЛЯЮТ ЕЙ ВОЙНУ,

ГРОЗЯТ ЕЙ СРЫВОМ, ПОНИМАЯ,
ЧТО В НЕЙ—ПОГИБЕЛЬ ИХ ПРЯМАЯ!

ДЕМЬЯН БЕДНЫЙ.

65, 66 The Five Year Plan was a period of sharpened class conflict against the alleged enemies of progress: rich landowner, *kulak*, drunkard, priest, bureaucrat, Menshevik, etc. Most serious of all, the hoarder (right): 'Down with those who keep food from the workers', a poster of *c.* 1930

against the *kulaks*. *Kulaks* soon ceased to be any distinct class or group; all those who resisted collectivization were *kulaks*.

Collectivization and the initiation of the Five Year Plan must obviously be considered as one and the same social phenomenon, even if the order of individual decisions suggests a more complex connection. In the next few years the achievements of the Five Year Plan provided the main content of news in the Soviet Union. Production statistics became the thought and life of Soviet society. For foreign communists and sympathizers the cautious self-regarding foreign policy of the Soviet Union, and the macabre horrors of the great purges to come, could be made intellectually bearable only by off-setting them against the industrial attainments of socialist Russia. The domestic stress on economic development was readily echoed by sym-pathizers everywhere, to explain the disappointing and, for many, downright reactionary, features of Stalinism, its cruelty and its apparently blind unpredictability. Rapid industrial development became the main goal of

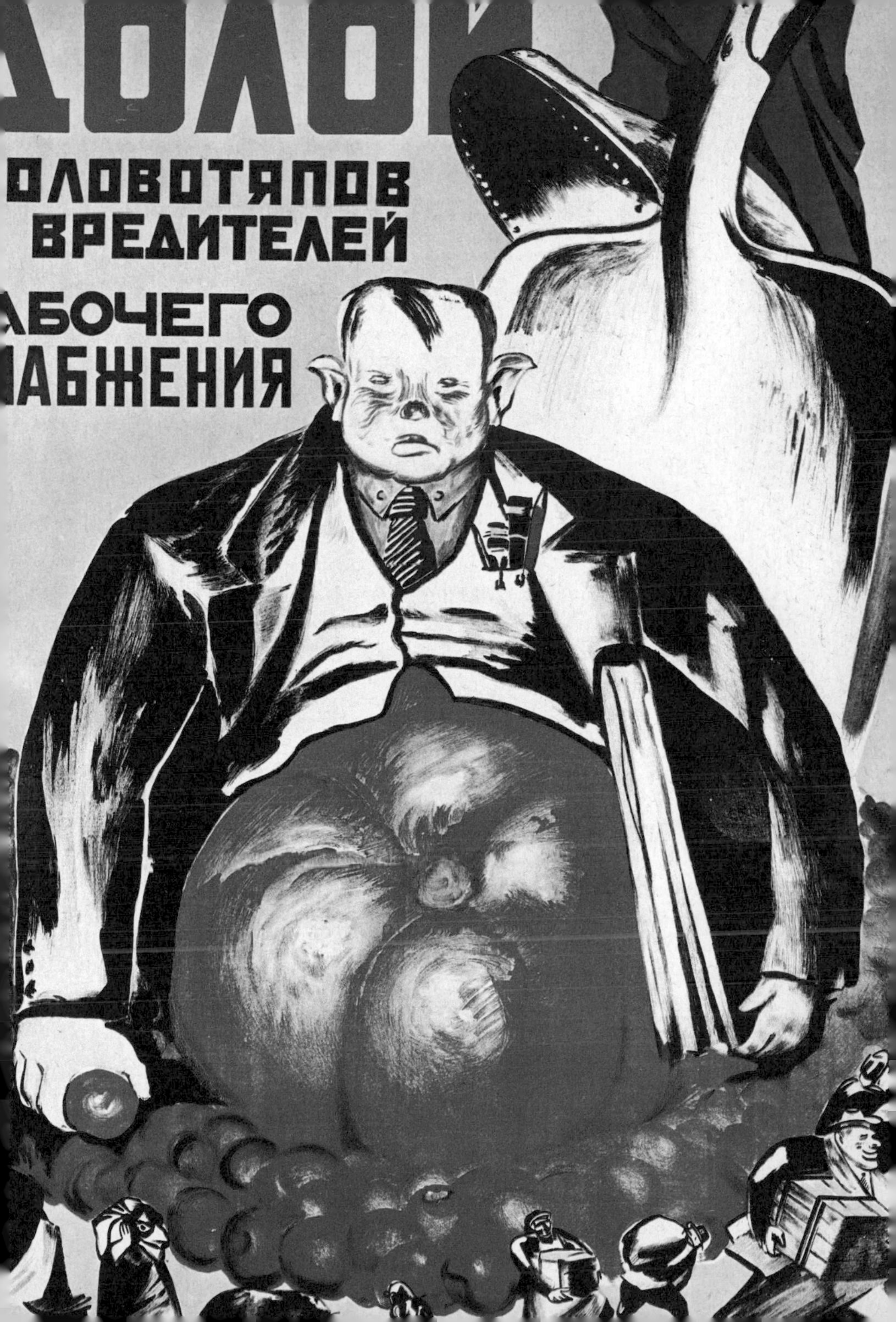
ДОЛОЙ
ОЛОВОТЯПОВ
ВРЕДИТЕЛЕЙ
АБОЧЕГО
АБЖЕНИЯ

Soviet society, its attainments a blanket justification for everything else. The nascent *ouvrièrisme* which had emerged so clearly in leadership styles from the Fifteenth Congress at the end of 1927 onwards now became the desired style at all levels of Party life. The final victims were the intellectuals, for whom a world of production figures in percentages could hardly be a creative environment. Since for most people figures are cold and unlovely things, the spirit of the 1930s in the Soviet Union was epitomized in popular culture by spectacular examples of production – the Dnepropetrovsk Dam and, perhaps most memorable of all, the Moscow Underground. No traffic analyst looking for a means of relieving pressure on surface transport would have plumped for this particular investment in a metropolis where automobiles were few, yet the 'Metro' came to epitomize heroic achievement in the face of physical and technical odds. All the decisions, down to relatively minute technical problems, were made by the Party rather than by the engineers. Given a willingness to work regardless of hours, and unshaken faith in the human capacity to triumph over any environment, no task was too great for the activists of the Communist Party if the will was there. This approach to the solution of technical and economic problems, known as *sturmovshchina*, governed official Soviet attitudes to production for several decades. It also set norms which all were enjoined to follow.

The real importance of the second revolution of 1928–30 was not so much in what it achieved, as in the radical change in the manner of achieving it. Figures for overall industrial production do not in fact show any marked increase between the NEP period and that of the first two Five Year Plans (though the rate of growth increased by about 2 to 3 per cent in the first few years); agricultural production actually declined for a time.[*] The second revolution as such can hardly be deduced from gross production figures at all. It was in the emphasis on *what* should be produced that the great change made its impact – the stress on heavy industry at the expense of consumer goods which was to be a prime feature of Soviet economics for the next twenty-five years. More important still, perhaps, was the change in outlook. Henceforward politics and economics were to be fused into one, and not divorced as they had been during NEP. Every political decision seemed to be shaped to a single end – more production, and still more. Marx had derided capitalist society as an inhuman engine for the production of profit:

***

[*] Statistics in the USSR for a long time presented a special problem, since they were intended to convey a minimum of accurate information to potential critics and a maximum of propaganda for supporters. Accordingly the analysis of Soviet industrial and agricultural statistics is itself a major academic exercise. Figures in this book have been selected from a wide range of possible alternatives as being the most informative in the view of the author. Recent Soviet statistics are of course a considerable improvement over those put out under Stalin.

67, 68, 69 Socialist competition – shock-workers and their achievements. Above, an appeal to all workshops to compete. Right, a women's 'shock brigade' at the Kharkov electric works, 1930. Below, construction of the Moscow Underground in 1936

'Accumulate, accumulate: that is Moses and all the Prophets.' Yet nowhere in any capitalist society was the entire weight of propaganda directed quite so firmly and self-consciously towards the end of capital accumulation as in the Soviet Union under Stalin. We shall meet this paradox again: precisely those features which Marx had characterized as typical of 'high' capitalism, and which he had condemned accordingly, reached their official apotheosis in the Soviet Union, legitimized only by the destruction of the private capitalist as a class and his replacement by 'the workers' state'. The motor of investment in capitalist development had usually been the agricultural surplus; in Soviet Russia this principle was pushed to its logical conclusion in that the agricultural 'surplus' was simply provided more or less by force. Finally the state and its institutional apparatus, whose destruction had been the first task of Bolshevik revolution, were strengthened beyond all measure in the Soviet Union of Joseph Stalin, and provided the cutting edge of 'the dictatorship of the proletariat'. The point in emphasizing this is not to convict communists of hypocrisy and insincerity (which are unmarketable commodities in politics anyway) but to show that self-conscious and rapid industrialization has a logic of its own to which ideologies and philosophies – capitalist and communist alike – have necessarily to be tailored.

In effect the second revolution transformed the whole of the Soviet Union into a single enormous firm. The management of the economy merged with the government of the country: managing director Stalin, the Politburo his board, and everyone else managers, technicians, public-relations men and workmen. The plan figures of 1929 had been merely indicators of what production levels were desirable, as was the practice during NEP; they now became overnight a legal norm – by statute. This did not make the figures any more attainable; it took many years of hard struggle and the dismantling

70, 71 The achievement of plans and work norms has always dominated official propaganda at home. Right, a poster of about 1930 on which the names of 'slackers, doubters and ill-disposed persons' could be publicly inscribed by their workmates. Left, the same problem as recently as 1965; a *Krokodil* cartoon entitled 'Rush job'

126

of an already outdated Stalinism before the technique of planning could finally be made to accommodate economic criteria of balance and preference instead of a set of behavioural rules which incessantly spurred and threatened. Many competent economists have devoted much time to exposing the irrationality of Soviet industrial plans, as well as measuring (on the basis of insufficient and often highly inaccurate figures) reality against expectation and propaganda. In a sense all this is beside the point. What mattered was the obsession with *more*. At the level of production of the USSR in the late 1920s there could hardly be a serious danger of over-production in physical terms, and the problem of balance was solved, at least for the next decade, by the concentration on heavy industry as a first priority. So everything was ploughed back into more production. The bottlenecks came mainly in distribution, and these were tackled, if not always solved, by the institutionalization of permanent crisis. Almost overnight the Soviet Union became 'plan conscious'; as children learn the Ten Commandments in Christian countries, so Soviet children learned the importance of fulfilling plans.

This involved a cultural and social revolution as much as an economic one. For the sake of production some very fundamental tenets of Bolshevism were sacrificed. The basically egalitarian approach to economic and social rewards, which had been a distinctive feature under Lenin and had been retained in the state sector of agriculture and industry even during NEP, was now abandoned. Inequality had not only to exist but to be seen to exist. Military ranks were once again introduced into the Red Army in 1936, when it was reconverted into a standing force, and with formal ranks came the more ornate courtesies and visible differentiation that go under the name of military discipline. But of course the resulting social rewards were quite distinct from the hierarchy of political power. The effective authority of commanders was reduced by the system of political commissars (*politruky*). A tense competition between commander and political officer developed which Stalin deliberately refused to resolve; apart from an inevitable but temporary relaxation during the war it was only in the 1950s that the military commanders finally obtained a clear decision on their own primacy in all matters pertaining to military discipline and control.

Planned as they were, prices had to give expression to the social priorities of the planners – both in artificially cheapening strategic materials and supplies, and in inhibiting consumption at the retail end. The inequalities of the price system therefore reflected, at least officially, the priorities of the government rather than the scarcity expression of the market – a special and not always rational form of inequality. The whole system of consumer supplies was, however, partially removed from the influence of the pricing

72, 73 Alexei Stakhanov (right) in 1935 explaining the system by which he doubled output per man. Twenty-five years later people were more sceptical. Above, a 1956 cartoon lampoons the miracle man who claims a 175 per cent fulfilment of his plan

system altogether. In times of crying shortage, special shops sold superior food and clothing to the privileged and the deserving – not against payment of money but against proof of status. Above all Stalin fulminated against wage levelling, and stressed the importance of rewarding workers in accordance with what they produced – a piecework mentality of an extreme kind. In 1935 a coal-miner called Stakhanov, under the full glare of publicity, succeeded with two assistants in producing 102 tons of anthracite in a work shift of five and three-quarter hours at the Irmino Coal Mine in the Ukraine. Stakhanovism had arrived: the perpetual pressure to overfulfil work norms and plans, with rewards of public esteem and material benefits in money and kind for success, and public condemnation or punishment for failure. Within a few months similar records were reported from many other industries. In spite of its unpopularity – during the mid 1930s shock-workers ran the risk of being killed by their workmates – the Stakhanovite campaign was never abandoned during Stalin's life, and was even copied in some of the People's Democracies in eastern Europe after the war. It may seem a heavy-footed, even absurd approach today, but it dominated the attitude to work of an entire Soviet generation.

Secondary and deeper effects soon made themselves felt. The Lenin period of freedom and experimentation was over, not only in the Party but in every sphere of life. The debates of the 1920s about the proper representation of

Party ideals in literature now gave way to direction from above, and the professional organization of writers with its link to the Party was transformed into an institution through which the Party could exercise tight control over literary production. We may ask whether forced industrialization, with its built-in pressures for conformity and commitment, can ever co-exist with an atmosphere of free criticism and comment; Stalin and his colleagues certainly did not believe this to be the case. In the course of his authoritative definition of Marxism-Leninism, artists, scientists and even architects had their tasks minutely allocated. Literature had to be solid and earthy and concern itself with the objective problems of socialist construction rather than idealist speculations about human nature. Painting had also to represent the ideal of socialist construction – this is the period of endless canvases of happy people working on building sites or on farms. Industrial art of a sophisticated kind is a perfectly feasible form of expression, as artists like Lissitzky showed; but direction on the subject-matter was not enough, content and form were specified as well. Both writing and art had to have pedagogical as well as highly representational qualities. The buildings of the period were grandiose, old-fashioned and heavy in exterior and internal design.

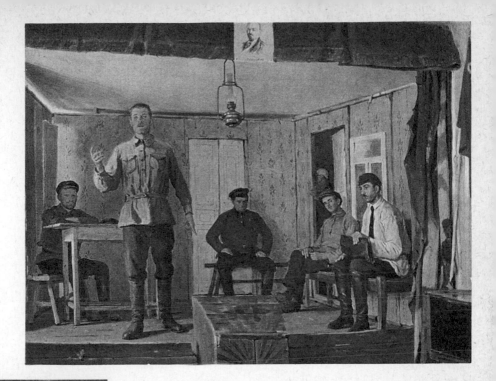

74, 75, 76 A crude form of socialist realism was the dominating art style during the Stalin era. Left, a feast on the Kolkhoz by Gerasimov, 1937. Above, a meeting of the village Party unit by Cheptsov, 1924. Lissitzky, however, continued in his abstract diagrammatic style, as in this sketch for a children's book, 1928

Nor did this incorporation of intellectual activity into the Stalinist version of an industrial society stop at the immediately expressive arts. The writing of history was examined critically according to the new criteria. Party history was already being re-written to suit the current political situation from 1930 onwards; after 1932 Stalin's pronouncements on the past as an integral part of the present became the stuff of Soviet historiography. Henceforward footnotes and references were not designed to do anything but give a scientific appearance to these proceedings – the writings of Lenin and Stalin became the main sources of all Party history. World history as a whole was put through the same mincing machine. The class struggle became the main component of history since the Neolithic Age. Science also was classified into Marxist and bourgeois concepts. Lysenko and the environmental school of biologists triumphed on political rather than experimental grounds – inhibiting advances in research for two decades. Even exact sciences like mathematics were analysed according to ideological content, and mathematical concepts were subjected to the 'correct' critical analysis. In the fields of both art and science the strait-jacket was laced tight; only physics and chemistry escaped unscathed in their basic approaches. The arts have not fully recovered to this day. The sciences lived off capital by concentrating largely on problems of application and technology for twenty years, and only the enormous revival of basic research less inhibited by ideological considerations after Stalin's death refurbished the partially depleted intellectual capital of Soviet science.

These developments should not be viewed as mere narrow-mindedness. We have seen that in the 1920s the fundamental question of a proletarian culture had been posed and answered mainly in the negative in accordance with Lenin's own strongly felt views. Stalin did not specifically subscribe to any notion of a proletarian culture, but he did believe that culture was a secondary consequence of the social environment. This was being visibly changed, and the control of and interference with free expression were designed to align the arts and sciences with the concrete phenomena of the new industrial society – a process of the firmest integration. There was accordingly a basic logic in this proceeding. Its failure, as Lenin in a sense foresaw, was due partly to the fact that science and art relate not only to the social processes of any one society, but form an international system of their own; unless the Soviet Union really could be hermetically sealed for many generations, this international system could not wholly be broken. More important, the relationship between social life and its intellectual reflection is not a simple step-by-step process but a complex and long-term one. No one can predict accurately the precise way in which cultural and intellectual changes will reflect those of society. The attempt, therefore, to integrate these two spheres merely resulted in the impoverishment of scientific and intellectual achievement: the substitution of photography for art, of technology for science – an impoverishment which Soviet scientists and writers were to feel all the more acutely when they had a chance once more to 'compare' themselves.

Yet the very impoverishment of quality seemed to make possible the vast increase in quantity, or at least the widest diffusion of a basic minimum. By reducing history, philosophy and science to a series of over-simple paradoxes, Stalin made them comprehensible to levels of society which hitherto had been quite untouched by them. Anyone reading today the famous *Short Course in the History of the Communist Party of the Soviet Union*, anonymously published but strongly influenced if not indeed written by Stalin, is struck at once by its falsifications, its simplifications and turgidness of style. Yet this was the book that hundreds of thousands of Party workers and agitators in the Soviet Union and abroad learned by rote, and which formed the basis of their approach to Marxism and its history. They in turn reproduced its heavy-footed simplicities to millions of listeners forcibly collected in study groups and Party cells. In judging its quality we should therefore bear in mind not what it represents as history, but its enormous success as a simple pedagogical instrument, the font of baptism through which the complex ideas of Marxism were sprinkled over a whole society. Not since the Bible has any single text had the same impact. In the absence of challenge, and with the irresistible push of authority behind it, the *Short Course* became the most important document of the Stalinist era.

Meanwhile 'socialism in one country' was to be applied literally and universally – and socialism for the moment meant industrialization. Everything that was conducive to higher production was stressed and supported. During the first flush of free thinking the institution of marriage had been left to the individual's private proclivities; in the 1920s divorce and abortions were easily obtained (at least as far as facilities allowed). Now the sanctity of marriage began once more to be officially reaffirmed, divorce became more difficult and in 1936 abortions were made illegal. The struggle against religion was no longer left primarily to Party agitation; the limited revival of overt religion during NEP was now met by the full force of Soviet law. The decree of 7 April 1929 forbade the Orthodox Church to own property or to teach. Only local Soviets could license a building for purposes of worship on a temporary basis. Some 2,000 monasteries and many more churches were closed during the two years 1929–30, and the new towns often contained no churches at all.

ЧЕРНЫЕ ВОРОНЫ ГОТОВЯТ РАЗБОЙНИЧИИ НАБЕГ НА С.С.С.Р.
ПРОЛЕТАРИЙ-БУДЬ НА ЧЕКУ!

77 Behind the frail, appealing
cross of Christ
lurk the big guns
of reaction.
This anti-religious poster of 1930
followed the
renewed militancy
of official atheism

The educational experiments of the 1920s at first received an enthusiastic further lease of life with the challenge of the new industrialization policy. Learning by doing, the Complex and Project Methods, and even the Dalton Plan seemed to acquire new relevance. But from 1931 a new and strictly conservative trend was initiated from the top. Experiments were quietly abandoned, and classrooms became disciplined centres for turning out the necessary army of conventionally qualified workers and technicians. Teachers were restored to full authority in their domain. Even equality of opportunity came to mean something different. Access to educational opportunity had been opened to the children of workers and, to a lesser extent, peasants, but the selection of those able to go on to higher education was henceforward increasingly based on the ability to excel in examinations. The education authorities went back to prescribing curricula in the minutest detail, as in Tsarist times, tailoring the educational system to serve the recruiting needs of the vast Soviet 'firm', not those of an experimental society in revolution. The technicians and scientists of whom Khrushchev was to be so proud in the 1950s were mostly selected and trained in the schools of Stalin.

But the second revolution succeeded where the first had really failed. Liberation by example and by cultural prescription had not been enough. Only by destroying the very basis of the old society and providing a universal infrastructure of literacy, by controlled mobilization into a social environment dominated by crude perspectives of production, could the basis of a new society be created. But no one could foresee the shape of the new. Perhaps it was this deliberate unwillingness to gaze into the future – to make the present seem as though it embraced both past and future, as though there would never be anything but this present – that actually made the future possible.

What was life like for ordinary people in the 1930s? The answer must be: grim and grey. If you were not a Party member for whom the present was made luminous by the logic of historical necessity and the conviction of being on the side of the future, if you were not a manager, technician or shock-worker with special privileges, the pressures must at times have seemed well-nigh intolerable. At the bottom of the process of industrialization, life is hard under any system, but even more so when all the basic received certainties of life – religion, friendship, tradition – were being questioned and changed at the same time. The myth of the good times under Lenin and NEP grew up in this period, particularly in the countryside. Some people even thought nostalgically of pre-war Russia, though of course they did not dare to say so. This was above all a period of dislocation, of movement into new regions and towns. Housing was in desperately short supply, and not high on the order of official priorities. Around many of the major cities of the Soviet Union, both in the old industrial Russia of the west and in the new towns in the centre and east, there grew a ring of improvised dwellings, often no more than holes in the ground, in which whole families crowded together. The provision of an adequate apartment was in fact one of the rewards for deserving workers and technicians, and therefore a major incentive. The hours of work were long. When they were over, social and political obligations started: meetings of factory groups or cells, trade union meetings and other activities in which Party and government plans were explained and – in an increasingly formalized manner – discussed. Informal social life virtually disappeared from the Soviet Union, for by the time all obligations of formal society had been discharged, only one's immediate family could enjoy the little energy and time that was left. Nevertheless, in spite of the fact that almost all women worked, and that the state assumed ever greater responsibilities for children, the family was the residual beneficiary; even more than in western Europe family ties were actually strengthened in this period. For every son who denounced his father to the police or the schoolteacher during the purges, a thousand failed to do so. The only successful splitters of the family in this era were the Nazis in Germany.

In general the Party was everywhere. Behind it, once the great purges began, stood the Secret Police. You learnt to trust no one. The naturally open nature of the Russians, to whom long and inconclusive conversations about the problems of life, and the offer of intimate confidences to almost complete strangers, were a normal part of life, gradually became enclosed in the new official culture of silence. The class enemy, one was constantly reminded, lurked everywhere, waiting and watching. With household names like Trotsky, Zinoviev and Bukharin suddenly revealed as bourgeois agents, English spies, whom could you trust? Did not Stalin call for incessant vigilance, which made surveillance of your neighbour a social duty? Whatever else the purges did, they taught the Russians the need for extreme reserve.

In the countryside things were worse, though for different reasons. The economic discrimination against agriculture made itself felt on all levels. The Communist Party made little headway among the collective farmers. Recreation, medical services, education hardly existed except on posters. The idiocy of rural life (Marx's phrase) found a grimmer realization in the Soviet Union. The depletion of the human and cultural as well as economic resources of the countryside in favour of the new industrial towns was only made worse by the absolute refusal of the leadership to acknowledge it – even though official policy was directly responsible.

Any objective evaluation of the Soviet standard of living during these years must take into account the substantial benefits supplied by the state to sections of the population who had hitherto been almost completely deprived. During the period of industrialization, there was an enormous expansion of medical and health services. Already by 1940 there were more doctors per thousand of population than in the United States, Britain, Germany or France. The system of polyclinics, whatever its medical pros and cons, certainly made access to facilities more readily available to greater numbers of people – especially since some of the sociological inhibitions which prevent people from visiting doctors were largely removed. It was in this period that relatively general sick-pay benefits were instituted, though an attempt to reduce the excessive labour turnover in the late 1930s tied these to a minimum period of service in any one enterprise. Sport became professionalized. Footballers, athletes, and above all chess players (the Russian national game *par excellence*) were induced to treat their performance as part of their plan fulfilment. Outstanding excellence was equivalent to the achievements of the shock-worker in industry. More important, however, was the popularization of these events in terms of mass participation. The commitment to the performance of teams and individuals, which still marks the Soviet Union today, is thus a compound of the natural loyalties of most *aficionados* for their favourite performers with the identification of support for sporting performance as a social duty.

78, 79 Facilitated and
planned recreation.
Above, chess players
in the Kirov Memorial Park
of Culture and Rest
in Leningrad.
Right, organized holidays
for workers in Baku

The system of paid holidays also dates from the mid-1930s. Naturally the
facilities in no way expanded as rapidly as the demand, but the principle had
at any rate been established, and was to survive as a sheet-anchor of the
Soviet approach to labour problems. It is significant that recent investigations
into comparative job satisfaction in the Soviet Union, on the one hand, and
the United States and the West on the other, show clearly how important a
part of the general attitude to work paid and organized holidays have become, and above all to what extent this institution is regarded as a fundamental and original aspect of Soviet life.

The first decade of industrialization thus witnessed substantial hardships –
though not without some very basic benefits, the results of which were only
to be reaped a generation later. Parallel to these official benefits were the
informal mechanisms with which the Soviet citizen learnt to defend himself
against excessive demands and controls. These were the result of the failure
of even the best of plans to provide for every eventuality, but in fact they
'humanized' the system and made it possible to function and live in it.
Blat, the unofficial lubrication of the wheels of production and supply
through hoarding, supplementary private purchase and bribery, was in some
ways 'higher than Stalin' – as the saying went. Managers of factories, caught
in the trap between fulfilling plans that were sometimes unattainable through

137

miscalculation or supply breakdowns (and would, if achieved, almost inevitably bring higher norms for the next year), and failure, which could mean severe punishment, learnt to circumvent the official channels of material distribution. They also hoarded material in short supply, which they did not declare in their returns of material balances – figures on which the whole edifice of planning depended. Such materials could only be obtained unofficially. To supply them a small army of fixers or *tolkachy* grew up, who handled the whole delicate business. Since government and Party insisted during the heyday of planning on laying down the precise amounts of each product which individual farms were expected to deliver – as though the very earth itself could be made amenable to the planners' will – collective farms were sometimes obliged to purchase at higher prices in the open market such amounts of grain and other produce as were needed to fulfil their delivery quotas. The farms had no mechanical equipment of their own, for the collectivized peasant could not be trusted with such valuables. Tractors and other machines were supplied by hire arrangements with state-owned Machine and Tractor Stations, whose job it also was to keep an eye on the honesty and efficiency of the farmers. Since peasants were not paid wages, but received a share of the total collective farm profit divided into so many labour days per member of the farm, they went short if the farm failed to make a surplus. This was no rare occurrence – especially in the marginal farming areas in the centre and south of the Soviet Union. Controlled, supervised and squeezed as farmers were, the job of collective farm chairman was not an enviable one, and it often proved difficult to find suitable candidates. Many of those who undertook the job were not attracted by the challenge but rather by the chance to exercise power or extortion, to squeeze the farm still further for their own and their cronies' benefit.

Probably the most important single factor of relief for the peasant was the existence of the private plot within the framework of the collective. A collective farm differed from a state farm in that it was legally regarded as the property of the members, rather than of the whole society represented by the state. This was of course of no advantage to the participants. Quite the contrary, it was a means of discriminating against them as compared to the state farmer or *sovkhoznik*. But the collective farmer did retain small peripheral plots of land in and around the new collective farms. Though the time spent on these for his own benefit, and the disposal of the produce, were strictly controlled by law, in practice these private plots afforded the *kolkhoznik* the only straw of private incentive. It was almost impossible to check accurately the division of his time between the private plot and the collective as a whole – especially in the many cases where the farm chairman and other

80 The perennial and insoluble problem of the private plot. Cartoon in *Krokodil*, 1939, showing the farmer cultivating his own land at the expense of the *Kolkhoz*

local authorities connived at the neglect of the farm for the private plot in return for 'contributions'. The removal of private plots was threatened at various times, but overall the system has survived – at times proliferating to such an extent that after the Second World War a quite disproportionate amount of food was produced privately.

The ability of the individual to bypass the endless regulations depended ultimately on the collaboration of others. There gradually developed throughout the Soviet Union a system of *quid pro quo*, through which one eye was shut to the misdeeds of others in return for a reciprocity of blindness – a system known as 'family relationships'. In a sense this system follows logically from the enormous apparatus of control built up during these years, in which everyone in a job or office from the lowly farmer to the highest official had somebody watching over him. These relationships were primarily based on the Party. In the provinces particularly the secretary of the local Soviet Executive Committee, the secretary of the Party Committee, the representative of the Procuracy (local law enforcement) and the representative of the police collaborated with managers, collective farm chairmen and other interested parties in a well-organized chain of mutual protection. The same type of relationship operated even in individual ministries at the centre.

The Party was well aware of this, and for the next twenty years eternal vigilance against such secondary 'families' was preached in the newspapers and at Party meetings. The systematic purge in the Stalin period may partly be explained as the only means available to break these informal ties. While it is not suggested that the first purges were in any sense due to such considerations, the vicious spiral of more control, more evasion, more supervision and still more evasion, could in the last resort be broken only by undermining all sense of security in personal relationships based on mutual interests. Mutual protection is a bureaucratic phenomenon in all societies. With the existence of a supreme and irremovable Communist Party as a fundamental part of the system, and the exacting demands it made upon the system's members, the institutionalization of such relationships became almost inevitable – and purges, or the threat of purges, the only way of somehow limiting them. It can therefore be argued that the Soviet system, as it developed in these years, threatened to block all known channels of change. Revolutionary fervour was certainly not enough; normal processes of turnover had atrophied with the reduction of elections to a mere formality. Only the institutionalization of insecurity could provide a safeguard. Even today, with terror largely dismantled, the basic insecurity as a built-in system of Soviet administration and Party life partly remains.

81, 82 Industrialization under Stalin. Left, Stalin himself inspecting tractors produced at the ZIS factory. Right, a propaganda photograph of ZIS cars manufactured in 1936

To us and our contemporaries in the Soviet Union today, preoccupied with welfare and rising standards of living, these times must in retrospect seem grim indeed. What was achieved? Let the unadorned figures speak once more. In general the year 1928, just prior to the first Five Year Plan, showed a level of industrial production very similar to the Russia of 1913 (adjusted for loss of territories after 1918). The enormous ravages of six years of foreign and civil war had been made good at last. By 1940 Soviet industrial output had trebled. The annual growth rate in these twelve years was almost 9 per cent per annum, compared to present British growth rates of less than 3 per cent. The beginning of Soviet industrialization, and the period of the first Five Year Plan, coincided with the great depression in other parts of the world, when output in the United States fell by almost a third. By 1940 the Soviet Union was a major industrial power. Yet at the same time the rate of growth, impressive as it appeared, was not significantly higher than during the recovery period of NEP from 1921 to 1927. We are therefore faced with two obvious questions, only one of which historians have really tried to answer. This concerns the means chosen to achieve full-scale industrialization in the Soviet Union. Could NEP have been continued and still have attained the levels of industrial output and the growth rates of the Stalin period? Not surprisingly historians divide ideologically over this question. Pointing to the growth rates of NEP, many Western economists and historians maintain that the system was 'taking off' in any event. The partial market factors of 'limited' socialism under NEP might have allocated resources more rationally, they say; there would have been more consumer goods, and a more efficient use of resources. Soviet historians naturally take a contrary view. Only the absolute priority for basic industries made possible the further growth rates of the post-Second World War period, and the attainment of the superior technological sophistication of the present day. Moreover they consider the question itself largely absurd. Socialism requires this order of priorities, the transformation of the economy from individual small-scale procedures to collective and integrated large-scale production. This problem had already been discussed in the early 1920s. Only fully controlled industrialization justifies planning, and *vice versa* – only full-scale planning can solve the problems of socialist industrialization.

This leads to the second question: why was the process of industrialization in this form begun in 1928? Was it a purposeful execution of a rational and deliberate decision, or did it just happen? It is still not possible to answer this question with any real authority, but I think that within the context of a desire to accelerate production and tighten the planning process, Soviet industrialization was to a considerable extent self-generated, feeding on itself politically and economically just as collectivization had done. However much Stalin covered his actions with explanations of historical and logical inevitability, he was a far less acute theorist and thinker than Lenin. His explanations were always retrospective rather than programmatic. The squeeze on the *kulaks* may have started as an attempt to obtain grain, but once the class-war justification for it had been articulated, a more fundamental solution to the problem developed mainly under its own steam, and this self-reinforcement was fed back up the line into the political process to become official policy. Similarly the dramatic switch from indicative planning to a full command economy became self-generating, with official explanations and justification hurrying alongside. Once the process was under way, the Soviet leaders embraced it wholeheartedly. The vision of a long next step towards socialism and finally communism opened out in the early 1930s, and transformed a series of particular policies into a fundamental philosophy.

There was one field especially to which Stalin had devoted a great deal of time and effort – Party manipulation and control. Both collectivization and the first Five Year Plan meant a greatly strengthened role for the Party, which was wholly in line with the wishes and intentions of the communist leaders. In the course of the economic upheaval the Party was to become formally integrated into Soviet life at every level – except in the agricultural countryside – in a way which hitherto had been impossible. By the time things had settled down after the purges and just before the Second World War, the Party was installed literally everywhere. Those who controlled the Party really controlled the Soviet Union rather than merely ruling it.

The great purges from 1934 to 1938 seem to be in flagrant contradiction to the demands of forced industrialization. If the Party was to lead society in its enormous production drive, it would surely need to be cohesive and united. But there are always two approaches to cohesion and unity: consensus or discipline, persuasion or terror. Stalin chose the latter alternative. Society and Party were galvanized simultaneously. Terror was applied to production. Its threat was a spur to fulfilment, and its victims were often reintegrated into the bottom of the production process as slave labourers who consumed only a fraction of what they produced – the ideal form of surplus accumulation. How then to galvanize the Party? Hitherto the struggle among the leadership in the late 1920s had had relatively little effect on the middle and lower Party levels. By 1929 the simple and gross condemnation of Trotskyism had worked its way right through, and following on the leaders the lower echelons were being purged as well – no longer because they were unsuitable, but because they were deviationists. By the mid-1930s recantation of error no longer made re-admission possible. Between 1928 and 1933 industrialization brought an influx of new recruits; the Party grew from one and a half to three and a half million members and candidates. But the numbers declined again sharply during the continuous purge of the next three years, and this time the mass purge preceded that of the élite. By the beginning of 1937 numbers were down to just below two million. The purge had got out of hand. From then on there was again to be an excess of recruitment over evictions. Most important, the character of the Party was completely changed during these years; it became on average substantially younger, and though the proportion of workers or sons of workers was still overwhelming, they were themselves increasingly members of the new intelligentsia, the product of Soviet schools and Komsomol.

The idea of different norms for Party and society, of keeping the two distinct though hierarchically connected at the top, had been fundamental to Lenin's thinking. He envisaged that the period of amalgamation between

83 Trotsky, by now becoming the arch-enemy of all things Soviet. This 1930 cartoon in *Krokodil*, called 'The opportunists' show is unsuccessful', already shows Trotsky manipulating all the critics of Stalin's policy, especially collectivization

Party and society would be a gradual and very long-term process. Stalin decided to shorten it; in the process Lenin's conception of the amalgamation procedure was radically changed. In the course of four years he eliminated a large part of Lenin's old Bolsheviks, the leadership of the foreign Communist Parties (physically if they happened to be in the Soviet Union, by eviction if not), and finally a nameless host of more or less innocent people who were caught up in the vortex of destruction. By the time it was over, the Communist Party of the Soviet Union had become a monolithic and disciplined instrument of control. But instead of being the vanguard of society, distinct and self-conscious, the Party had become a social and political élite, with all positions of importance and power in its hand. The non-Party specialist, engineer, professor or lawyer had effectively ceased to exist in any position of importance.

Though the channels of discussion and participation in the Party became replaced by mere ritual, new channels of social mobility were opened up instead. With the destruction of a whole generation of old Bolsheviks, whose main experience had been the clandestine political life before 1917 and the pioneering spirit of the early years, a new generation moved into positions of power, to whom these early years were sacred legends rather than actual adult experiences. These were people to whom concern about basic problems was unfamiliar and therefore secondary, who accepted the industrializing perspectives of the Stalinist leadership as a part of their life, and whose activism was revolutionary not so much in a political as in an economic sense. Though solid Party members all, whose whole *raison d'être* was encapsulated within the Communist Party, they viewed their privileged position increasingly as connected with specific know-how in different fields. Instead of debating the first principles of Marxism, they applied Stalin's interpretation of Marxism-Leninism to production, planning, military strategy and management. Most of them were not technicians in the ordinary sense (though a few were), but rather politicians whose politics consisted of the ability to move rapidly from one technical sector to the other. They were political professionals specializing in management. Each of them saw himself as the beneficiary as well as the expression of the historical wisdom residing in the Party as a collective. But they regarded membership of the Party in terms of something they possessed rather than something which they created. Khrushchev was typical of these men. Beneath and below them there was to grow up yet another generation of *real* technicians, silently awaiting their turn – but this comes later.

At the approach of the 1930s, Stalin, Bukharin, Rykov and Tomsky were uneasily expressing their conflicting views about collectivization and Party policy behind closed doors. If Bukharin and his friends opposed the principles of collectivization and the first Five Year Plan, they certainly were not going to create the same open split for which they had condemned Trotsky and Zinoviev. Nonetheless Stalin moved firmly against them. The Party men who had supported the General Secretary at the Fourteenth and Fifteenth Congresses, the loyal Central Committee and purged Politburo, now supported him again. It was Stalin's particular expertise to draw arbitrary lines across overlapping shades of opinion; Bukharin, Rykov and Tomsky had to go, Kalinin remained untouched. By the end of 1929 all three had been removed from their top posts in the Soviet state and the Comintern. Bukharin was expelled from the Politburo; his vague *pourparlers* with the previously routed 'left' were loudly denounced as yet another attempt to form an opposition bloc – the Party crime that had become unforgivable. Bukharin now began to realize what so many other Bolsheviks would yet discover: Stalin, the grey, silent and inscrutable bureaucrat, who had always appeared as the very embodiment of a self-effacing Party official, was in fact an unprincipled intriguer who subordinated everything to his appetite for power. 'Whenever necessary he will from one moment to the next change his theories in order to get rid of someone. He will strangle us all.'

Stalin now had an absolutely reliable majority on the Central Committee, the Orgburo and the Politburo – not merely allies but direct and often dependent supporters. The Sixteenth Congress in July 1930 enthusiastically supported his call for unremitting struggle against right-wing opportunism. Organizations at lower levels, who had voted with the opposition, were dissolved or purged. The collectivization drive was at its height – and so was resistance to it; opposition within the Party suggested all too clearly and directly an alliance with the recalcitrant class enemies of the régime.

We do not know exactly when police terror as such really began. Khrushchev, in his anti-Stalin speech at the Twentieth Congress in 1956, cited documents to show that in Stalin's view the purges of 1936 came four years too late. Nor can we assess the attitude of the Politburo, in effect the ruling institution of the Soviet Union. It is at least possible that some of those who had backed Stalin solidly against the more individualistic and enterprising intellectuals might still have baulked in private at the use of this ultimate weapon indiscriminately and generally against the Party as a whole. One effect of the industrialization drive, with its emphasis on rigid obedience and loyalty, was that many former Mensheviks who had joined the Bolsheviks after 1917 and had been left to occupy important posts were now flushed out again as an 'objective' danger to security. Those former Mensheviks who wanted to survive had to distinguish themselves by their superlatives in

Stalin's service. Vyshinsky was one of them – the gruesome and unlovely Fouquier-Tinville of the great trials, to whom fell the task of prosecuting and annihilating men far more distinguished than himself. In March 1931 a group of Mensheviks, including the eminent economist Groman and the historian Sukhanov, were sentenced to long terms of imprisonment for treason. Riazanov, perhaps the most distinguished Marxist scholar in Russia and former head of the Marx-Lenin Institute, certainly a Bolshevik of independent mind, was implicated and evicted from the Party: he was to be one of the first to perish in the purges. From 1933 onwards the purges of the Party were no longer carried out by regular Party organs like the Control Commission or the Central Committee, but by a group of new Party men like Ezhov whose career *was* the NKVD, the Commissariat or Department of the Interior. This organization in July 1934 integrated the secret police (GPU), which in the 1920s had replaced the Cheka.

At the time, these events seemed no more than an unusually heavy and prolonged squall. At the Seventeenth Party Congress in early February 1934 it looked for a moment as though the worst excesses of collectivization were over and industrialization safely on its way. This congress of the victors had about it some of the air of reconciliation and mutual satisfaction. Even condemned oppositionists like Bukharin, Zinoviev and Kamenev, who had been savagely attacked at previous Congresses, were now able to appear and speak in an atmosphere of apparent good will. The idea of mass trials, terror and death was unthinkable, fantastic.

Ten months later, on 1 December 1934, Kirov, a rising member of the Politburo and head of the Leningrad Organization, was murdered by a young communist called Nikolaev. This was at once labelled as the joint work of the opposition – all of them lumped amorphously together for purposes of condemnation. In fact it may have been the single and unsponsored action of an individual. Possibly Stalin had a hand in it: at least in 1956 Khrushchev was to hint strongly at Stalin's complicity. It may be, as one commentator has alleged, that the relaxation and apparent harmony in Party affairs between 1932 and 1934, and the reintegration of the former oppositionists, was due to Kirov's 'new line', according to which the oppositionists had been punished enough and the industrialization drive now required Party harmony. With support for Kirov coming from within Stalin's own Central Committee Stalin was faced with both a restriction on his own freedom of action and a possible alternative leadership. The assassination of Kirov was thus extremely convenient for Stalin, ridding him of a powerful opponent and giving grounds for the liquidation of the oppositionists. The great purges followed directly from this event. It became 'the

84 Andrei Vyshinsky, one of the few former Mensheviks who survived and prospered under Stalin. He was state prosecutor during the purge trials of the 1930s, and from 1949 to 1953 was Minister of Foreign Affairs. He is shown here as chief Soviet delegate to the UN

basis for all the mass acts of abuse against socialist legality', in Khrushchev's words. During many of the fabricated cases the accused were charged with the preparation of terroristic acts. This deprived them of any possibility that their cases might be re-examined though they stated before the court that their confessions had been secured by force, and in some cases even managed to disprove the detailed evidence against them in a convincing manner. By the time Nikolaev and his alleged accomplices had been executed their activities were being publicly linked with Zinoviev. At the beginning of 1935 charges were laid against Zinoviev and Kamenev: they were sentenced to imprisonment. For the first time the law was used openly against Lenin's peers and colleagues. In January 1935 Kuibyshev died suddenly; in June 1936 Maxim Gorky, Lenin's friend and the revolution's best-known writer, also died. The then police chief, Yagoda, initiator of the mechanism of the purges and himself a later victim, was to be accused in due course of having poisoned them. In any case these deaths removed two of the last potential public obstacles of conscience to the full fury of the great purges.

Just as the purges were getting under way a new Soviet constitution was being worked out. All through 1936 Stalin, Bukharin and Radek co-operated with many other future victors and victims in producing a draft of what was proclaimed, at the meeting of the Supreme Soviet of 5 December 1936, to be the freest constitution in the world. Designed to embody fully planned state ownership of industry and collective farming as the twin bases of Soviet society, the constitution guaranteed solid liberties to the citizen, rights of

147

independent decision-making and even secession to the Federal Republics. For the first time in Soviet constitutional history, the Party was formally mentioned – as 'containing the most active and politically conscious citizens . . . the vanguard of the working people in their struggle to build a socialist system . . . and the leading core of all organizations . . . both public and of the state.' Stalin himself described it as 'the only completely democratic constitution in the world. Its international significance is without parallel.' But the heavy irony of the timing of this charter of Bolshevik democracy emanates from a sense of right and wrong peculiar to our present time; for many Soviet citizens, and particularly for foreign sympathizers in the new left-wing Popular Front against Fascism, this well-publicized document helped above all to make the great trials and purges plausible. In such an atmosphere of triumph and achievement, with Stalin (in the words of *Pravda*) 'the genius of the new age, the wisest man of the epoch', was there not bound to be something in these charges against the major accused, however monstrous they sounded? Did not the defendants admit to almost all the accusations against them? Above all, was the Soviet Union not somehow generically different from the rest of mankind, so that normal judgments of right and wrong did not apply?

By the end of 1936 a wave of arrests with and without subsequent trial was swamping the Soviet Union. The most distinguished old Bolsheviks were being arraigned and executed in batches. Perhaps a formal trial was the only concession to their rank; for every one of these, hundreds and thousands of people simply disappeared into the prisons and labour camps of the secret police and thence all too often to the grave. No one really knew how it had all started, and certainly no one knew how it was going to end. Safety of a very uncertain kind lay in denouncing others, and so the gruesome immolation went on for two years. The record, like all records of such enormity, loses its impact by the sheer quantity of well-known men who died: in August 1936 the trial of Zinoviev, Kamenev and fourteen others on capital charges, in September 1936 the suicide of Tomsky, in January 1937 the suicide of Ordzhonikidze, hitherto one of Stalin's closest collaborators (according to Khrushchev once more, he was forced to shoot himself). In June 1937 the secret trial and execution of Tukhachevsky with a galaxy of the most senior Red Army commanders – German spies all. In March 1938 the trial of Bukharin, Rykov, Yagoda and eighteen others on capital charges. Each time the arch-villain was Trotsky, grinning behind the scenes and manipulating corrupt Bolsheviks into their treacherous practices. By the time the last trial had taken place even the solid Stalinist majority of the Central Committee of 1934 had been almost wholly liquidated; the leadership of the army, of the

Komsomol, and of every other major institution of the Soviet Union had been turned upside-down.

Then, quite suddenly, the fury of the terror died down to a dreadful whisper. As in the case of collectivization, the purge was rotting away the foundations of those very sectors of society which it had meant to cleanse and strengthen. The Party hierarchy was running out of replacements. In January 1938 the new Central Committee met and issued a stern warning against excesses. It was time to make an end. By December 1938 Ezhov, whose name has become notorious in Russia through the word 'Ezhovshchina' by which the great purges are usually referred to, had quietly disappeared. The men now around Stalin, with a few exceptions, were relatively unknown: Molotov, Zhdanov, Khrushchev and Beria, Kaganovich and Mikoyan. The aftermath of the purges was in fact truly Thermidorean: the liquidation of the secret police, a purge of the purgers. In the meantime, however, the prison population, especially of the labour camps, had swollen to the size and importance of a state within a state, and went on making its contribution to socialist accumulation. People began to wonder if the growth rate and the whole system could in fact survive without them, whether the real reason for the purges was not the need for a cheap supply of non-consuming labour.

After five years, in March 1939, a new Party Congress assembled at last, the eighteenth. The new leaders could review the purges as a necessary attack on counter-revolution, open and disguised, and take stock of its consequences. They decided to admit that there had been excesses; it fell to Zhdanov to berate the assembled delegates on this account. At the same time the class struggle which allegedly had necessitated all this was still not resolved: 'Many of the real enemies remain unscathed.' The delegates agreed and applauded the reams of figures, the cost of so many lives, as a necessary price for the continued advance of all the main economic indicators. In spite of Zhdanov's cautionary warning against self-satisfaction there was certainly a hope that the terror had now perhaps served its function and would never happen again. But when Stalin himself announced to the Congress that the Soviet Union was now stronger than it had ever been, he almost certainly did not realize how soon its strength, indeed its very existence, would be challenged by the onslaught of Nazi Germany. Whatever the delegates at the Eighteenth Congress thought about the future – and who dared any longer to speculate too closely upon it? – the idea that within twenty-seven months the nation would be fighting for its very existence, not against internal opposition, but against the German invader, can hardly have occurred to them. Even if there had been such a danger, Stalin was sure to know and guard against it.

The dramatic changes of course from 1928 onwards, justifiably called a second revolution, naturally affected the foreign policy of the Soviet Union. By the mid-1920s the country had emerged from its international isolation; with *de facto* recognition from most of the major European powers, it could trade in goods rather than in subversion. For the Communist Parties abroad the years 1923–7 were a period of consolidation and internal reorganization. Just as the Soviet Union was becoming increasingly preoccupied with its internal problems, so 'Bolshevization' of the international communist movement was directing attention towards problems of internal discipline and structure within foreign Parties. The Comintern was ceasing to be a channel for transmitting the demands of the international movement to the Soviet leadership, and providing a link between different but equal Parties. Instead it was becoming an instrument of Soviet control for the direct furtherance of Soviet policy. As such it quickly reflected the issues and struggles that were taking place in the CPSU.

Collectivization and intense industrialization were, we already know, theoretically conceptualized in terms of a sharpening of the class war. Stalin never tired of connecting *kulak* resistance and internal Party opposition with the machinations of international capitalism. In this new atmosphere the foreign technicians imported in the pragmatic period of NEP now found themselves regarded with suspicion as potential if not actual foreign agents; many of them were evicted and some put on trial for espionage. As early as December 1927, at the Russian Party's Fifteenth Congress, Stalin surprised the delegates by his statement that the period of stabilization of capitalism had come to an end, and a new and more aggressive policy on the part of all communists was called for. Foreign parties were to launch an all-out attack on the class enemy and their Social Democratic collaborators under the slogan of 'class against class'. Stalin characterized the international situation as one in which a new wave of imperialist attacks and preparations for intervention against the USSR were inevitable. In this way he heightened the domestic atmosphere of crisis. Collectivization and industrialization at home were matched by a major change of course abroad, and the two aspects were not only related but made interdependent. Thus the defeat of opposition at

85 The benign father of his people. Stalin in wartime ▶

home and the victories on the production front became a direct contribution to the international class struggle. Sympathizers were induced to believe that world communism was being advanced primarily through the witch-hunt against Trotskyites and Zinovievites in 1929–30, and later even through the purges. Here then we have some evidence that Stalin in fact may have been considering both collectivization and industrialization late in 1927. But the new Comintern course also follows from the failures in China, Britain and elsewhere. The most that can be said with certainty is that these fulminations about a sharpened international situation provided the right climate in which to justify the harsher measures at home – whatever they might be. By the time the purges reached their high point ten years later communists in the Soviet Union and abroad had become so accustomed to allegations of capitalist machinations against the Soviet Union that the idea of plots at the highest level did not seem absurd any longer.

In practice the new aggressive line for Communist Parties in the West had little effect on the overall domestic situation in these countries. Communism was simply not strong enough to achieve anything but some ripples of alarm in left-wing circles, and a new embitterment of relations between Communists and Social Democrats. The mobilization of European communism in the end consisted of an all-out attack on Social Democracy. The curtain-raiser for the new course was provided by the Comintern's needling of the Chinese communist leadership, starting with Li Li-san, even though the Chinese Party had been gravely weakened by Chiang Kai-shek's onslaught. Similar tactics were ordered against leading communist conciliators in Europe. The slogan 'class against class' meant that only communists represented the working classes, while the more moderate parties were depicted as 'the moderate wing of the bourgeois Fascist bloc'. Stalin dealt with the new phenomenon of Fascism quite simply: 'It is not true that Fascism is a militant organization only of the bourgeoisie. It is a militant organization of the bourgeoisie based on the active support of Social Democracy. Objectively Social Democracy is the moderate wing of Fascism. Fascism is the shapeless political bloc of the two basic organizations of Social Democracy and the bourgeoisie. These are not antipodes but twins.' What then of proletarian solidarity or unity? This was dealt with by a paradox, captured in the slogan of 'unity from below'. Unity could be achieved, not by collaboration with the Social Democrats, but by reaching down into the mass organizations and stealing the masses from the grasp of their false leaders.

This policy was to have tragic consequences. At a time when National Socialism in Germany was riding the crest of a dangerous wave, when Trotsky in exile was warning the world of the menace of this new phenomenon before which the well-publicized dangers of imperialism and capitalism were child's play, the policy of 'class against class' reduced Fascism to a mere slogan without special significance. The German Communist Party's attitude was summed up in the contemptuous reassurance of 1932: 'Fascism? But don't we already have the Fascism of the Social Democratic government of Prussia?'

This abandonment of any sustained attempt to view the international scene in broadly progressive or reactionary terms marks the definite end of the Lenin–Trotsky phase of the International. In spite of all their differences Lenin and Trotsky – as well as Zinoviev and Bukharin, who had effectively presided over the execution of Bolshevik policy in the Comintern – had never lost sight of the cause of the international left as a whole. Whatever the needs and manœuvres of Soviet diplomacy, the international movement had never been totally subordinated to it. After 1929 these restrictions simply fell away. Soviet diplomacy henceforward fished liberally in any troubled waters – no lack of these in the 1930s – for the benefit of the Soviet Union *tout court*. It was not Stalin who broke with Hitler, but Hitler with Stalin. The German officers training in Russia were recalled; Rapallo was replaced by the Anti-Comintern Pact. Only after he had failed to induce Hitler to sign a non-aggression pact did Stalin begin to turn to the Western Powers. So far as the Soviet Union was concerned, the brief flowering of German communism in the 1932 elections, at the height of the depression, had little significance. The Comintern under Manuilsky was more concerned with internal orthodoxy than with any revolutionary perspectives. Stalin was already in the throes of the mistrust and pessimism about the chances of foreign communism which were to remain with him for the rest of his life.

Thus the policy of revolutionary egoism which had caused such heart-searchings among the Bolsheviks over Brest Litovsk a few short months after their seizure of power had now reached a consummation which no one could have foreseen, though to us it may appear as the logical end. And it was by no means without its reward. While production indices everywhere were falling catastrophically during the great depression in Europe and America, those in the Soviet Union were going up – an important factor in an international movement whose *raison d'être* was now almost wholly anchored in the progress of the Soviet Union itself. After the breakdown of diplomatic relations with Great Britain in 1927, following the raid on the Soviet trade delegation in London, and a near-breakdown with France, the Soviet Union had become internationally acceptable once again in the early 1930s. In 1933 even the American government finally recognized its *de jure* existence. A year later the USSR joined the League of Nations. Another switch of policy in the International was now imminent. The policy of 'class against class' was abandoned as suddenly as it had been instituted, and the Popular Front era took its place – unity of all progressives in the fight against Fascism. European communists for the first time in a decade enjoyed the support of a sizable left-wing intelligentsia – no mean factor in a country like France. There particularly the communists now came within the orbit of government, offering qualified support to the socialist government in the National Assembly. But it was an uneasy alliance soon doomed to failure; the now wholly *ouvrièriste* leadership of the French Communist Party found direct collaboration with the hated Léon Blum impossible after a few weeks. The Popular Front was more stable and effective in the ideological formulations of Moscow than in practice in Paris.

The next five years were the period of Maxim Litvinov, old Bolshevik and dedicated internationalist, married to an English wife. Litvinov spoke in a voice familiar and acceptable to France and Britain. Western diplomats in the Soviet Union were treated with increasing attention and courtesy: everyone suddenly discovered a reasonable and statesmanlike Stalin – so different from the bloodthirsty monster of the popular tale. In March 1935 Eden, then a junior minister, was received by Stalin and listened to a Soviet orchestration of 'God Save the King' played at a banquet. Russia concluded mutual assistance pacts with both France and Czechoslovakia. Had she at last become a member of the concert of nations, a 'normal' nation like any other?

Hopes in this direction rose to their highest point during the Spanish Civil War. While the purges in Russia were at their height, international attention was partly diverted to Russia's role as sole champion of the Spanish government, seemingly the only effective bulwark against the advance of Fascism. In fact the Soviet intervention in the Spanish war was not as simple and clear-cut as propaganda would have it. The factional preoccupations during the great purges were only too well reflected by the activities of the Soviet emissaries in Spain who seemed as much concerned with the liquidation of anarchists and POUM deviationists fighting alongside them as with the defeat of Franco's army. But here again the unedifying details known to those directly involved were unknown to the outside world. In the eyes of many left-wing intellectuals the brutality of the purges was to some extent muted and overlaid by Soviet intervention in Spain. Many Americans who had drifted into the communist orbit during the great depression, and half a generation of well-born young Englishmen, accepted the Soviet Union as the doughty champion of democracy. Some of them would have cause to repent their enthusiasm before the investigations of Senator McCarthy and

his friends in the early 1950s.

Stalin now appeared to be conducting a diplomatic offensive in all directions. On the face of it he exploited the emerging image of the Soviet Union as the main bulwark against Nazi Germany. In the Munich crisis of 1938 it was Russia alone among the great powers that offered armed assistance to the Czechs, in accordance with its obligations under the 1935 Soviet-Czechoslovak Treaty. Perhaps this represented merely a gesture to world opinion – for the activation of the Treaty required simultaneous French backing, and the Russians had every reason to expect diplomatic difficulties in obtaining permission to cross either Polish or Rumanian territory to reach Czechoslovakia. But Stalin was also drawing his own conclusions from the hesitant appeasement of Britain and France, and the aggressive determination of Nazi Germany. Though negotiations with a British and French military mission continued in Moscow through the spring and summer of 1939, Stalin began to cast about for a concrete alternative. If Soviet security could not be assured through membership of an alliance against Germany, then the whole international anti-Fascist posture would be thrown overboard in favour of an arrangement with the arch-enemy at the expense of the West. The fact that several previous approaches to Hitler had been rebuffed did not deter him for one moment. The enthusiasm with which Soviet participation in the international fight against Fascism had been greeted by communist supporters and sympathizers, the fact that the period of Popular Front tactics had significantly increased communist membership everywhere in the West, counted for little as compared with the problem of Soviet security.

On 3 May 1939 Litvinov was dismissed and disappeared into obscurity. His place was taken by Molotov, the iron pillar of support for Stalin throughout the many changes and tergiversations of the previous decade. Within three weeks negotiations with Germany were opened simultaneously with those in progress with Britain and France. Stalin was nothing if not cautious; the longest possible delay in committing himself to either side in the widening rift between Germany and the Western Powers suited his policy very well. In the end he made up his mind. The shamefaced French and British negotiators were sent packing, and on 23 August 1939 the formal non-aggression pact between Germany and Russia was signed – secret clauses and all.

It was, as we now know, not simply a non-aggression pact, but in fact a delimitation of mutual spheres of interest, an agreement to divide eastern Europe. Stalin now recognized that war was inevitable. He believed that this would involve a long drawn-out struggle in the West between two more or less equal groups of adversaries. By assuring Germany of her benevolent neutrality, the Soviet Union would be able to stay clear of the conflict and

86, 87 Two differing phases of Soviet foreign policy and the men who personified them. Maxim Litvinov (left) was Foreign Minister during the period of the Popular Front and anti-Fascist policy. Vyacheslav Molotov (right) inaugurated the Nazi-Soviet pact and symbolized the unyielding attitude of Stalin's isolationist period

to make one more clean break with the nationality policy of Lenin and of the then Commissar for Nationalities, Joseph Stalin. In the name of Soviet security the Baltic states, the eastern part of Poland, and Bessarabia in the south could simply be annexed, Finland invaded for refusing to cede strategic territory considered vital for the safety of Murmansk and Leningrad. Soviet security thus finally subsumed the problem of revolution in neighbouring countries. Henceforward revolution in this area would not come primarily through the sharpening of class conflict, but in large measure through the direct intervention of Soviet armed forces, or at least close Soviet super-vision – as in Czechoslovakia in March 1948. Such revolutions as were to succeed elsewhere by virtue of their own internal strength would be viewed with scepticism and disfavour by Stalin – as the future history of Yugoslavia and China was to show.

The Soviet Union tried initially to crush the determined Finnish resistance throughout the winter of 1939–40. While the white-clad Finns were beating back the attacks of vastly superior Russian forces in the snow and ice, the Western Allies denounced Soviet intervention and sent food parcels. The Germans kept diplomatically quiet. To some extent the exposure of Soviet military failure was overlooked by the belligerents in the West, who had their own preoccupations. The Soviet Union and its communist supporters elsewhere denounced the Second World War as yet another imperialist struggle in which they had no direct interest and in which they would take no sides. By the summer of 1940 the Finnish problem had been settled.

156

Surveying the scene at the beginning of 1941 Stalin could legitimately claim that Soviet interests had been well served: peace and industrial expansion at home against a background of a major European war. All this fishing in troubled waters appeared justified. If there was unease at the unexpected speed of German victory in the West and in the Balkans, faith in the non-aggression pact with Germany provided reassurance. Against all this the agony of foreign communists, now compelled after so many difficult adjustments to accept even a Russo-German alliance, was simply irrelevant.

The German attack on the Soviet Union was, on the surface, not entirely a surprise. Warnings had already been received – specific ones from Churchill and an accumulation of Soviet intelligence reports about German troop movements on the border since the early spring, as well as messages from Sorge, the Soviet master-spy in Tokyo. But in fact the shock was funda-mental – beyond any mere error of tactics or even strategy. Stalin's policy had always been based on consolidation. The diplomatic activity of the previous decade had not been designed to give Russia a greater role in inter-national affairs for its own sake, because of any desire for diplomatic prestige, but to obtain a measure of security for the communist leaders to deal with the all-important domestic problems, economic in aim and political in means. Stalin had never expressed great faith in the potential of the Inter-national, or in the revolutionary viability of foreign Communist Parties; their main function was to give second- and third-line support to the Soviet Union. When Stalin spoke of being an Asiatic this was not intended to be an ethnic description nor a form of intellectual deprecation but rather con-veyed his firm intention not to play the European diplomatic game for its own sake, not to demonstrate European concerns or European attitudes. It also meant a refusal to accept the European rules of the game. Lenin had seen the Soviet Union as part of Europe, the advance guard of a new revolutionary Europe in which the Bolshevik Soviet Union was the dynamo spreading revolutionary energy outwards in all directions. Accordingly Lenin had played the diplomatic game upside down, with the main emphasis on the Comintern. Stalin played it in a more orthodox fashion, yet as a means of keeping Europe at bay. 'Socialism in one country' was perhaps the only one of Stalin's policies which involved a deep and personal commitment. It meant that diplomatic activity in European affairs was mainly designed to keep Europe as far away from the Soviet Union as possible. Now, on 22 June 1941, the whole scheme was shattered in an instant. Russia was to be firmly involved in Europe and its problems. All possibility of manœuvre and manipulation had gone; overnight the Soviet Union had necessarily become the client of its new allies, Britain and then the United States.

The map legend reads:

German Front 1941-42

●●● 22 June 41		═══ 5 Dec. 41		
●●● 9 July 41		═══ May 42		
■■■ 30 Sept 41		- - - Nov. 42		

0 _____ 400 M

88 Map of Russia at war, 1941–2

For the first fortnight after the invasion, Stalin kept completely silent, and it was Molotov who broadcast the news on 22 June. When Stalin did speak to the nation on 3 July the dramatically changed situation of the Soviet Union at war reflected a less obvious but equally dramatic change in the whole outlook of the Soviet government. Already on 6 May 1941 Stalin had, by what now seems an unintended coincidence, taken over formal as well as effective power in state and Party. Instead of managing the vast enterprise of the Soviet Union as Secretary of the Communist Party, he had also assumed the Chairmanship of the Council of Peoples Commissars. Though he now asked 'his people to rally round the party of Lenin and Stalin', he depicted this Party as a national leadership rather than that of a social class. And the forthcoming battle for the very existence of state and nation was no longer primarily a communist struggle. 'It was as if the Russia of 1812 had resurrected and spoken through Stalin's mouth', says one of his biographers. The tactics were the same: defensive retreat, the purchase of time through the cession of space, the determination to leave the invaders nothing except scorched earth. In the same broadcast Stalin announced a new apex to the political structure. Supreme economic powers of co-ordination and control were vested in the Economic Council of Peoples Commissars, called Ekonomsoviet. 'It acted', in the words of one historian, 'as an inner cabinet co-ordinating the whole economy.' Parallel to it was the supreme political and military body, the State Committee of Defence, which was ultimately charged with the military conduct of the war. Its members were Stalin, Molotov, Voroshilov, Malenkov and Beria.

89 Hitler in the footsteps of Napoleon. This *Krokodil* cartoon entitled 'On the old Smolensk road, 1812–1943' illustrates the Soviet appeal to the likelihood that history would repeat itself

In summarizing briefly the impact of the war on the government of the Soviet Union, we are at once faced with a paradox. On the one hand the emphasis on the defence of the Russian patrimony provided, strangely enough, a relief for the population – a sort of intellectual liberation. The new references to the motherland were couched in a language which people could understand. The unfamiliar, linguistically and intellectually awkward constraints of Stalinist ideology disappeared. Even the Partisan bands which were soon forming behind the German lines were as much in the tradition of Russian territorial defence as they were technically organized in accordance with the principles of communist cells. No doubt efforts were made to maintain Party supremacy and to prevent any dissolution of Party discipline in a purely patriotic context. But on the whole they had little relevance; as in the civil war the 'who's who and who does what' of the highly organized Bolshevik Party gave way to the absolute priority of fighting the war. Party leaders at all levels had to do any job that the situation required.

Yet at the same time it was the Party which effectively dominated the war effort from top to bottom. Here, too, the tradition of the civil war was fused with an older Russian tradition. If the symbols were based on the Napoleonic Wars, if 1812 suddenly became the most important historic date and the names of generals like Kutuzov became the immediate example to the commanders and soldiers at the front, the guidance of the struggle, the control of critical regions and areas, were firmly clasped in the hands of Party leaders *en mission*. These men were the Stalin loyalists of the purges, and they took up the role of their civil war predecessors with enthusiasm and devotion.

90, 91, 92 The Soviet Union at war. Below, young partisans of the Kotovsky detachment receive their arms in 1943. Above, an anti-aircraft battery looms up against the Soviet Army Theatre in Moscow in 1941. Right, a vegetable patch in a square opposite St Isaac's Cathedral during the long siege of Leningrad

Molotov, Kaganovich and Voroshilov among the older generation; Beria, Malenkov, Zhdanov, Khrushchev, Mikoyan, Bulganin and Voznesensky among the new. In particular we find that three of Stalin's most trusted advisers took overall responsibility for the three major sectors of the front: Zhdanov based on Leningrad for the north-west front, Bulganin on the western or central front, and Khrushchev in the south-west, the Ukraine and later the Stalingrad area. Military commanders changed frequently, but the Party proconsuls were to remain firmly entrenched in their areas throughout most of the war. At the grass roots, too, the Party and the workers achieved a new unity in diversity. When the Germans reached the outskirts of Moscow, brigades of shock-workers with rifles (and tools for those who had no rifles) flowed out from their factories to defend them against the invader; these worker brigades or *Opolcheniye* were formally constituted in July 1941.

There were exceptions – dissident national minorities seduced by false German promises of independence, a number of officers and men for whom the irresistible German advance and the appalling Russian losses and retreats spelt inevitable German victory. But overall the government of Stalin got a resounding vote of confidence – not in any obvious electoral terms, but through the stubborn and determined effort of the Soviet population. When it was all over, and Stalin on 24 May 1945 thanked 'the Russian people for their confidence in their government' this was but a minimal recognition of the truth. The Germans had helped to make his task much easier. They showed unparalleled brutality to the population of the occupied territories, to the many prisoners they had captured. Their clear expression of contempt for the inferior Slav peoples, above all their determination to exploit the Soviet Union as a source of food and slave labour for the German war effort, undermined the effectiveness of anti-communist propaganda.

93 One of the innumerable German atrocities. Soviet photograph of citizens near Leningrad burned alive by Nazi troops in 1944

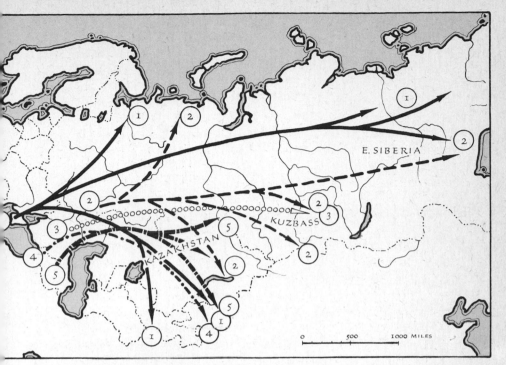

94 Map showing the Soviet deportation of various national groups during the war (1 Crimean Tatar; 2 Volga German; 3 Kalmyk; 4 Karachai–Balkar; 5 Chechen–Ingush)

Only in the Baltic states, incorporated into the Soviet Union a mere eighteen months earlier, among disaffected minorities in the south-west of the Soviet Union and a few remote tribes in the interior, could any substantial numbers be induced to give aid and comfort to the enemy. In many ways the solid response of loyalty was more than had been expected. The Soviet government took severe and often brutal precautions to resettle the Volga German community over a thousand miles to the north-east; for all intents and purposes this minority group henceforward ceased to exist as a distinct ethnic entity. In many cases retribution was more terrible than precaution; any evidence of collaboration with the abhorred invader, as in the Crimea and the Caucasus, led to mass deportation to Siberia and large-scale executions. Beria and his enormous NKVD apparatus became the angel of official vengeance and the extractor of surplus labour in the ever-replenished work camps around the Arctic Circle.

The first six months of the war were an unmitigated disaster for the Russians. Official British opinion had estimated that the Russian resistance could last two months at the most. Recent analyses by military experts of the early period of the war, and more important still the revelations from the Russian side since Stalin's death, show clearly how ill-prepared Stalin had been, and how close the Soviet government came to bankruptcy during these early months. Militarily the Russians were unable to deploy their basic superiority in manpower with any effect, so that the Germans outnumbered the Russians often by four and five to one in any particular engagement. In addition the retreat was disorganized rather than planned, so that very large numbers of Russian soldiers fell into German hands – estimates reach up to a million during the first six months of the war, together with many thousands of tanks and other precious equipment. The Soviet air force suffered enormous destruction – on the ground.

The Germans advanced all along the front. By October 1941 they were at the gates of Moscow and Leningrad; almost the whole of the Ukraine had been overrun. Russian military losses were enormous, especially in the south where the Germans had moved altogether too fast for their opponents and their armoured pincers sliced off large parts of Budenny's armies with their equipment. But the Russians were more successful in saving their industries. If the Soviet Union was indeed one large firm devoted to economic enterprise, it concentrated primarily on the removal of every asset that could be transported eastwards. Factories were moved wholesale in so far as the strained transport system and German bombers permitted. Train upon train lumbered towards the east with its industrial cargo, and a remarkable amount of equipment was safely transferred behind the Urals. With it a huge shift of population took place, often to necessarily appalling living conditions. Industries cannot be transported and produce at the same time; the reduced figures for industrial production from the end of 1941 to 1943 illustrate not only destruction and loss of territory, but also this mass transfer eastwards of industrial capacity.

Most significant of all perhaps was the rapid dismantling of all the barriers of self-sufficiency in the international field. A British-Russian Mutual Assistance Pact was signed on 12 July 1941, followed by pacts with the Czech and Polish governments-in-exile, and shortly afterwards a Polish army was formed in the Soviet Union. From then on with pedantic regularity Stalin began to call for a second front to relieve pressure on the Soviet Union. Although the United States was not yet a participant in the war, the Hopkins Mission which arrived in Moscow on 30 July 1941 began the negotiations which, after Pearl Harbor, were to lead to full-scale lend-lease aid, and in

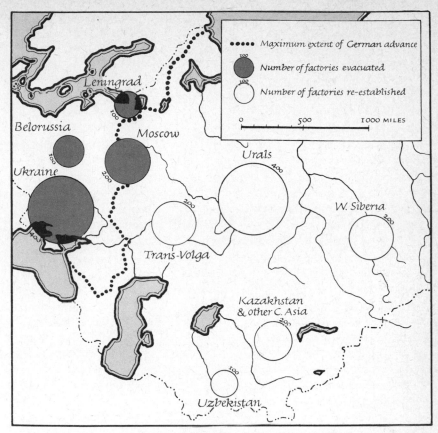

95 The eastwards evacuation of heavy industry in the USSR during the war

return for which the Russians made diplomatic and ideological concessions, culminating in the dismantling of the Comintern on 22 May 1943. Stalin at this time was perfectly prepared to have both British and American troops fighting in the Soviet Union if he could get them.

It was a war of rapid movement, of tanks and motorized infantry – and aircraft, which thrust ahead of the armies and transformed the towns and cities of western Russia into rubble on the pattern the Germans had already made familiar in Poland and Yugoslavia. It was the first truly mechanized war, and the Germans were at first infinitely superior to the Russians, both in what they possessed and in the skill with which they used it. German industrial and technological experience showed up the rawness, the largely experimental nature of the young Soviet industries.

165

Many of the Soviet commanders were dismissed after this first holocaust of failure, their places taken by new and almost unknown generals like Koniev, Rokossovsky and Zhukov, who had made their career since the civil war. Apart from Voroshilov and the Party generals who had come up primarily through Party channels, almost the entire General Staff of the Soviet Army with fighting experience had been wiped out in the great purges. Was this part of the reason for the early failures? There were moments of near panic, both at the top and among the bewildered soldiers streaming back over endless miles of precious territory. In November the Germans mounted their all-out offensive to capture Moscow before Christmas, as Hitler had promised. The government as a whole departed eastwards, and under the canopy of the capital's leaden, snow-filled skies billowed the smoke of burning archives, the nerve-centre of twenty-five years' centralized planning and control. But Stalin did not leave. Having deliberately evoked the spirit of 1812 he went one better than his predecessors; this time Moscow would not be surrendered even as a burnt shell.

Many German generals have since claimed that the failure to capture Moscow at the end of 1941 was the first real failure of the German war machine in action. More than this, the Russians were determined to turn their native winter to advantage and mounted a counter-offensive against the German army around Moscow early in the New Year. It did the Germans no great damage, but it did force them to retreat. There were history-suffused voices in the German High Command calling for a retreat right up to the Polish border, a notion which made Hitler burst into a paroxysm of rage. In a sense the pattern of the war was already becoming set: Hitler firmly determined to impose his will and his technological power on the inhospitable environment and the subhuman Slavs produced by it. (Stalin was depicted as the personification of darkness and evil, though privately Hitler expressed admiration for and envy of Stalin's immense power.) On the other side Stalin himself was cautiously and determinedly profiting by the self-destructive arrogance of his adversary, which together with the doggedness and self-sacrifice of the Soviet population made up in the end for all shortcomings and mistakes on the Russian side. He stayed in Moscow, spinning the web of national defence from the Kremlin throughout the whole war, invisible and curiously impersonal.

Khrushchev's later indictment of Stalin's wartime leadership pinpointed not only a basic indecisiveness but also a number of specific strategic errors: the loss of over half a million Russian troops because Stalin overruled the decision to pull out of the Kiev salient in September 1941; the ill-judged offensive on Stalin's orders near Kharkov in May 1942. Throughout the

96, 97
Marshal Zhukov,
who led the
counter-offensive
which saved Moscow;
and Marshal Beria,
the feared and hated
head of internal security

spring and summer of 1942 only the defence of Sevastopol inflicted com-
mensurate losses on the Germans. Perhaps the culmination of Russian military
failure was reached in the summer of that year with the fall of Rostov and
the implicit official admission that the Red Army had lost its nerve and
abandoned the town against the specific orders of Stalin. Two days later
Stalin's 'Not another step back' order was read to all units.

'The Rostov affair' led to the ruthless stamping out of cowardice and
disobedience, and to a series of sweeping reforms in the army. Younger
officers were quickly promoted *en masse*, military decorations for officers
and more distinctive uniforms were introduced, and above all the hated
system of parity between political commissars and commanders was replaced
by giving the military commanders clear and unequivocal control – at any
rate over military decisions. The lowest ebb of military fortune thus coincides
with perhaps the high point of retreat from communist orthodoxy. Ideologically the interpretation of the war turned increasingly into a Russian-
German dichotomy. Love of the Russian motherland was matched by hatred
of the German invaders. Its clearest expression was in the literary efforts of
Ilya Ehrenburg, who had previously been on the verge of deviation through
his pre-war warning against the menace of Nazi Germany (he himself later
came to wonder why he had not been purged), but now became unofficial
poet laureate of the Great Patriotic War. Party was now subsumed under
nation in an entirely new way, and the old priorities were reversed. Entry
into the Party was made correspondingly easy so that membership trebled
from two to six million members and candidates between 1941 and 1944.

It is almost impossible to date with any accuracy the swing of the war from
involuntary retreat to the recapture of initiative and counter-offensive by the

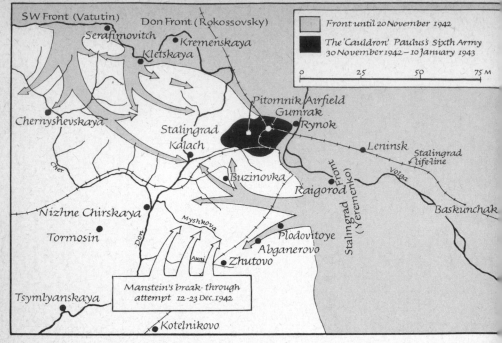

98 Map of the battle for Stalingrad

Russians. Traditionally the successful defence of Stalingrad and the subsequent pincer movement on 19 November 1942, resulting in the capture of the German Sixth Army more or less intact, is taken as a crucial date. Certainly it represented a turning point – but militarily perhaps more from the German side than the Russian since it was the first failure of Hitler's particular intuitive strategy. Yet psychologically the effect on the Russians was enormous. It gave them their first irreversible victory – a victory made all the more uplifting by its association with the name of the Soviet leader, henceforth endlessly eulogized as a military genius. But two other events were of significance in turning the war. The three-year defence of·besieged Leningrad, in which over a million people died, both epitomized Soviet capacity for resistance and tied down substantial German forces. Every war needs its martyrs – places as much as people. Perhaps the crucial moment of Soviet military resurgence came in July 1943. It was now Hitler's turn to need a spectacular victory to make up for the losses and retreats since Stalingrad, and much of German strength was directed to a counter-attack at Kursk, some five hundred miles north of Kharkov – chosen by Hitler precisely because it was a point of Russian concentration. Yet again the Russians succeeded in breaking the counter-offensive and inflicting heavy losses on

ОКНО ТАСС № 640

ЕВРАЩЕНИЕ „ФРИЦЕВ"

99, 100 Wartime propaganda.
Far left, poster showing
'The Fritzes Transformed';
left, cover
of *Krokodil* in 1943
showing the shadow
of the Stalingrad
victory over
the German soldiers

, 102 The devastated
centre of Stalingrad
in February 1943
(above).
An anti-aircraft
battery during
a Nazi air-raid
on Leningrad in 1942
(right)

the Germans. After this defeat at Kursk the Germans did not mount another major offensive and the Russian advance continued unchecked, except for minor delays, all the way to the gates of Berlin.

Already in March 1943 Stalin had assumed responsibility for Russian successes by adopting the title of Marshal. In July and August of that year the first large-scale trial of Russian collaborators took place at Krasnodar in the northern Caucasus, and the formation of the Free German Committee signified the first attempt to get to grips with the future problems of a defeated Germany – a concept which made sense only when the prospects of Russian victory seemed assured. It was to be a long and hard-fought road back through the vastness of western Russia, conquered and devastated by the Germans, the invasion of German-held eastern Europe, and finally the entry into Germany itself. From the summer of 1943 onwards, however, the Soviet government was able for the first time to raise its sights beyond the immediacies of the fighting, and review its general position both at home and abroad.

103 Map of the Soviet counter-offensive which drove the German troops back towards the west

104 The triumphant Soviet soldier in 1944, a somewhat grand-opera conception

In the second half of 1943 the first cautious changes in emphasis were beginning to appear at home. Once the problem of post-war Germany had been raised, the simplifications imposed by the need to defeat the invader were adjusted to accommodate a more specifically communist perspective. By 1944 Ehrenburg was being played down, and in 1945 Stalin began officially to differentiate between the social phenomenon of Nazism and the democratic potential of the German people – just as official communist policy had always done in the early 1930s. In September 1944 recruiting into the Party was sharply cut down, and the ideological threshold for entry was raised. The government did nothing to discourage the feeling of relief and joy over victory, and the desire to reap the benefit of the long and hard struggle – yet; it was not until 1946 that the bleak prospect of what was to be called Zhdanovism began to darken the horizon.

On the diplomatic front, too, the new self-confidence in impending victory made Stalin less forthcoming in his relations with his allies. Lend-lease had operated effectively and smoothly. The Soviet leaders were well aware that without it the industrial base of the Soviet Union might not have been capable of producing victory in the time. But divergences over post-war reconstruction between the Allies were beginning to appear. In particular Soviet relations with the Polish government in London were deteriorating. They received a nearly fatal blow when the Soviet forces, encamped on the

171

east bank of the Vistula, watched the almost complete destruction of the Polish Home Army in the Warsaw uprising of 1 August 1944, and the Soviet Union refused landing rights to Allied planes for supplying and assisting the Polish rebels. Whether the official Soviet explanation – that the German defence had stiffened and the Soviet forces in the eastern suburbs of Warsaw were unable to attempt a crossing of the river after a long and rapid advance – is true or not, the fact remains that the only real rival to the Soviet-sponsored Lublin Committee was effectively destroyed by the Germans in these few weeks. Of course the argument works both ways, since the orders in London for the uprising in Warsaw may also have been intended primarily to create a situation in favour of the anti-communist elements before the Russians arrived. In any case it proved an important moment in the crystallization of Stalin's conception of post-war eastern Europe. Hitherto he had vacillated and resisted Polish communist plans for more direct support, but now he plumped more openly for the Lublin Committee and against the London government sponsored by his British allies. As so often, Stalin's decision seemed forceful and decisive though in fact it followed events he had not himself brought about.

Stalin's determination to organize eastern Europe under Russian influence was the major cause, apart from the question of the future of Germany itself, of the break-up of the war-time alliance. It can be understood only if the extent of Hungarian, Bulgarian, Rumanian and Baltic participation in Hitler's invasion of the Soviet Union is fully understood. Whether they were reluctant allies or enthusiastic supporters of the German solution of the Russian question, is irrelevant. As far as the Russians were concerned, some of the worst excesses against the Russian population had been committed by these auxiliaries, and their units had fought bravely alongside the Germans at Stalingrad and elsewhere. The result was that Stalin viewed eastern European participation in the war on the German side as a total commitment, and determined that future arrangements for this part of the world must make a repetition of this alignment impossible.

In the course of a meeting with Churchill in Moscow on 9 October 1944 this crucial problem was discussed. Its provisional settlement took the form of elementary horse-trading. Churchill himself describes how the whole question of south-eastern Europe was 'settled' between them in a few minutes; Russia was allocated 90 per cent influence in Rumania, 75 per cent in Bulgaria and 50 per cent each in Yugoslavia and Hungary. The figures themselves were not to have great consequence (obviously, since influence cannot be apportioned in percentages), but the very notion that Britain – in Stalin's eyes speaking for the West as a whole – accepted Soviet primacy in eastern Europe was henceforward interpreted as the right to a free hand. As it turned out, Stalin's assumption that Churchill represented more than Britain in these negotiations was an important error – one that led directly to some of the most frozen cold-war recriminations and attitudes. For American views on the post-war world were well summed up in a message which Roosevelt sent to Stalin in 1944: 'There is in this global war literally no question, either military or political, in which the United States is not interested.' This denied the very concept of spheres of influence, and put paid to Churchill's horse-trading. The later differences in the conceptions of Churchill and Roosevelt as to the post-war world were already implicit in these negotiations, though at the time, the collaboration between the major Allies in the war against Germany, characterized by personal contact, was one of the most encouraging features for the post-war future.

The Yalta Conference, which opened on 4 February 1945, marked the high point of Allied collaboration and also, if dimly, indicated the shape of the coming peace. The war with Germany was nearly over. The Russian contribution to the Allied victory was universally acknowledged as outstanding. Public opinion everywhere glowed with tribute to Soviet achievements. Names like Zhukov, Malinovsky and Koniev, places like Stalingrad, Voronezh and Kursk became as familiar to millions of Englishmen and Americans as Lincoln and Wellington, Gettysburg and Waterloo; the Soviet Union was becoming familiar as never before. The odious Comintern had been dissolved in 1943 – the last link with a regrettable past of Soviet isolation and international conspiracy. The Allied leaders were meeting for the second time on equal terms and with apparently common aims. The Oriental strangeness of the Soviet Union encapsulated in its mysterious Marxist philosophy had given way to a more familiar Russia beating back and pursuing the common enemy right to the gates of his own capital, Berlin. As in 1918 there was widespread hope that the price of the holocaust would purchase a different and a better world.

Unlike 1918, however, Communist Parties in countries outside the Soviet Union were no longer a hunted and feared minority; they had been among the doughtiest and often the best organized fighters against the Germans, and now emerged as the cornerstone of a new left-wing alliance. In France the communists had recovered from the extreme doldrums of the Nazi-Soviet Pact of 1940 to head the resistance movement against the Germans; it was natural for them to be included in De Gaulle's first post-war government. In Italy they did not join in the post-war government, but succeeded in splitting the opposition socialist movement, and obtained the tactical adherence of the majority group of socialists under Nenni – an electoral alliance that was to last effectively until 1964. Admiration for the Soviet Union coupled with popular demands for social change gave the communists substantial if temporary advantages almost everywhere. Perhaps even more significant was the situation of Communist Parties in newly independent countries. Here they became identified from the start with the immensely popular fight for national independence. Indonesia, India and other ex-colonies started their newly independent existence with built-in and strongly supported Communist Parties, which were shortly to overreach themselves by attempting a bid for power in what was still a revolutionary situation. Whatever Western governments might think, the world position of international communism had reached an all-time level of popular support and opened up serious perspectives of power. Moreover, these commanding positions had been attained not through Soviet assistance, but from their own resources. The war of 1939–45 had provided perhaps the first occasion since 1918 when Communist Parties were able to act independently and successfully. Nevertheless, as the situation became more stable, and the United States began to shore up the war-worn economies of the West, the future of European and Asian communism began to be linked more directly once more with the attitude and policies of the Soviet government. In the event almost no assistance whatever was forthcoming from that quarter.

For the Soviet Union was quickly relapsing into its pre-war isolationist emphasis on self-sufficiency. Stalin was in a very real sense only a reluctant member of the Three-Power Consortium for world management. His acceptance of the primacy of the United States, Britain and the Soviet Union was not based on any real expectation that these leading nations could collaborate successfully, that their interests were analogous. Once victory was in sight, Stalin quite automatically reverted to the successful tactics of his own struggle for leadership and for the later strengthening of the international position of the Soviet Union: isolating his rivals from their supporters, and relying on them to cancel each other out. If he opposed the suggestion that France should become an equal fourth partner in the Consortium, it was because she would probably become merely a reliable ally or client of the British. If he suggested that the newly created United Nations should dispose of its own armed forces stationed on members' territory, it was not in order to make an international policy more effective, but to obtain a valuable bargaining counter in the delimitation of spheres of influence. The important thing was to ensure that the Soviet Union obtained every advantage in the coming international settlement, which Stalin envisaged as a parcelling out of spheres of influence between the three great world powers. The concept of imperialism, which meant that powerful and advanced capitalist countries exercised hegemony over smaller neighbours, readily suggested the institution of spheres of influence in which the USSR could participate. If the Soviet Union could henceforth ensure that its frontiers were protected by a shield of friendly and dependent nations, two basic objects would be achieved: the Soviet Union would be secure from surprise attack (the immediate lesson of 1941), and it could revert more easily to the withdrawn and self-regarding situation which was Stalin's preferred and natural habitat. In moving heaven and earth for a Soviet-controlled eastern Europe, Stalin claimed that he was only doing what his allied opponents would automatically be seeking to do for themselves.

He accordingly showed very little sympathy or understanding for British pleas about pledges towards Poland, and for opposition to the installation of reliable governments in Hungary, Rumania and Bulgaria. These were manifestations of unwarrantable interference, evidence of continuing aggressive designs on the part of the 'interveners' of 1919. As we shall see, Stalin did not seriously attempt to influence British and American actions in the areas allotted to them; equally he did not expect them to interfere with him. Soviet participation in the final campaign against Japan was an unexpected bonus. Stalin appears to have been surprised that a Soviet contribution at this late and easy stage in the war against Japan should be so strongly solicited by Roosevelt. Accordingly the Soviet invasion of Manchuria was presented primarily as an historic *règlement des comptes* for the defeat of 1904. 'An event for which our older people have been waiting for forty years' – actually a patriotic falsification of Party history, for at the time Lenin and the Bolsheviks had rejoiced in the Tsarist defeat. As to China, Stalin was perfectly prepared to accept Chiang Kai-shek and the Kuomintang as the legitimate government. It was not Stalin who needed persuasion to open negotiations for the settlement of Russian border problems with China, but the ever-wary Chiang Kai-shek, on whom the Americans had to bring strong pressure.

Roosevelt and Churchill differed considerably in their evaluation of their Russian ally, but both failed in the last resort to appreciate Stalin's real motives. To Roosevelt Stalin had 'evolved'; the isolated, introspective and paranoiac dictator of the purges had been forced into helping to create the new world order – always provided that his most immediate and legitimate security interests were satisfied. Churchill took a more sceptical and old-fashioned view. The international victory of communism was still the primary motivation of Soviet action. Stalin might orchestrate his wartime responses and attitudes with Russian voices, but beneath all this was a deep commitment to the world revolution proclaimed by Marx and Lenin, whose disciple Stalin had always claimed to be. The Soviet desire to manipulate the governments of eastern Europe was seen by Roosevelt as unfortunate evidence of excessive traditional caution, by Churchill as a return to the bad old ways of international subversion. Both were right, but at a surface level. For Stalin the attainment of international status had never been a goal but a means. The war was an unfortunate interruption to the introspective development of 'socialism in one country' which Stalin had pursued so laboriously from 1925 onwards, at home and abroad. Now that the war was coming to an end, the advantages of victory would be turned to good account – not in order to enable the Soviet Union to attain a new and dominant role but in order to buttress the old and familiar pattern. Whatever the Western press with its enthusiasm for Russian bravery might say, Stalin saw the cleavage between the Soviet Union and its capitalist allies as basic and unbridgeable. The only difference was that Russian victories in the field, and her powerful voice in international affairs, would now make her position more secure. The new might of the Soviet Union would be used not so much as a springboard to further action but rather as a bulwark to ensure her safety and distance from predatory and powerful opponents.

In practice Stalin returned to the same dual form of international policy which he had evolved before the war: the pursuit of Soviet interests abroad which co-ordinated both Soviet diplomacy and organized communism into one coherent instrument. No risks were to be taken in the pursuit of impossible revolutionary tasks. If in practice this often meant consigning Communist Parties in the West or in developing countries to the mercy of capitalist governments, then this was no worse than the treatment these parties had received before the war. Stalin was just as sceptical after the war about communist chances abroad as he had been in the 1930s. He hardly expected the resurgence of communism in western Europe which resulted from the communists' control of a large part of the resistance movements in France and Italy; when Togliatti returned from Moscow to Italy in 1944, his colleagues were staggered by Stalin's sealed instructions – recognition by the communists of the monarchy, and service under Badoglio, no less! Stalin underrated the alliance between communism and nationalism in countries like India and the Middle East. Above all, he sold the Chinese communists short. While he certainly expressed no public enthusiasm for capitalist forms of government, his analysis of the world situation assigned the new wave of left-wing radicalism even less chance of success than it had had after the First World War. In any case he was not going to risk Soviet interests on its behalf.

Was he correct? Was there a real chance of communist-inspired socialist revolution in the West? The answer is almost certainly no – and communist

105, 106, 107 Soviet view of the cold war. Left, during the Korean War in 1951 the United Nations were regarded as the instrument of US policy. Below, the accusation of germ warfare. American imperialism in the form of an aeroplane scattering bugs over the countryside. Bottom, from the White House the United States reaches out to encircle the USSR in Korea, Iran, Turkey, Formosa and Vietnam

analysis of the situation exaggerates the importance of American support for the existing governments. For there were more profound social reasons for the failure to turn a widespread desire for a better world into a revolutionary situation. Underneath the radical ferment at the end of the War there lurked a basic and highly conservative longing, however inchoate, to return to peace and stability, often expressed in a determination to dismantle all forms of control and rationing. Change might be desirable, but only within the framework of the known system, not through a series of further upheavals following on the demands of full-scale war and, in many cases, German occupation. There was thus a contradiction between the general if vague desire for social improvement and the more immediate reluctance to accept the necessary measures that this involved. In these circumstances the only alternatives for Communist Parties were either co-operation and a share of power on essentially bourgeois terms, or a return to the wilderness. For Stalin the latter was the self-evident choice. If Communist Parties were unable to gain complete control there was little point in assisting them for any other purpose. He was more concerned with re-establishing discipline, which had been diluted as a result of alliance with other groups in the Resistance. Hence Communist Parties in the West were once more relegated to a non-participating role of structural though impotent opposition, leaving the diplomatic field clear for the Soviet Union.

Though he probably predicted the long-term chances of communism in the West correctly, he did not appreciate the revolutionary potential in developing countries. In fact he failed to distinguish between these two different sets of conditions. Instead of dividing the world into capitalist and developing countries, in effect and for practical purposes he saw only the contrast between the area of his own power, the socialist bloc, and an amorphous, more or less hostile mass made up of all other countries. As a result, the partially justified pessimism about revolutionary chances in advanced countries was indiscriminately applied to what came to be known as the Third World as well. Here the revolutionary situation initially created by the upsurge of anti-colonial independence movements was neglected by communists, and left to be exploited by nationalist groups who consolidated their new power at the expense of their uneasy communist allies. In the absence of firm guidance the local leadership vacillated and became divided. Above all the pre-war pattern of belated insurrection after the chance of success had already passed was once more repeated.

Quite different was the situation within the Soviet sphere of influence. If Communist Parties were actively helped by Soviet occupation forces, and their allies in the anti-Fascist bloc manœuvred first into impotence and later into either destruction or a docile shadow-like existence on the fringe of political power, this was not primarily due to any ideological commitment to the success of international communism. These were simply the obvious and well-tried means to hand. The only form of control which Stalin knew and trusted was the highly disciplined Party. The communist leaders who emerged in the People's Democracies of eastern Europe had mostly been trained in Moscow – the safe and trusted remnants who had survived the purges of the 1930s. To them fell the task of creating a socialist revolution from above – with the help and under the surveillance of the Soviet occupation forces and, behind them, the Communist Party of the Soviet Union – while having at the same time to satisfy heavy Russian demands for goods and services in payment of the war debts incurred by their predecessors. The help these countries received from their great socialist neighbour was political and ideological; on the economic side the Soviet Union did not give but rather took – and a great deal at that. Throughout the remaining period of Stalin's life eastern Europe was to a large extent integrated into the Soviet economy as a source of cheap goods for the Soviet Union. The structure of economic organization imposed a permanent form of tribute on the People's Democracies. Punctilious fulfilment was treated as equivalent to political orthodoxy; indeed such orthodoxy tended in part to be defined in terms of economic subservience. The so-called movement for liberalization in eastern Europe since 1953 was therefore essentially a revolt against economic exploitation by the Soviet Union, from which flowed a number of unexpected but secondary political consequences. Stalin's suppression of national deviations in eastern Europe after 1945 was concerned not only with ideological heresies but also with signs of economic independence. And *pari passu* the resurgence of nationalism in eastern Europe, and the articulation of different national paths to socialism, similarly have their roots in the desire to keep the benefit of industrialization at home instead of integrating it into the larger conceptions of Soviet economic strategy.

The construction of a communist-dominated eastern Europe in the decade after 1944 cannot be understood in terms of a new wave of revolution which threatened to engulf western Europe. The fact that the securing of Soviet influence in the East coincided with the high point of communist influence and an occasional simmering of the revolutionary pot in the West, India and Indonesia was largely a coincidence. In fact there was a certain conflict between these tendencies, for Soviet imposition of socialism from above in eastern Europe in a sense undermined both the validity and the chances of success for communists elsewhere. Vital as the Marshall Plan came to be in the quick reconstruction of the economies of western Europe, its primary purpose was to shore up these countries against the lapping tide of subversion from the East – a tide which in fact did not exist. If anything, the Soviet Union viewed capitalist western Europe as lapping at its own socialist shores; security consisted of protecting these shores by creating a strong east European sea wall. This was very different from a policy of active subversion of western Europe. There is a clear distinction between Soviet ends and Soviet means. The end was security – the creation of tributary and subservient states within a Soviet sphere of influence. The means, on the other hand, were the only ones conceivable to a generation of Russian leaders brought up in both the ideology and the techniques of Soviet Marxism – a dominant Party industrializing from above, eliminating its opponents one by one, and creating the basis of a socialist society in a hurry. Any government that could not be controlled represented a threat, and communist governments were far easier to control than others. The only possible exception to this simple system of classification was Finland – hence the widely believed myth of Stalin's special affection for that country, sometimes generalized into a quite erroneous belief that Stalin had sympathy for all small powers. Instead the Finnish case may be seen as a demonstration of Stalin's realism; for the subversion of Finland might well have provoked a second intervention by the Western Powers.

Stalin's disinterest in the export of communist revolution as such and his sense of priority for economic problems and control can best be illustrated by the variations from the Soviet model in many of the People's Democracies. In Poland, Hungary, Rumania, and later Czechoslovakia as well as East Germany, only the structure of the Communist Party and the overall emphasis on industrialization were precisely copied from the Soviet model. From this followed mandatory acceptance of collectivization, emphasis on heavy industry, purges, great power for the leaders combined with total insecurity, and finally the all-pervasive presence and power of the police. For the rest Stalin was not very interested. Important differences in social policy among members of the Socialist bloc continued to exist throughout this 'uniform' period. Except for Yugoslavia, where it was inevitable, no attempt was made anywhere to copy the Soviet federal structure – not even in Czechoslovakia where it would have been feasible. Perhaps the most important departure, however, was the maintenance, however formal, of party coalitions in Poland, Hungary and the German Democratic Republic, but not in Yugoslavia, Rumania or Czechoslovakia. This meant that while single-party rule had been the sacrosanct cornerstone of politics in the Soviet Union for over twenty years, a number of People's Democracies were in appearance ruled by a bloc of parties, the reliable elements of the immediate

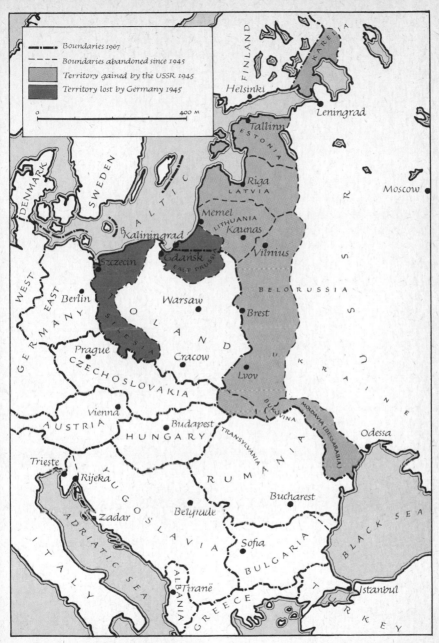

108 The boundaries of eastern Europe, 1925–67

post-war anti-Fascist alliance. Though the communists' partners were strictly controlled and always in a weak minority position, they were able to seek electoral support and maintain an organized existence of their own. The precise organizational structure of industry was also left to the discretion of the local leaders in each country, always provided that the delivery quotas to the Soviet Union were fulfilled. The Cominform, founded in September 1947 to replace the defunct Communist International, had from the start a marked stress on economic control. The transformation of the largely agricultural and backward countries of eastern Europe, except for the relatively advanced societies of Poland, Czechoslovakia and later East Germany, into a rapidly industrializing belt along the western frontiers of the Soviet Union was therefore a residual benefit arising from the means adopted as much as the attainment of a deliberate goal.

The limits of the Soviet sphere, and the extent to which it was amenable to close control, were not of course pre-ordained, but emerged by a process of trial and error. The eight years extending from the end of the war to Stalin's death should be viewed as an attempt to test the reality of Soviet power and its effectiveness in controlling its immediate environment. The map shows the extent to which the position of Czechoslovakia after the war was something of an anomaly – a bourgeois émigré government returning to take control of a country in the midst of the Soviet sphere of influence and lying across Soviet communications with East Germany and Hungary. Though the Czech coup of March 1948 was a gamble, it was a good one from a geo-political point of view, and imperative for the effective control of the new socialist bloc as a single unity. The risk was minimized by the fact that Soviet forces were not involved; the Czech Communist Party succeeded in taking over the country with only the sympathetic surveillance and advice of the Soviet Embassy. Though the communist take-over in Czechoslovakia set the pattern of the coming cold war, and confirmed the West in its darkest suspicion of Soviet intentions, it was in fact a closing operation to complete the organization of the socialist bloc rather than the beginning of a new offensive against capitalist states. Czechoslovakia could, with some justification, be considered to lie within the Soviet orbit of influence. However much a communist seizure of power might be deplored on ideological grounds, it did not seriously alter the balance of power.

But occasionally events at or outside the periphery of the Soviet sphere did get out of hand. Stalin was quite prepared to sit back and wait to see whether he could benefit, provided he was not called upon to incur any direct risk of involvement. We now know that far from encouraging the Greek insurgents to capture power in 1944–5 he actively discouraged them, and certainly did nothing to help them. All the effective foreign help for the Greek rebels came from Yugoslavia. The evidence indicates that the insurrection had its roots more firmly in the background of Greek politics than in the history of international communism. In Iran, on the other hand, the enthusiasm of communist sympathizers certainly received some initial noncommittal support; but once it was clear that the Shah had the support of the Western allies the restoration of the Teheran government's authority over the northern provinces was accepted as inevitable. Much the same pattern applied to the abortive communist risings in India and Indonesia shortly after independence, where there were indigenous efforts to apply the methods of Bolshevik revolution. Even the much more serious Korean war of 1950–3 was no exception. Stalin did not encourage the North Koreans, though he armed them and did not hold them back. The impending American withdrawal from South Korea offered a useful opportunity of testing the United States' willingness and capacity to react, and embroiling it in a peripheral affray (without any direct corresponding Soviet involvement) which could not but deflect its attention from the much more important European and particularly German theatres. In all these cases Stalin's support for the communists was confined to a certain amount of material help and much diplomatic stone-walling at the United Nations. The Soviet Union was certainly not prepared to risk its own armed forces for a single moment.

All these events served to test the strength of the adversary, to delimit areas of control and influence, to help convince the Russians yet again of the unbridgeable gulf between the socialist and the capitalist worlds, and finally to reinforce Soviet security by firmly instilling in the minds of Western statesmen and their electors a healthy fear of communist military, economic and ideological potential. But in both the Greek and Korean affairs a new and unexpected variable had made itself felt for the first time. The Yugoslavs and Chinese had been the communist powers closest to the conflict and had actively taken on themselves the furtherance of a cause which they presumed was also that of the Soviet Union. Both in their different ways drew significant lessons from the unenthusiastic and self-interested policy of the Soviet leadership. Eventually both rebelled against Soviet hegemony. Their revolt was to take place at different times, take very different forms and be based on different reasons – but both the Yugoslav and Chinese Party leaders came to realize that their immediate interests could no longer be served by total identification with the Soviet Union. It was now proving as untrue to say that what was good for the Soviet Union was good for world communism in all its aspects as it was untrue that what was good for General Motors must automatically be good for the United States. But while the Yugoslavs forced hot-tempered and open conflict with Stalin, the Chinese appeared to swallow Stalin's lack of interest in their revolution and failure of support at crucial times – indeed the whole long history of Comintern mistakes in China. As recent history has shown, however, these were buried but not forgotten, and would be disinterred whenever this should prove desirable. In the end the Chinese challenge to Soviet leadership proved far more serious than the open split with Yugoslavia which paranoiacally dominated Stalin's last few years.

Tito's breakaway in 1948 appeared to Stalin himself and to the world as the Soviet leader's greatest failure. This was a domestic rebellion within the sphere of control, the likelihood of which Stalin had totally misjudged. Once again the issues had been primarily economic, but had soon degenerated into recriminations and threats about Soviet supremacy, socialist discipline and the real basis of co-operation between the USSR and Yugoslavia. Even after the Yugoslav leaders had begun to show defiance in the high-level discussions behind closed doors, Stalin still believed that he could easily deal with a recalcitrant Tito, as he had always liquidated opposition within his orbit. 'I will shake my little finger – and there will be no more Tito, he will fall,' he said to Khrushchev at the end of 1948. But the Yugoslav leader, hitherto the strongest and most reliable of Stalin's associates in eastern Europe, was also the only one who had attained power by his own efforts and not by courtesy of the Soviet armed forces. He had behind him a tough and loyal Party forged in a war to the death against the German invaders. Short of armed intervention, there was no way of getting rid of the rebel. Internal Party manipulations, as well as the attempt to isolate Tito from the other Communist Parties of eastern Europe, only served to strengthen his position at home. If socialism could flourish on its own in one country, as Stalin had shown, then it could equally well flourish in another country – without and in spite of the USSR.

109 He who is not with us is against us. A cartoon of 1950 shows Tito saying to Churchill, 'We have common interests now, Mr Churchill – the Americans.'

110 The leaders of two People's Democracies meet in June 1957 in East Germany. Walter Ulbricht (left), head of the German Communist Party, and Władisław Gomułka, First Secretary of the Polish United Workers Party

The lesson that Stalin drew was typically cautionary. What had happened in Yugoslavia could clearly happen elsewhere. The answer must be more purges, no relaxation of any kind. The enemy (never made specific but always generalized) had now taken on the guise of nationalist deviation; its leaders were foreign communists who did not fully accept that even the implicit interests of the Soviet Union must override all domestic considerations. A whole series of prominent victims were arraigned all over eastern Europe. Some were shot, like Slansky and Clementis in Czechoslovakia, Rajk in Hungary and Kostov in Bulgaria. Others, like Gomułka in Poland, were merely imprisoned without trial – to emerge again as the dismantlers of Stalinism a few years after his death. Stalin threatened the whole Polish leadership if they did not bring Gomułka to trial; 'everybody', he told them, 'has trials except you.' By now the very business of staging dramatic demonstrations of subservience had become more important than the nature of the victims themselves. But in the meantime Tito went from strength to strength at home.

It was Germany, however, which proved to be the crucial frontier and testing-ground of the Soviet sphere. In July 1945 the leaders of the three major Allied powers had met once more, and for the last time. Appropriately this reunion had taken place in Potsdam, the rococo but tough-minded capital of Frederick the Great. The war was over, the basic decisions about the peace had already been made; all that remained was to agree on the future

185

of Germany. But by now it had become clear that the fluid discussions at Yalta only a few months earlier had already become constrained by newly set attitudes and conflicting policies. Perhaps communism had not changed its spots after all – and nor had capitalism either. Churchill invented the phrase 'Iron Curtain' – to describe the restrictions thrown around British representatives in the Balkans. Stalin retaliated by objecting to the British determination to restore the King of Greece. There were further fruitless appeals by the West against Russian support for the Lublin Committee as the legitimate government of Poland. What then of Germany? It had been decided to leave Germany intact as one country, but to deprive it of all its acquisitions since 1937, and to leave the areas beyond the Oder-Neisse line under Polish control. Western remonstrations about the expulsion of Germans from the Sudetenland and Silesia merely annoyed Stalin as a demonstration of gratuitous hypocrisy. Administratively Germany was now to be divided into four zones of occupation. Common policies were to be co-ordinated in Berlin by the four-power military government.

On paper the arrangement was clear enough. But in practice the four zones soon crystallized into individual spheres of influence, reflecting the East–West cleavage at its most marked. All the Allies were determined that Germany should never again be a menace. But while Stalin envisaged future security against Germany through the destruction of her economic power and a heavy long-term obligation to pay reparations, the West had in mind something less radical. Whatever expectations the Russians may have had of benefiting from the dismantling of Ruhr industry were soon disappointed. The full burden of providing reparations for the USSR therefore fell on the Soviet Zone. As in the Soviet Union the end was economic, the means political. The development of a communist-controlled society in East Germany was not the result of a doctrinaire pursuit of ideological aims, a springboard from which the rest of Germany could be revolutionized, but the secondary consequence of installing reliable and efficient supporters of Soviet economic policy whose main skills were those of transforming societies from above as prescribed by Soviet practice, and as they had learnt in the Soviet Union. It is useless to ask, as many historians have done, whether the breakdown of joint Allied military government in Germany, or indeed of the wartime alliance, was particularly the fault of East or West. Both were the prisoners of their knowledge, experience and ideology. The West eventually saw its requirements satisfied by the temporary removal of Nazis and their replacement by known anti-Nazis – at any rate at the top; a prosperous Germany was both harmless and less expensive for themselves. The Russians, on the other hand, were unimpressed by the substitution of a few top leaders. Adequate control was possible only if social conditions were right; if necessary these had to be created. The fact that the German Democratic Republic could thereby achieve socialism was almost a bonus for which the beneficiaries were expected (but hardly showed themselves) to be duly grateful to the Soviet Union.

Control of East Germany was crucial. A resurgent Germany was the greatest menace that Russians, Czechs and Poles could conceive. The more the Soviet occupation authorities exploited East Germany, the more the Western Powers enabled West Germany to build itself up, and in turn the more determinedly did Germany's eastern neighbours feel the need to cling to the Soviet Union for their safety. Stalin the 'Asiatic' was not in the least worried about American domination of Japan; he was perfectly prepared to cede those overcrowded and industrious islands to the American sphere of influence. But not Germany. When the Russians exploded their first atomic bomb on 25 September 1949 the citizens of the Soviet Union and eastern Europe not only took pride in socialism's technological achievement. They also knew that military parity with the West was in sight and that the problem of Germany would at last begin to lose its peculiar significance – at least as long as there was no question of Germany's possessing control of nuclear weapons.

111 Germany remained the major source of contention in Europe after the war. This cartoon of 1951 shows the godfathers of western German militarism – the US, Britain and France – crowing over their fledgling

We tend to think of wars as the most important agency for generating major changes. In the field of technology and its management this is patently the case, and the technological breakthroughs called forth by the inventive exigencies of war do often lead to major social changes – in the end. But the immediate social and political consequences of war are often not so much innovating as restorative. In government circles this shows itself in a desire to return to traditional processes at the first available opportunity. Stalin was no exception.

On 24 June 1945 Stalin attended the victory parade in Red Square and thanked the Russian people for all they had done. It was the last time that he appeared in the role of great military leader of a united nation. Communist perspectives had been played down during the war. There were no narrowly political purges; the criteria were loyalty to the state and efficiency in executing allotted tasks. The special sufferers had been national minorities of doubtful loyalty, especially in the newly liberated or annexed territories in the south and west. Religious and class differences were pushed into the background. Indeed the war witnessed a substantial religious revival in the Soviet Union, both Greek Orthodox as well as Jewish. Recent evidence suggests that the early pressure, while the war was still in progress, to form communist-dominated organizations to take over in Poland, East Germany and elsewhere, did not come primarily from Stalin, but that these were at least in part the result of pleading and lobbying by groups of Polish and German communists in the USSR who were afraid of being sold out to the exigencies of Soviet wartime alliances. In the event, all this proved to be a series of concessions permissible and necessary in a period of great national danger. As a more permanent government policy they suited neither Stalin nor his colleagues – nor indeed the many minor officials and functionaries for whom the Party was their sole career and means of social mobility. Soon the slogan was 'back to class vigilance'. In effect this meant a return to Stalinist political economy. However greatly the Soviet Union had suffered during the long war, much as people may have longed to retain the new emphasis on solidarity rather than coercion, the system to which the Soviet Union returned was precisely that of 1941. It was a conservative restoration in the most literal sense of the word.

Within two years, by 1947, almost all the wartime concessions had been withdrawn. The military leaders were quickly reduced to their place, and political control of the army intensified. The increasing stress on the wartime role of Stalin and the Party diminished in retrospect the contribution of those much-decorated generals whose names had graced all the victory communiqués. Stalin began to regard them with particular venom.

112, 113 Ilya Ehrenburg (left), the distinguished journalist who survived all the shifts of official attitudes towards the arts, and published his memoirs in the 1960s. Right, Andrei A. Zhdanov, the architect of Stalin's ideological rigidification after the war

Khrushchev tells us that by 1952 even the venerable Voroshilov was under suspicion of being a British agent, no less. Although himself a member of the Politburo, he was obliged to telephone before each session for permission to attend, and this was granted or refused in accordance with Stalin's whims. Zhukov was demoted from command of an army to that of a minor military district in the Urals, and returned to an important position at the centre only after Stalin's death in March 1953.

The immediate post-war period was particularly the era of Zhdanov, the epitome of the anti-intellectual *apparatchik*, dully devoted to the enforcement of total orthodoxy. The war had been a means for Soviet writers to express their strongest feelings in honest and yet acceptable form. But as early as 1945 Ehrenburg, a Jew and relatively cosmopolitan, was being publicly attacked for failing to distinguish between Hitler and his Fascist gang on the one hand, and the essentially democratic and peace-loving German people on the other. Zhdanov now attempted to impose new and hitherto unattained standards of dullness and conformity on the writers and artists of the Soviet Union. It was a return to socialist realism with a vengeance: dreary stories of realizing production norms, devoted collective farmers threshing wheat, and above all fulsome – indeed gruesome – praise of Stalin as the all-seeing genius of Marxism-Leninism. The emphasis on patriotism during the war had not of course been confined to Russia in the narrow sense; Ukrainians, Georgians and others had benefited in so far as they had remained loyal to

189

the Soviet Union. Even so, at the end of the war pockets of originally German-inspired but by now fierce indigenous resistance to re-incorporation in the Soviet Union were still in existence. A nasty little war on the new Polish-Russian border in the Ukraine dragged on for two years. And had not one or two whole nationalities been disloyal to the Soviet Union during the war itself? That was the period when entire tribes and nations like the Kalmyks and the Balkars were deported, when the autonomous republic of the Chechen and Ingush was 'liquidated'. 'The Ukrainians only avoided this fate because there were too many of them and there was no place to which they could be deported. Otherwise Stalin would have deported them too', Khrushchev told the delegates to the Twentieth Congress in 1956. The terror now fell not only on the citizens of a few selected nations, but on the spokesmen for a great many more. The nationality policy of the Soviet Union, of which Lenin had been the initiator and Stalin himself the first architect, began to appear as a sorry farce – yet that policy had been one of the proudest achievements of a federated Soviet Union, whose very origin had been a protest against decades of Russian oppression.

The large proportion of Jews among the early Bolsheviks had always represented a cosmopolitan element in the Communist Party which to some extent counterbalanced the 'Russian' perspectives of 'socialism in one country' and later the isolationist and self-regarding policy of industrialization. At any rate Stalin came to regard Jews collectively as potentially dangerous internationalists, with only a few specific exceptions in the case of men like Kaganovich. It is therefore not surprising that the number of Jews among Party officials declined steadily from 1924 to 1941. After the war the cultural ice age of Zhdanov fell particularly heavily on such self-conscious Jewish culture as remained. One of the first purges of 1947 more or less closed down the activities of writers and actors who used Yiddish as their medium of expression. Among these was Mikhoels, a senior Bolshevik as well as a famous actor, liquidated in 1949. Many of those who had been enlisted to organize Jewish international assistance in the United States and elsewhere on behalf of the USSR during the war now found themselves accused of illicit connections and espionage, and were purged accordingly – an aspect of Stalinist oppression which Khrushchev did not mention in his indictment. The evidence for Stalin's suspicion of Jews, even those who had proved completely loyal supporters, is by now overwhelming. But this manifestation of an archetypal Russian reaction can also be explained, even if it cannot be justified, by policy considerations. In 1948 the State of Israel came into existence, and the Soviet Union voted for its creation at the United Nations. But it soon became evident to the ever-vigilant eyes of the Party that many Russian Jews wanted to join the hundreds of thousands who flocked to the newly welcoming shores. Substantial if unpublicized desertions of Jewish soldiers among Russian occupation forces in Germany had taken place since 1945. Here, then, was at least a potential manifestation of that national separatism which had always been Stalin's special bugbear – supported, moreover, by the active assistance of a foreign state. The reaction was typical and brutal: suppression of all possible signs of ethnic separateness, and the gradual removal of as many Jews as possible from positions of power. The political demands of security quickly set off a profound echo in a society in which anti-Semitism, dormant or open, had always been strong.

Zhdanov died on 31 August 1948, but the policies associated with his name continued. By 1949 there was every prospect of a renewal of large-scale purges, and those in the highest positions felt particularly vulnerable. Perhaps the most distinguished of those shot during these years was Voznesensky, Chairman of the State Planning Commission, head of Gosplan, at one time Deputy Chairman of the Council of Peoples Commissars and wartime member of the very powerful *Ekonomsoviet*. In the same purge Kuznetsov, Chairman of the Council of Ministers of the Russian Federal Republic, disappeared together with many others. Four years later, in 1953, an even larger purge appeared to be in the offing. The arrest of several prominent doctors, many of them Jewish, for plotting to kill members of the government, seemed to be the beginning of a widespread shake-up, possibly involving the liquidation of the entire top leadership – the same menacing tip of an unfathomable iceberg which Kirov's murder in 1934 had proved to be. Stalin personally directed the affair and planned the victims. 'He told the then Minister of State Security, Ignatiev: "If you do not obtain confessions from the victims we will shorten you by a head"; he personally called the investigating judge and told him what methods should be used: "Beat – beat and once again beat."' The assembled members of the Politburo were told, with Stalin's particular mixture of avuncular and menacing patronage: 'You are blind like young kittens; what will happen without me? The country will perish because you are unable to recognize our enemies.' Khrushchev also stated that the intended victims were to be Mikoyan, Voroshilov and Molotov; it is possible that Beria and Khrushchev himself may also have been intended for this fate. But these men were no Thermidoreans determined to overthrow Robespierre before he could destroy them; they could only sit and fearfully wait.

Many of those who studied the Soviet Union during the post-war period came to the conclusion that, far from being an exceptional event due either to Stalin's megalomania or to the dynamics of a great and long drawn-out upheaval like the French or Russian revolution, violent purges must be accounted a normal part of the Soviet process of government, the standard form of élite self-renewal. They may well have been right. A society in which other channels of choice and change are blocked, where all major decisions as well as the interpretation of orthodoxy are in the hands of one man surrounded by servile colleagues, must become rigidly static, like the Byzantine or Chinese empires in decline. The Soviet Union, however, was dedicated to rapid industrialization and to a social revolution managed from above. How, then, to combine a commitment to movement and action with a system of endless checks and balances, a rigid bureaucratic hierarchy and enormous power only at the top? Notions like 'the permanent purge' and 'terror as a prophylactic' (both titles of books about the Soviet Union) suggest the answer: a system of absolute insecurity, in which terror and uncertainty counteract the natural phenomenon of bureaucratic complacency which develops in the absence of democratic control – whether of the liberal or revolutionary variety. In such circumstances a continuous purge – or fear of purge – becomes the only means of preventing social arthritis, of keeping things moving and making men perform their allotted tasks. In addition, purges provide the means of social mobility, by which the new replace the old, the junior the senior – above all, by which the expectation of advancement is kept alive. Stalin himself seemed to confirm this when he put forward the general proposition that 'political bureau members should always be replaced by new ones'. The great purges had enabled millions of younger men to aspire to top positions, and in 1951 the statement sounded ominously as though another upheaval was due.

In the economic sphere, too, there was a complete restoration of the managed political economy. War losses had been enormous. Estimates vary, but industrial production was probably down by over 30 per cent in 1946 as compared with 1940 – the consequence of war losses as well as the slow change-over from war production. Something like one-fifth to a quarter of the capital assets of Soviet industry had been destroyed. Agricultural losses were probably on a similar scale. The extent to which the survival of the Soviet economy depended on wartime lend-lease from the United States may be judged from the fact that while the total production of Soviet industry was valued in 1940 at around £3,000 million, the value of lend-lease shipments was about £1,100 million – more than one-third of the value of Soviet pre-war industrial production, or the equivalent of the actual loss of production during the war. Long-term losses in housing, social services of all kinds, even population itself (a reduction of twenty-four million according to official statistics between 1940 and 1945, instead of a projected rise of fifteen million), were immense. It was a situation somewhat similar to that faced by Lenin in 1921, if proportionately less severe. But this time there was no relaxation, no concession; the socialist economy had proceeded too far and become too deeply ingrained in the consciousness of the Party. In fact the pre-war tenor and rhythm of the economy were reinforced after 1945. Strong emphasis was again placed on primary industries. Once more the drive was for more rather than better. New and spectacular industrial projects, particularly in the new development areas of Siberia and on the Volga, were initiated. By 1953, halfway through the second post-war plan, the pre-war levels of production in industry had been surpassed. Stalin's refusal of Marshall Aid appeared justified by the enormous resurgence of Soviet industry.

All this was taking place under the aegis of meticulous and bureaucratic planning at the centre. The post-war period witnessed a vast extension of the apparatus of control. Moscow had become a labyrinth of technical ministries supervising and directing the activity of combines and groups of factories all over the Soviet Union whose only channel of communication was with the centre. Though the economy was becoming increasingly complex, even the simplest transactions were planned and supervised by the centre; local officials and factory managers were mere executants – at least on paper. In fact the whole system was beginning to creak – only the organized breaking of rules made it possible to achieve the production aims. The government and the Party leadership were well aware of these deviations, but the well-tried answer was always the same – not change, but more control, more supervision, more insecurity.

In 1952 Stalin wrote *Economic Problems of Socialism in the USSR*, his last and most definitive statement on Soviet economics. He re-emphasized in full his commitment to the salient features of industrialization of the early 1930s – strongly differentiated prices and wages, emphasis on socialist planning principles as a means of pricing goods (rather than the market, let alone the consumer), absolute priority for heavy industry, the extension of detailed planning to keep pace with the growing complexity of the economy, no change in the structure and control of agriculture. The recipe had worked before, and Stalin was convinced that it, and it alone, would continue to work. Whole generations of Soviet technicians, economists and workers had been trained under its auspices, and were dedicated to its survival. By 1952 the very successes and achievements of the Soviet economy had begun to bring forth a number of suggestions from some of his closer colleagues, particularly the younger ones. They wanted to adjust the management of the Soviet economy to its present state of high production and complexity, to improve efficiency and above all productivity. One such proposal was made by Khrushchev and concerned the latter's particular hobby-horse: agriculture. Khrushchev pointed out that the most urgent need was to raise agricultural production in order to bring it in line with the growth of industry and the increasing movement of population into the towns. For this purpose the *kolkhozy* or collective farm organizations should be strengthened, their numbers reduced and their acreage increased. Above all they should now be given control of tractors and mechanical equipment, previously organized under the politically more manageable Machine and Tractor Stations. In short, it was a partial recognition that agriculture had come of age, both politically and economically, that the collective farms were no longer to be treated as socially untrustworthy. But Stalin refused. His recipe was to put more pressure on the peasants under the existing system. Even to make a proposal like this required courage; it may well have been that suggestions of economic reform had hastened Voznesensky to his doom. Stalin stuck to his system – all or nothing. Improvements could only come through more of the same. This was the tenor of his last Party Congress, the nineteenth, held in October 1952.

114, 115 Two architectural monuments of the Stalin era. Moscow State University (below) and the Bratsk hydro-electric power station in the Irkutsk Region (right) ▶

On 5 March 1953 Stalin died of a haemorrhage of the brain. Once more, as in 1923–4, nobody could quite foresee what the disappearance of the outstanding leader would mean. The Western world had by now almost come to accept the Stalinist phase of the Soviet Union as permanent; the experts foretold the violent emergence of another leader of the same mould. In the Soviet Union itself there was shock and respectful mourning. The leaders who carried the coffin to its resting place had the grave and reserved expression suitable to the occasion; they gave nothing away. On both sides of the Iron Curtain it was difficult to picture the Soviet Union without the man who had so firmly imprinted his image and his ideas on his country and the whole world.

116, 117 More recent Soviet architecture shows some signs of a more modern conception. Above, a new town of the Siberian branch of the USSR Academy of Sciences in
the Novosibirsk Region. Below, the Kremlin Congress Palace in Moscow built in 1961

What was the Soviet Union like when Stalin died? It is only fourteen years ago yet it already requires a distinct effort of recall; history moves very fast in the Soviet Union. Moreover the sense of dissociation from the past is shared by the foreign observer and the Soviet citizen himself. Yet without doubt all the developments since 1953 were built on Stalin's foundation – re-shaped and modified, it is true, but totally dependent on what he had created between 1929 and 1953.

The Soviet Union had grown both stronger and bigger. In the west new territory had been acquired: the eastern, Ukrainian-speaking parts of Poland as well as the northern half of German East Prussia; Bessarabia, the strategically important route of access to the Balkans; the wild and backward area at the eastern end of Czechoslovakia; parts of the Karelian peninsula and the strategically vital strip of land north of Leningrad. The Baltic republics were finally extinguished as independent states and had now become federal republics within the Soviet Union. In the east, Outer Mongolia, though independent, had been firmly drawn into the Soviet orbit, both politically and economically.

The centre of economic gravity had begun to shift eastwards – not, to be sure, through any tendency towards decentralization or regional autonomy, but through the physical displacement of industry on a vast scale. The wartime shift to the east had merely accelerated a pre-war tendency to locate the new growth points in the centre of the country rather than in the west. Names that had been mere dots on maps to mark transit stations now became associated with enormous industrial complexes. This planned shift to the east created its own special problems. Housing and other social amenities lagged far behind the construction of industry, and life in many of these new towns was stark and grim. Stalin had tapped the pioneering spirit of revolutionary enthusiasm which made many young people willing to accept immense hardships for the sake of building the new society – new in the literal sense that factory chimneys now dominated the tundra and steppes where there had only been emptiness before. This enthusiasm had been supplemented by coercion. Much of the development in the north and north-east was based on huge labour camps of prisoners. Their inmates consisted of deported nation-alities from inside the Soviet Union (together with Polish and German prisoners of war as available) and the never-ending stream of directed labour and candidates for socialist re-education – political and ordinary criminals in their enforced search for rehabilitation. By the time Stalin died this process had become self-generating, with the economic demand for cheap labour dictating the supply of the guilty. The labour needs of this industrial infra-structure required a continuous supply of prisoners which the courts and the NKVD (now MVD) provided. By 1953 the MVD was not merely a power-ful enforcement organization but had become a subterranean empire of economic production, paying minimal wages and providing as much ac-cumulation as low productivity and high wastage through disease and death would allow. Though few people in the Soviet Union had any notion just what was involved, and official statistics made no allowance for this un-remunerated labour, the planners in the early 1950s might well have won-dered how the growth rate could be maintained in future without this contribution.

The opening up of the Russian heartland suddenly brought the local inhabitants, their traditional way of life still hardly touched by 150 years of Russian domination, face to face with the modern world and the rapidly increasing influx of Russians. Though official policy continued to emphasize the full equality of all languages, creeds and cultures, the arrival of large numbers of Russian workers and technicians with their families inevitably made inroads on the local culture. A career, whether political or technical, in the Soviet Union had by now become unthinkable without complete com-mand of the Russian language. With few exceptions, only Russian-language schools provided the new technical and scientific education which was fast becoming the exclusive avenue for managerial and technical careers – as it had been before 1917. Official policy with regard to minority cultures had begun to take on something of a romantic quality which tended simply to ignore the hard facts imposed by an increasingly Russian-speaking era of modernity. There were, of course, genuine concessions to national feeling; for instance, in the staffing of top Party and government posts Russians often alternated with leaders of local origin. But during the twenty-five years of Stalin's rule such locally born leaders had in practice become entirely 'russified' through common Party experience. Genuinely local leaders had been eliminated almost entirely in the early 1930s. In any case, within a few years of Stalin's death, Soviet delegates at an international philological con-gress were putting forward the claim that if English had been the language of commerce, French the language of diplomacy and German the language of nascent science, Russian would undoubtedly become the language of modern industrial technology and society. Only a language secure and supreme at home could afford to make such international claims. Not for the Soviet Union the linguistic schizophrenia of other multi-lingual societies like India or even Belgium.

The restoration of educational orthodoxy in the schools in the 1930s had by now produced a highly selective educational system. The basic period of schooling was from the age of seven to fifteen or sixteen years. Great emphasis had been placed on the primary school in the early years of industrialization. For one thing it was a more easily controlled means of inducting the young into the new society than the socialization provided by parents, many of whom had been brought up before 1917. At the height of the purges the school was treated as a distinct antithesis to the home. Children were encouraged to bring forward instances of domestic criticism or dissatisfaction. The teaching profession accordingly came to be regarded as very sensitive, and teachers were among the first for whom Party membership was almost essential. But many writers who have thrown up their hands in horror at this deliberate introduction of politics into the classroom have ignored the secondary result – the almost complete conquest and eradication of illiteracy, at least in the Russian-speaking areas. By the time Stalin died literacy rates in the Soviet Union could compare respectably with those of most of the advanced countries of Europe.

Earlier notions that everyone should be entitled to higher education, that existing facilities should be shared as widely as possible, had, since the 1930s, fallen victim to the principle of differentiated rewards for skills. Higher education had in fact become limited to the demonstrably able, selected according to strict examinations, and to the sons of parents who had attained an élite position in state or Party and could pay the maintenance fees demanded for the last three years of secondary education. Studies of the social composition of students at Russian universities in the late 1950s show clearly that the re-introduction of fee payments and the careful selection of entrants on academic merit had brought about a positive correlation of educational access with parents' status. It was far easier for the sons of scientists, managers and Party functionaries to obtain places at secondary schools and especially at institutions of higher learning than for all others. (One of the first major acts of de-Stalinization in the mid-1950s was a return to a system of secondary education without payment of fees. Since the effects of social changes are long-term, the results of this move cannot yet be assessed – though Soviet commentators specifically claim to have achieved the most democratic educational system in the world.)

The bright, devoted and politically sound student was privileged and carefully tended in the Soviet Union. This is important because it meant that the straightforward class correlation which we find among students at universities in England, France and Germany was modified. Many of the students at Russian universities in the 1950s had parents who, though of high status themselves, were clearly of working-class origin. The Soviet educational system might be creating a new form of inequality in the long run, based on the possession of intellectual capital, but it did not reinforce existing lines of class differentiation established in the past.

By the time Stalin died the content of Soviet education was strictly laid down and centrally controlled – at least at Union Republic level (education being the responsibility of the individual republics). Any sufficiently powerful régime in an industrializing society can dictate the substance of what is to be taught in proportion to its generality and intellectual content. The more technical and applied the teaching becomes the less the extent of possible ideological control without reaching a point of absurdity. Stalin had at one time or another attempted to mould the basic principles of almost every scientific and humanistic subject in the cast of his particular interpretation of Marxism. The teaching of biology had to accord with the excessively environmental bias of Lysenko. There was a Marxist interpretation of physics, mathematics and chemistry – all emphasizing the dialectic principle of conflict and synthesis. In the arts a foreshortened form of class-relatedness had become established, so that the study of literature, music, history and philosophy was simplified far beyond Marx's broad and sophisticated epochs of historical development. Stalin simply allocated events, situations and processes to an historical period by fiat and that was that. The impact of official dogma made itself particularly felt in all socio-economic areas of study – philosophy, history and economics. While science, at least in its applied form, was becoming increasingly specialized and technical, the more sensitive subjects were left almost deliberately amorphous. Under the guise of stressing the relationship between history, economics, philosophy, art, etc., tight Party control was exercised over these subjects and all authoritative formulations were made, not in the academies or schools, but by the Party institutes, for whom the rigorous application of Stalin's every word had become the main criterion. Every even mildly contentious question was referred to the Central Committee if not to Stalin himself. The Marxist notion of universal inter-relatedness had become an intellectual porridge of universal simplification. Inconvenient phenomena or concepts simply disappeared. So, in fact, did inconvenient subjects, like sociology. The exciting Soviet start in this field in the 1920s gave way to a simple interdict on fact-finding and analysis of current Soviet society except for the endless procession of figures by and for the planners. By the time these emerged for public consumption they had become mere columns of crude percentages. The never-ending secrecy of Soviet officialdom, justified by constant warnings against hostile elements and spies, hardly encouraged any research into or disclosure of facts about the Soviet Union. There is, for instance, an almost complete absence of all population figures between the beginning of the war and 1956; even these were treated as official secrets. In short, the state of Soviet higher education and research was becoming greatly impoverished as far as basic theory was concerned, but surged ahead in the solution of applied and technical problems of production. This lack of correspondence between basic research and applied technology became one of the major preoccupations of Stalin's successors.

Since 1953 the Soviet press has been full of complaints about the excessive demands made on people by Party, union and other organized group meetings after long hours of work. But after the twenty-five years of Stalinism a high identification of work with pleasure remained the dominant ethos. Recent investigations in the Soviet Union show that the level of job satisfaction among respondents to questionnaires is significantly higher than in other industrial countries – even though this may not be evidence of anything but a commitment to the notion that this is how it ought to be. The heavy pressure on writers and artists to conform to socialist realism may have been an ideological constraint on artistic self-development, but it ensured the provision of books, paintings and music which could be and were appreciated by broad masses and not merely by an intellectual élite. Reading and knowing the classics was accepted as evidence of being cultured; the range of foreign classics available in cheap Russian editions has never ceased to surprise visitors to the Soviet Union. *Kultura* in Soviet Russian carries the exactly opposite connotation to the German word *Kultur*; it signifies a generally accepted standard instead of a sign of élite differentiation. Though Stalin had definite ideas as to what constituted good reading and music, and did not, for instance, hesitate to express visible disapproval at public performances of what he considered to be cacophonous work by Shostakovich, the offering of classical ballet, theatre and concerts was always generous by any standard. Just as in England the provincial jaunt to London has traditionally included a visit to the theatre, the privilege of a precious seat at the Bolshoi Theatre constitutes one of the most sought-after rewards for provincial workers who have earned a visit to the capital.

Sport was both highly organized and lavishly provided. Standards of training and performance were laid down like industrial norms. Watching a

118, 119, 120
Books, especially
popular editions of
Russian and foreign
classics are made
available cheaply to
the Soviet public.
Left, an illustration
for Tolstoy's
Anna Karenina,
and below,
two woodcuts
by Goncharov
for a Russian
edition of *Hamlet*

football match was in some ways like a tour round a factory: a form of privileged participation in Soviet achievement, with social as much as individual benefits. Holidays were as a rule allocated to sectors of industry and individual factories. If you worked in a particular factory or area your holiday entitlement would be at a particular place and time, often at a place reserved for an industry or a particular institution. Since facilities were limited, access to them was naturally a matter of reward for effort or for status. The chance of a much sought-after holiday on the Black Sea coast, the Russian Riviera, or a visit to Moscow or Leningrad, was not available to the majority of the population; only the posters and the descriptions of the press could be savoured by all. Even so, the institution of the collective holiday brought a scarce facility within the reach of many who on any other basis might never have benefited from holiday travel at all.

The obsessive and all-pervasive ideology on one hand, and the effects of industrialization and widespread basic education on the other, naturally produced great changes in the social and personal characteristics of those involved. During the purges everyone had learned to keep grimly quiet. The Russians, who tend to achieve satisfaction in strongly subjective face-to-face contact with other people, had become inhibited. The very subjects they would most want to talk about were often those on which even silence was barely safe. There were significant increases in the figures of alcoholism in the late 1940s and early 1950s. Initially this was regarded almost entirely as an integral part of the unsolved problem of 'incomplete' socialism. Those who drank were characterized as relics of a pre-socialist era who had failed to adjust to the new collective orientations and to the devotion to work which defined the new Soviet man of the Stalin era. Only in the last few years have Russian social scientists and officials concerned with welfare recognized that excessive consumption of alcohol is a specific problem requiring specific remedies and control.

In general the effects of 'the second revolution' on the broad mass of the population may be summarized as constraining rather than liberating. The Russians today, in the more relaxed atmosphere of the last decade, have reverted more to their national characteristics than to the requirements of prudence and silence. At the same time the spread of education, the beginnings of common social benefits and services provided a basis for both future demands for, and future supplies of, satisfactions which – however inchoate – were to make their irresistible impact in the fourteen years following Stalin's death.

The period of intense industrialization had certainly sharpened the contrast between town and country. This is an almost inevitable consequence of industrialization. In most democratic capitalist countries the political over-representation of the countryside has as a rule helped to bring about a distribution of resources which, though largely earned in the towns, is disproportionately spent in the country. In the Soviet Union, by contrast, the countryside had by 1953 become politically almost the forgotten three-quarters of the community. Though efforts were made towards the end of Stalin's life to bring the agricultural sector more squarely into political life by extending the efforts and resources of Party work in the countryside, the Communist Party and its youth branch, Komsomol, remained an over-whelmingly urban organization however much it claimed to speak for the countryside as well. Senior Party members of peasant background could traditionally count on the built-in advantage of being a relative rarity; their prominence – with their origin noisily emphasized – was considered a useful demonstration of the Party's all-inclusiveness. Ironically Stalin, who had been denounced by left-wing communists during the heyday of NEP in the mid-1920s as a peasant Napoleon, had in fact precious little interest in the state of the countryside as such. Agriculture's task was simply to provide investment capital and food. Even to speak of completing the process begun with collectivization by nationalizing the land and increasing the number of state farms was heresy. The state farms (4,859 compared to 93,300 collectives), though favoured with resources and equipment, comprised no more than $7\frac{1}{2}$ per cent of the total land sown to grain. Any proposals for change, however technical, were unwelcome and dangerous. It almost seemed as if Stalin had shot his bolt with collectivization and then lost interest as long as there were no major agricultural crises. The war and lend-lease both helped to mask the increasing imbalance of town and countryside; the figures of agricultural production from 1945 to 1952 were particularly mendacious (as Khrushchev was later the first to admit).

There was accordingly little change in the Soviet countryside between 1936 and early 1953. Political control and political stimulation of productive effort were served by a single channel of communication, the Machine and Tractor Stations, which, aside from their main function of providing equipment for collective farms, acted, in the absence of an adequate Party organization, as the political arm of the government. It was an odd and inefficient arrangement. The equally inefficient system of payment for collective farm members, based on a division of the farm's residual income after the stipulated deliveries and payment of variable costs (depending on such unknowns as weather, harvest, accuracy of controlled planting, etc.), was defended on the grounds that it embodied the co-operative nature of the Kolkhoz. The private plots which each member could work on the collective farm, and whose produce largely disappeared into the open or black market, were viewed with considerable suspicion, and suggestions were made at various times to do away with them. But this, it was argued, might strike a serious blow at morale and consequently food production. Accordingly the government attempted to deal with the problem of the private plots by locating them within the plan, limiting by law the time and effort to be spent on them, ordering what was to be produced and where it could be sold and at what price, and generally threatening and coercing the farmer. In short, agriculture stagnated, leaving what was to prove the most crucial problem of all for Stalin's successors. The relative neglect of the agricultural sector was naturally reflected in the quality of rural life; by 1950 migration to the towns was not so much an economic consequence forced on an agricultural reserve army of labour as the only means of making a career, if not simply a living. The government in turn tried to contain it; all during the Stalin period the dispatch of ideologically stable and enthusiastic town dwellers to Machine and Tractor Stations and other Party assignments in the countryside was one of the most feared and resented forms of pressure on Party members.

The greatest impact of the Stalin era could probably be seen in the new élites in politics, industry, education and the government apparatus. The destruction of the Bolshevik old guard in the great purges involved not only the disappearance of a host of individuals but of a type; the highly individual Marxist revolutionary, who had made his commitment as a result of a personal decision, and who accepted the collective and depersonalizing emphasis of Bolshevism because he believed in the Party as the highest form of historical wisdom. The new generation accepted the collective as a natural, inevitable, sacrosanct phenomenon, not something they had created, but which had created them. They had reached maturity and often status in a period of rapid political realignment and a restructuring of priorities – processes which incessantly stressed the consistent correctness of the Party and the ever-repeated fallibility of the individual. The type of person who emerged was therefore colleagual in a very special sense. He had no affection and little sense of comradeship in shared dangers and achievements, but was instead a watchful and wary member of an organization which provided the sponsorship of every social action in the Soviet Union. He was educated into simultaneous consensus and conflict, unanimity and deadly disagreement – all within a single organization which encapsulated him completely, and without which life simply could not be imagined.

These new men were reserved, cautious, and careful. Lenin's democratic centralism meant for them not so much a political principle as a way of life. Under Stalin the whole concept of collective decision-making had become a foregone conclusion by the time it reached the vast majority of Party members. The process of discussion, acceptance and acclaim had become formalized from top to bottom. Just as the Central Committee and even the Politburo awaited the official line from Stalin or his immediate spokesman, so every Party meeting down to the factory cell received the official formulation of policy ready-made and clothed it with the seal of collective approval. Here the new type of Soviet administrator excelled – provided the line was clear. The average administrator may often have interpreted his duties less decisively, and the bureaucrat unwilling to put his signature on even the most routine piece of paper without backing from higher up became a popular figure of fun as well as a social menace.

Two parallel tendencies among the ruling group of Party members can be observed – towards increasing social cohesion and also individual alikeness. Whether you were in charge of a university, a Party office or a factory, whatever type of person you might be, your official attitudes and behaviour would be almost identical. The individual with different attributes and idiosyncrasies, the eccentric, had long since disappeared from the hierarchy. This process of homogenization was reinforced by Stalin's principle of substitutability; any Party member must be able to do anything adequately, and technically anyone could replace anyone else. Stalin had not invented this attitude. But whereas in Lenin's time it had applied only to the very top élite of his Party and was viewed as a necessity as long as the Bolsheviks were in a small minority, it had by now become normal practice in a Party of three to four million members. It was this relative facelessness together with the application of total power which gave rise among Western political scientists to the concept of totalitarianism which George Orwell epitomized in *Animal Farm* and *1984*: the transformation of individuals into completely substitutable units with numbers. Yet we must distinguish between the real and the apparent. If Stalin had lived for a hundred years the Soviet Union might really have become as it appeared to be. At the time, however, much of this facelessness and substitutability was merely the reticence most Russians adopted deliberately in order to achieve promotion or merely to survive. Since 1953 some of this attitude has already begun to be discarded, however slowly and cautiously. Much of Khrushchev's personal success (and in a sense his ultimate failure) resulted from his total reversal of type, his determination to give rein to his own highly individual personality in Soviet politics.

The point of Stalin's system of purges now becomes clear. The facelessness, the immobility, the fear of action, which only the war had temporarily interrupted and which were all enthroned again in the conservative restoration after 1945, could easily lead to a completely static society unable to meet

Приемка дома
состоялась...

Рисунок И. СЫЧЕВА

КРОКОДИЛ

№ 17 (1739) • ГОД ИЗДАНИЯ 43-й • 20 ИЮНЯ 1964

121, 122 Since Stalin's death, Soviet satirists have turned their pens increasingly against malpractices in government, especially among the bureaucrats. The *Krokodil* cartoon, above left (1965), satirizes the amount of paperwork involved in daily life, and at right the manacled bureaucrat says 'How can I show any initiative?' (1964)

the pace of industrialization. This total insecurity required a special apparatus of eternally duplicated supervision to ensure that wherever or whoever you were somebody was keeping an eye on your performance and your loyalty: the Party, the police, the procuracy, or just your colleagues at work, at play or in bed. Stalin had no high opinion of human nature. Ambition and greed as well as revolutionary enthusiasm between them would serve to keep the system moving and to provide candidates for the posts vacated each time a reshuffle took place. A Party career still offered the greatest rewards though it also provided the greatest risks. The system was a matter of degree; by destroying the autonomy of the Party, Stalin had reduced it almost to a chain of command, and the essentially dynamic quality of the

Party had in large measure given way to a bureaucratic structure, which merely duplicated the official Soviet bureaucracy and the system of economic administration in ministries, combines and factories. Once the great effort of industrial mobilization had begun to slacken, and the system of terror and insecurity began to be dismantled, bureaucracy at once became the Soviet Union's major problem.

In March 1953 Western scholars disagreed profoundly about Soviet perspectives. Some predicted the inevitable collapse of totalitarianism on democratic or humanitarian grounds, using Nazi Germany as an analogy. They were challenged by economists impressed by the phenomenal rate of industrial growth and post-war reconstruction. All agreed, however, that the only way to analyse and understand the Soviet Union in the short run was in terms of the personal conflicts of leaders and immediate followers. Kremlinology, which viewed the position of leaders in photographs as though they were planets or stars moving in fixed and predictable orbits, was then at its height. Such apparent trivia as the order of seating at official functions, the amount of clapping for the speeches of leaders at congresses, and the order of precedence at Stalin's funeral, were all fed into the Kremlinologists' crystal ball (computers had not yet arrived) in order to enlighten Western leaders and their public as to who would inherit the enormous power which Stalin had held. Looking back now it is easy to pour scorn on this type of political commentary. The real problem was that an historical era was coming to an end. The social and political structure of the Stalin era had almost outlived its own purpose. An industrial society had been forged, but the grosser methods of industrialization were out of date. A political apparatus of control and activation had been created, but its effect was too crude for the type of control and decision-making that was now required. A great deal of national wealth had been accumulated, but the order of investment priorities was no longer supportable by those who were accumulating it. The process of industrialization had taken place behind an iron curtain which prevented all standards of comparison other than one's own yesterday, but this too no longer served the purpose of the next stages of development. The task of Stalin's successors was essentially to adapt the second most powerful state in the world to the modernity which had now been made possible but had not yet been achieved, to find different means which would preserve and improve what had been created without renouncing the basic heritage of Stalinist industrialization. The personality of the leaders, their particular policies and ideas, important as they are, were becoming secondary to this basic problem which had irrevocably imposed itself on them all.

★　　　　　★　　　　　★

Yet the immediate insecurity among the leadership became even greater immediately after Stalin's death. Hitherto the ruling group had at least known what to fear – the danger of a further purge, which appears to have been imminent during 1952. Without the sheet-anchor of Stalin there was suddenly a void of dreadful ignorance about each other. The note of reassurance struck in the announcement of a reorganization of Party and government on 7 March 1953, two days after Stalin's death, was hollow. No signs of 'disorder and panic', which it was designed to prevent, were to be found anywhere. To emphasize the collective inheritance of Stalin's power a new Praesidium of the Council of Ministers was instituted, and the Party Praesidium reduced to almost half its size. The two supreme bodies contained all the well-known names: Beria, Malenkov, Molotov, Bulganin, Kaganovich, Voroshilov, Khrushchev. The man who seemed at first to emerge on top was Malenkov, reputedly Stalin's most trusted adviser since the death of Zhdanov. The Soviet press, by now thoroughly attuned to the niceties of personal leadership, accorded Malenkov the full treatment indicated for the man who combined both the posts of Party Secretary and Chairman of the Council of Ministers. A week later, however, the Central Committee, acting as a genuinely deliberative body for the first time for many years, released Malenkov from his post as Party Secretary. The problem of the control of both Party and government, which Stalin had combined effectively since the late 1920s and formally since 1941, emerged as the first of many important constitutional issues. The Party now set itself the task of rapidly liquidating the unpleasant and unfinished business of the latest purge; the doctors' plot, implicating so many of the new leaders, was quietly abandoned, the accused released and some of the accusers arrested shortly afterwards.

But only a few months after Stalin's death came the first major challenge to the precarious stability and cohesion of the new collective leadership – a threat from an entirely unexpected quarter. On 17 June 1953 the least self-reliant and in many ways the least attractive of the peripheral socialist governments was shaken by a revolt in Berlin. Only the intervention of Russian troops and tanks saved the government of the German Democratic Republic from a public humiliation. With Stalin gone, early concessions to the demands of workers goaded beyond the endurable – and having a prosperous West Germany for comparison – had resulted in the rapid heightening of demands. For the first time a communist government was faced by something like a domestic revolution. These events served to precipitate the unresolved conflict in the Kremlin. At the end of June Beria was suddenly arrested on the orders of his colleagues and on 10 July 1953 shot without judicial ceremony. Dramatic stories of Party Praesidium meetings, more reminiscent of a Wild West saloon, made the rounds: middle-aged ministers and Party functionaries pulling revolvers on each other. The old Stalin arsenal of preposterous accusations was raided once more. Beria was alleged to have been in the pay of British intelligence for the past thirty years. It was later established that the real ground which made his colleagues round on him was their fear of the enormous police apparatus he controlled. Besides, he had been Stalin's particular henchman and fellow-Georgian, a sycophant well-hated by all. The execution of Voznesensky and the preparation for the new purge at the end of 1952 could with justice be laid at his door. The Kremlinologists triumphed, for with Beria went Abakumov and many luminaries of the police establishment who had depended on the chief. The secret police as an institution was downgraded and in March 1954 was separated from the Ministry of Internal Affairs, to be controlled in future by an inter-departmental committee of state security. It was the first major breach in the Stalinist system.

We need not follow the various moves and countermoves in the leadership for the next few years. They had been important in the early Stalin period because they were instrumental in the emergence of Stalin himself, and of the system associated with his name. From now on they represented less and less the substance but rather the surface froth on more fundamental events which put them, and the school of Kremlinology who lived off them, into the limbo of history. Between 1953 and 1955 Malenkov seemed to have become the most significant figure among the Soviet leaders. The Kremlinologists considered him as the nearest approximation to Stalin, yet he came to be associated with a policy almost completely the reverse of Stalin's economic priorities. In 1953 for the first time the *rate* of growth of consumer goods production overtook that of heavy industry (though not, of course, the actual amount), and indeed the government deliberately underlined this switch of emphasis. More significant, perhaps, was the accompanying semi-public debate about the relative merits of priority for heavy industry or the satisfaction of long unsatisfied consumer demand. Problems were thus raised which under Stalin had been unthinkable. Churchill, who was always shrewder in his *obiter dicta* about the contemporary world than in his policies for implementing them, now began to stress the importance of the changes taking place in the Soviet Union. A general feeling of spring was in the air – only to be dashed when a session of the Supreme Soviet on 8 February 1955 suddenly replaced Malenkov as Chairman of the Council of Ministers. For the moment, the advocates of Stalinist orthodoxy on the question of heavy industry appeared to have won.

210

123 The post-Stalin régimes have made efforts to increase production of consumer goods. The crowds in the ornate GUM department store in Moscow find more to buy than ever before since the Revolution ▶

124 A food counter in GUM

The real interest of these events lay in the way they happened rather than in the personalities of the coming and going contenders for office. Under Stalin the formal institutions of both Party and state, like the Central Committee and the Supreme Soviet, had become rubber-stamping assemblies whose task it was to applaud decisions already taken elsewhere and in secret. Now these unwieldy, oversized bodies emerged from cold storage and became arenas, if not yet of genuine discussion, at least of more overt decision-making. The resignation of Malenkov and his displacement as Chairman of the Council of Ministers by Bulganin, which really meant more power for Khrushchev as Party Secretary, took place at a session of the Supreme Soviet. Malenkov sat silent while a statement apologizing for his inexperience and, by implication, inefficiency, was read on his behalf. No doubt the decision was not taken there and then, but the fact that the Supreme Soviet became the *forum* of a formal leadership change was already a substantial departure from Stalinist practice.

Only shortly afterwards an even more significant event provided evidence of a new vitality in the larger elected organs of the Party. In July 1955 a conflict over foreign policy between the new leadership and the supporters of a more traditional line headed by Molotov was resolved by the defeat of the latter in the meeting of the plenum of the Central Committee, to which an apparently private or secret discussion in the Party Praesidium (the former Politburo) had been appealed. Two years later, in June 1957, the struggle between the rising Khrushchev and his opponents was fought out and, for the time being, settled in an extraordinary meeting of the full Central Committee of the Party. Having been outvoted in the Praesidium, Khrushchev took the matter to the larger body where he obtained a triumphant reversal. It was the first time for over thirty years that the small and select collectivity of the Party leadership had been outvoted by its formal superior, the Central Committee consisting of 255 members and candidates. What had always been true of Soviet democracy in theory, namely that small executives should always be directly responsible to their larger parent bodies, now began to apply in practice.

It was in this atmosphere that Khrushchev emerged as the leading figure of the Communist Party and Soviet government. He and his close colleague Mikoyan set the tone at the Twentieth Party Congress which met in Moscow from 14 to 25 February 1956. The quiet, partial and piecemeal dismantling of the more baroque aspects of Stalinism in policy and organization now gave way to a formal and full denunciation of Stalinism as a system – though in the form of an attack on Stalin as an individual, and on the personality cult. It is possible that Khrushchev and his colleagues intended to confine this assault on their great predecessor to the confidential circle of Party delegates. Certainly no full report of the proceedings appeared in the Soviet press. But more probably the diffusion was calculated, in full expectation that such momentous denunciations must seep right through the vast network of Party organizations throughout the Soviet Union and abroad. In any case it did not take the Western intelligence service and the press very long to obtain detailed texts of Khrushchev's speech.

125 Malenkov,
Stalin's immediate successor
as Chairman of
the Council of Ministers in 1953.
By 1955 he had been demoted,
and was later relegated
to a minor post

The peculiar combination of broad moralism and narrow legalism with which many Western historians and commentators regard the Soviet Union has often raised the question why Khrushchev, a close collaborator of Stalin who made his career largely thanks to Stalin's favour, did not choose to denounce himself together with his master's works. Apart from the rather odd basic assumption about politicians' behaviour, such an expectation is pointless in the context of Soviet thinking. The notion that having shared in a policy now to be reversed constitutes any kind of admission of past failure is alien to Soviet practice. Besides, Khrushchev's problem was current and political; he was not concerned to produce an objective historical assessment of the Stalin period.

One of the essential differences between Soviet and liberal democracy is that, in the latter, change is usually associated with, and can only be understood in terms of, a change of people who *personify* policies; a change of policy can best or only be implemented by a change of leadership. In the Soviet Union this is not the case. The legitimacy of any leadership, whether personal or collective, is not seen in terms of individual policies. Since it is held that any policy at any time must be correct (otherwise it would not have been accepted in the first place), so changes in policy must also be 'correct'. Since Lenin, mistakes have rarely been admitted. What is usually at issue is a change in 'objective circumstances'. Accordingly the listeners at the Twentieth Congress, delegates from all over the Soviet Union assembled at a formal and honorific occasion which hardly presaged much drama, may have been startled to hear Khrushchev condemn Stalin in his long speech. For the first time in many years, many of the resentments, fears and concerns which had been worrying them privately were placed openly on the agenda. Some may well have disagreed with Khrushchev; some of his immediate colleagues certainly did, and attempted to limit and then partially reverse the progress of de-Stalinization. But nobody would have questioned the right of Khrushchev, former Stalinist and Party emissary in the Ukraine during the war, to announce a new policy, and to denigrate the old even though he had been one of its architects. Unless this is clear, no real understanding of political processes in the Soviet Union can ever be attained.

It is also important to understand precisely what Khrushchev was doing. His denunciation of Stalinism was in no sense an all-round indictment of Stalin and his whole period. Then, and since, a sharp line has been drawn between the 'collective' elimination of Trotsky, Zinoviev and Bukharin and the old Bolsheviks on the one hand, and the later purges known in the Soviet Union as the *Ezhovshchina*. This division is important, though it may not at first sight make much sense to Western readers. In reviewing the

126 The audience of Khrushchev's virulent denunciation of Stalin. Delegates to the Twentieth Congress of the CPSU in 1956

history of the Party, Khrushchev and official historians since have postulated that the majority decisions of the various congresses and Party meetings from 1924 to 1934 were correct expressions of the Party's will. Trotsky was and still is considered to be the arch-enemy of collective leadership in the history of the Party, and the arch-opponent of correct Leninist principles. The others had all been deviationists of various sorts; all of them had opposed the will of the Party on significant occasions. The actual charges of treachery and sabotage at the behest of imperialist secret services, which had formed the main part of the indictment against them, were quietly ignored, since everyone realized they were factitious. The fact that those men had been killed was accepted as an excess. The line of demarcation thus falls approximately in the year 1934, by which time a genuine collective leadership had emerged. But then Stalin developed his cult of personality, and the next round of his victims were precisely those men, like Ordzhonikidze, Chubar, Eikhe, Kossior and hundreds of others, who had helped to defeat the deviationists and establish the collective leadership of the Party in the entirely 'correct' collectivization and industrialization drive. These men were now specifically rehabilitated, their destruction labelled a crime. Given the circumstances and attitudes of the time, this analysis is not hard to understand. The emergence of Stalin was not, as we know, based on a preference for him as leader, but

215

rather on the certainty that he – calm, uninspiring, dogged and formalistic – represented more accurately the collective and impersonal will of the Party than any of the more individualistic, possibly charismatic and certainly distinguished, figures of the earlier Lenin era.

A substantial group of Party leaders thought Khrushchev was going too far, that the very basis and legitimacy of the Soviet system were being shaken. Questions about the priority of heavy industry as opposed to consumer industries had now been posed since 1953. Reforms of agriculture were in the offing which could seriously upset the tradition of accumulation on which the industrial investment programme had been based. But in rallying opposition to Khrushchev, problems of foreign policy were more important. Already the earlier tussle with Molotov had been brought to a head by Khrushchev's visit to Yugoslavia in May 1955, during which the Soviet leader loudly and publicly declared a *nostra culpa* for the rift with Tito in 1948, conveniently blaming everything on Beria and Stalin. The next clash, about which we know little, probably came over the problem of the Austrian Peace Treaty and the termination of the occupied status of that country – another departure from Stalin's policy of ceding nothing. In 1956 serious trouble began to arise in both Poland and Hungary, the former on the verge of open rebellion against Soviet domination and the latter in the process of it. In both countries Party and state leadership were in the hands of men recently rescued from the Stalin-inspired dungeon.

In June the Polish government of Władisław Gomułka had to face riots in Poznan and a veritable torrent of criticism of the past in the official and unofficial press. The public was reacting with a vengeance against the Stalinist era, and only a firm assertion of Polish independence could prevent a rebellion the extent of which was quite unpredictable. In October Khrushchev and a strong Russian delegation appeared in Warsaw out of the grey autumn skies, and some harsh discussions took place behind closed doors. But the Poles refused to give way. Mainly because of their successful and well-publicized stand against the Russians, the Polish leadership and Party managed to maintain their hold on the country, and even pushed back the domestic ferment and the demand for greater intellectual freedom. In a sense renewed Party control – though not on the previous scale – was traded for some economic relaxation and a greater sense of national independence. In Hungary, however, things had gone one step further over the brink. The Hungarian Prime Minister, Imre Nagy, acceded to popular demands for Hungarian neutrality and the virtual abolition of exclusive rule by the Communist Party. Here Soviet forces acted swiftly and brutally in order to set a terrible example. Nagy was replaced by Kadar, who turned out to be Hungary's

127 Budapest 1956, the most serious rebellion in a Communist country. Soviet tanks help to suppress the insurgents

real Gomułka. To save the basis of communist rule his government called for Soviet assistance. In the course of two weeks the revolt was exterminated by force of arms – but not before something like ten per cent of the population and twenty-five per cent of the intelligentsia and technical élite had availed themselves of the temporarily open frontiers and escaped abroad. Nagy and the military commander, Maleter, were more or less abducted from their refuge in the Yugoslav Embassy and later executed for treason.

The opponents of de-Stalinization could not unjustifiably point to these events in the People's Democracies – if not the Soviet Union itself – as evidence of Khrushchev's recklessness. The split in the Party leadership came to a head, and Khrushchev was almost defeated. Only by appealing to the full Central Committee, a procedure unused since Lenin's day, was he able to defeat his opponents. Members of the Central Committee, wooed assiduously by both factions, played a role of considerable importance once again. On 29 June 1957 an 'anti-Party group' consisting of Malenkov, Kaganovich and Molotov (both the latter senior supporters of Stalin at a time when Khrushchev was still politically nowhere), Shepilov (Foreign Minister since 1955 and editor of *Pravda*) and soon after Saburov and Pervukhin (whose name had been specially connected with the economic planning organizations) were formally expelled from the Praesidium of the Party. At the time, they were not evicted from the Party as well, but merely relegated to obscure posts in the provinces or abroad. It was still a political felony to oppose the majority, but the style of punishment had completely changed since Stalin's day.

At the end of the year another and, for the moment, final conflict in the Party Praesidium took place. One of Khrushchev's main supporters and mobilizers of support, during 1956 and 1957, had been Marshal Zhukov, himself recently rehabilitated from the obscurity into which Stalin had thrust him. But in December 1957 Zhukov was suddenly expelled from the Praesidium and Central Committee. In backing Khrushchev against his opponents, he had presumably represented the aspirations and interests of the professional army – and no doubt also of other institutions that expected the new leadership to show greater deference to technological, scientific and professional know-how at the expense of purely political considerations. As so often in the past, the victors in fact quietly adopted many of the demands of the vanquished; the process of professionalization in the armed forces did not stop, but quietly continued behind the scenes. The best evidence for this is not Russian but Chinese – the frequent and outspoken warnings by the Chinese communists over the next few years against adopting the Russian example of excessive professionalization in the armed services at the expense of political priorities and Party control. The point is that in the Soviet context any distinction between professionalization and Party control was ceasing to be meaningful. The Party was no longer a separate autonomous political entity standing apart from the higher managerial or technical strata of society. Where Zhukov seemed to be posing the problem in terms of profession versus political perspectives, the Party now claimed to *contain* the necessary professional point of view, and hence to accommodate all forms of competition for resources between 'its' institutions. This implied a very different type of Party from that of either Lenin or Stalin.

The victory of Khrushchev between 1953 and 1957 was the victory of the Party in its post-Stalin resurgence. The Central Committee and Praesidium immediately after Stalin's death in 1953 had necessarily consisted of those whom he had helped to promote. But on the basis of institutional representation, the Party apparatus as such was then represented in the leadership only to a minor degree. For the rest, the places were filled by the administration, the police and other institutions. In Stalin's days this representational aspect did not matter much; all were alike in their subordination. Now, however, it had become less the personal than the institutional aspect of representation in the top Party positions which began to count. When we look at the fifteen members of the Praesidium in December 1957 and find two-thirds of them to be full-time Party secretaries, this represents an important re-structuring of the representational basis of the leadership.

This new resurgence of the Party was to be significant for the whole Khrushchev era from 1957 to 1964. Though the form of decision-making *within* the Party had been broadened, the Party itself now claimed the status and power of which Stalin's personality cult had helped to deprive it. This factor corresponded to a change in the composition of the Party at the top, and even more at the bottom. The Communist Party which claimed and took full power in the Soviet Union after 1957 was already beginning to be quite different from that over which Stalin had established his personal ascendancy.

At first sight it seems strange that the man who came to bury the personality cult in the Soviet Union should display a much more distinctive personality than Stalin ever had. Stalin's beginnings had been obscure, his period of power monumental, his statues martial and stiffly avuncular. He had spoken and written in elephantine paradoxes, repetitious inversions and heavy platitudes. His contact with people had always been carefully stage-managed and had been as unspontaneous as befits or befalls a ruler of a far-flung empire, protected and exalted by a bureaucracy. Khrushchev was entirely different. He had few pretensions as an interpreter of Marxism-Leninism, and left to others the task of aligning his practical policy with the official ideology. Unpredictable in his personal behaviour, he would often cause his bodyguard great concern when, at home as well as abroad, he suddenly leapt across the street or marched distinguished visitors down the main street of Moscow while lapping a huge ice-cream cone. He played the role of a man of the people with verve and humour; his spontaneous slogans and jokes reeked of the farmyard and the peasant household. Agriculture was also his pet political preoccupation. But he transformed its problems into simple and direct imagery, not into blankets of pseudo-Marxist reasoning: 'What kind of communist society is it that has no sausage?' he exclaimed during a visit to central Asia.

This was no simple public relations stunt. Khrushchev brought a style of voluntarism into the political leadership of the Soviet Union which it had never known – for though Stalin made his decisions in his own peculiar way he always dressed them up in the official language of Leninist ideology. And when Stalin became abusive, which he frequently did, the descent from theoretical heights to personal insults was carefully calculated to strike his hearers with chilly horror. Khrushchev too was often abusive, but it irritated or amused rather than terrified; people did occasionally stand up to him even

in public. In November 1962 he shouted at an exhibition of sculpture: 'Filth, disgrace, dogshit – who is responsible?' The assembled dignitaries of the Union of Artists trembled. Somebody pointed at the sculptor Neizvestny, who shouted back at Khrushchev: 'You may be Premier and you may be Chairman but you are nothing here. I am Premier and we shall talk as equals.' Security men seized the intrepid artist and one of Khrushchev's ministers threatened him with the uranium mines. Then followed a long argument at the top of their respective and substantial voices. It ranged over the whole problem of Soviet art. Khrushchev shook hands and departed with a jocular remark, both compliment and threat.

Khrushchev was unpredictable in other more important ways. Plans for agricultural reform, the elaboration and then dismantling of a plan for peaceful co-existence with America in 1959, the vast reform of the administrative structure in the summer of 1957 – all seemed to spring out of his head like a Renaissance painting of Genesis. And yet this was the man who told his colleagues in a speech to the Central Committee in December 1958 that 'spontaneity is the deadliest enemy of all'. Khrushchev's paradoxical situation can best be understood in terms of three distinct factors. First, the release of creative energy and inquiry in the Soviet Union during the decade following the death of Stalin, which put a premium on the new, the daring and the unexpected – in terms of content but even more in terms of style. Secondly, Khrushchev's own personality, which seemed to fit this type of situation: ebullient and mercurial, shrewd and calculating, open-minded and modern, above all accessible and quite free from personal pomposity and self-esteem.

128, 129 Khrushchev proud and Khrushchev angry. Left, with three of the much-publicized Soviet astronauts in 1963. Right, hectoring the United Nations General Assembly in New York

Finally, the fact that the Stalinist tradition of an individual at the apex of Soviet power was structurally still in evidence; without him there would have been a void. Soviet government had developed many of the qualities of a parade and a person was required to head it. People had become used to identifying with an individual – in the Soviet Union as much as abroad. All these factors combined to project Khrushchev into a personal role which was strongly marked and contoured – at the very time when he was pursuing his campaign against the personality cult. But the power behind the personal role was infinitely smaller than Stalin's. Khrushchev was well aware of it. 'If you put fifteen of us [in the Praesidium] end to end, it would not make Stalin'; and to the Indonesian Foreign Minister he declared that 'Stalin was a god; he could make and unmake men and things; we can't.'

Not that Khrushchev was averse to basking in reflected glory. When the first Soviet satellite was launched in 1957 – in many ways making an impact on the rest of the world as profound as the October revolution forty years earlier – he above all others profited from the enormous prestige it secured. His tours abroad – and he loved touring – were reported as triumphs both for him and for the Soviet Union. He had an insatiable propensity for giving informal television accounts of his journeys. Khrushchev represented the often inchoate wishes and sentiments of the Soviet population and particularly of the Party. The new contact with the outside world, even with the arch-imperialist United States, was genuinely welcomed everywhere. The doctrine of peaceful co-existence, according to which communism would succeed by demonstration of superiority instead of the revolutionary or military destruction of its opponents, was only a theoretical justification for the determination of the newly educated and professional groups in positions of power not to live any longer in an inbred, isolated world of their own. The incessant call for reform and modernization, for the exploitation of the enormous industrial potential of the Soviet Union, struck a deep chord among all these groups. Above all, the self-confident articulation of Soviet power challenging American technological and political domination contrasted favourably with the fearful and defensive isolationism of Stalin. In all these directions Khrushchev represented the future, and had the support of the most progressive groups in Soviet society.

Like Stalin, however, Khrushchev could also calculate coldly. Not everything fell into his lap by force of circumstance. Frequently he found himself faced by situations which he disliked but could not control. Though the immediate break-up of the socialist bloc was prevented at the end of 1956, and there was a reaction against excessive liberalization in politics and thought both in the Soviet Union and in the People's Democracies, the loosening of Soviet control over its sphere of influence continued apace in spite of all declarations of complete solidarity. Khrushchev had to put the best possible face on it. He rushed off to various eastern European capitals in order to admonish, lecture and sometimes threaten, but the loosening of Soviet control continued. The emergence of polycentrism, the creation of various and often competing centres of power in an alliance, was a cardinal feature of the Khrushchev era, so far as the socialist bloc is concerned.

Khrushchev recognized formally that the Soviet path to communism was not the only possible one, and accepted – often with bad grace and truculence – the criticisms of the Soviet past and present that now frequently emanated from eastern Europe and soon from Communist Parties in western Europe as well. The process of de-Stalinization of the leadership in the People's Democracies was anything but uniform. In Poland and Hungary it was in full swing by 1956. In other countries Stalinist leaders like Novotný in Czechoslovakia, Ulbricht in the German Democratic Republic, and for a long time the old leadership in Rumania and Bulgaria all remained in power. Such divergences of pace would not have been tolerated under Stalin, but now these had become matters for each Party to sort out for itself. Undoubtedly Khrushchev hoped to align Tito more formally with the Soviet bloc after his expansive gesture of reconciliation in 1955. When Tito's reformism and independence persisted, not only in international affairs but in internal organization, the Soviet Party leadership again expressed its strong disapproval, and relations took a turn for the worse. But Khrushchev would not let matters come to a break; here also he accepted the inevitable.

The great dispute with China, which had been simmering since 1955, finally burst into the open in 1958, the official running being at first made by the Chinese. The Soviet Union attempted for a time to find a formula for agreement, and at least tried to keep the dispute private. Not that Khrushchev was in the last resort prepared to compromise the Soviet Union's basic interests or the main tenets of Soviet Marxism; as with the United States, the surface patina of sweet reasonableness often cloaked an unwillingness to make substantial concessions, but made the opponent appear as the intransigent party. Once the dispute was out in the open the Russians gave as good as they got and finally withdrew all their substantial military and industrial aid without much regard for existing commitments. But within the Party framework of international socialist solidarity Moscow was now prepared to allow a great deal of leeway both to communist governments in power and to Communist Parties in capitalist countries. Unable any longer to control the situation, Khrushchev determined to live with it as best he could – and accustomed his colleagues to do so as well.

The style of diplomacy in the Khrushchev era differed substantially from that of the past. Self-confident in its achievements and growing military power, the Soviet Union now claimed its rightful place in international decision-making, the place that Stalin had never wanted to occupy. Co-existence implied some notion of parity, and it was parity with the United States in the international arena that Khrushchev now claimed. He attended two sessions of the United Nations General Assembly, transporting his individual free-wheeling style into its debates by banging the table with his shoe in protest when he was procedurally frustrated. Stalin had regarded the UN as a useful means of defence, a holding operation. Khrushchev wanted to turn it into a weapon of offence, and tried to enforce a reorganization of the top secretariat to conform with his view of a tri-polar world: Atlantic Alliance, socialist bloc, and the (as yet) uncommitted nations of the Third World. In putting forward this new authoritative redefinition of international reality he took the initiative out of President Eisenhower's tired hands. The days of a bi-polar world in which neutralism was a form of aberration that could be overcome by persuasion or self-interest were definitely over. Though neither American nor Soviet ideology could easily accommodate the notion that neutrality between these conflicting and competing systems was feasible or could be lasting, the three-part world now became the accepted classification. Khrushchev threatened to disrupt the United Nations organization from time to time, but in fact Soviet participation in many of its activities was consolidated during his years of power and became an established fact of international political life.

Apart from the new participation in international relations, there were two major departures from Stalinist tradition in foreign policy. One was the new Soviet approach to the Third World of developing countries, the other the relationship between the Soviet Union and the United States. After the failure of his policies in China and elsewhere in the mid-1920s Stalin had lost interest in the active pursuit of communism abroad; the achievements of foreign parties, whether European or Asian, were their own, not that of the increasingly degenerate International (a fact which historians and Western statesmen obsessed with communist dogmatism in the Stalin period often overlooked). As its control over European communist decision-making relaxed, the Soviet leadership under Khrushchev gave increasing weight to the importance of the Third World (and did so distinctly earlier than the Western countries). An overall strategy emerged which related the economic growth of the underdeveloped countries to the Soviet Union's world-wide competitive struggle against the United States.

This often produced apparent contradictions. For example, extremely reactionary régimes which supported the Soviet Union internationally, like the Yemen and later Morocco, rated as partially progressive. As a consequence the Communist Parties in these countries had to adjust their internal tactics in accordance with a dual standard based on the international situation as well as domestic considerations. It was not desirable for communists in, say, Egypt or India to oppose too vehemently a government enjoying Soviet support. The situation differed from the Stalinist period mainly in the greater autonomy in decision-making left to individual Parties, and also through the elaboration of the new concept of the National Democratic State which provided theoretical justification for the collaboration of communists with local anti-imperialist (or anti-American) nationalists. The Soviet Union encouraged these nationalist leaders directly; Nasser in Egypt, Nkrumah in Ghana, and Sekou Touré in Guinea all benefited substantially from Soviet support once they had come to power. Support consisted of international backing in the struggle against the former colonialists ('neo-colonialism and neo-imperialism') and of heavily publicized and carefully directed develop-ment aid, often of a spectacular rather than an obviously rational kind – football stadiums, for example, rather than agricultural irrigation.

Military aid also figured prominently. The resonant but inexpensive Soviet backing for Egypt during the Suez crisis in October 1956 firmly established the Soviet Union as the Third World's friend – while the Americans, whose intervention was probably more effective in restraining the Anglo-French invasion, derived little or no prestige out of the affair. As far as the Third World was concerned, Soviet support during the Suez invasion completely outweighed the events in Hungary. It was from that moment that developing countries began to take the Soviet model of industrialization increasingly seriously.

Soviet policy also had its own contradictions. As Chinese competition developed, the Soviet Union tended to find itself in a position of backing existing governments against more orthodox left-wing claims supported by the Chinese. The Soviet posture of apparent conservatism in the international field was sharply challenged during the Sino-Indian dispute of 1962, in which the Soviet Union remained neutral and continued to supply the kind of military and industrial aid to India which it had previously cut off from its rebellious ally. These developments were leading to an open split in the international communist movement: a distressing prospect for the fiftieth anniversary of the October revolution.

The competitive confrontation between the Soviet Union and the United States was now becoming immediate and direct as it had never been before. Stalin's *cordons sanitaires* were being rapidly eliminated. But the notion of peaceful co-existence also permitted, indeed encouraged, direct intercourse between these countries on a political level of public debate as well as on a technical level of exchange of knowledge and information (not to speak of the greatly enhanced mutual efforts at espionage, which now shifted away from political penetration and the capture of potential sympathizers to straightforward theft of scientific, technical and military information). The high point of this relationship was reached during Khrushchev's visit to the United States in September 1959. For a moment the world's expectations from the personal and private dialogue at Camp David between the leaders of the world's two greatest nations were raised to the same level of optimism that had accompanied the communion of Stalin, Roosevelt and Churchill during the war. In the last resort people take an Olympian view of how intractable problems can best be solved. And in a sense the optimism was more justified than appeared at the time. The aftermath of the meeting was bitter; the destruction of the American U2 spy plane, the pilot's trial and Khrushchev's uncompromising hostility at the Paris Summit meeting in May 1960 seemed to dash all momentary hopes. Part of the difficulty and interest of the Khrushchev era is that he was as unpredictable to his American opponents as to his colleagues. Locked in their opposing hard-line ideologies, Dulles and Molotov had finally understood each other's limits and ultimates, and in a sense had shared a common fervidly gritty style; the Geneva conferences of 1954–5 were not without workmanlike and beneficial results. Eisenhower and Khrushchev radiated amiable accessibility but misjudged and misinterpreted each other wholly, as did Kennedy and the Soviet premier – and the world veered on at least three occasions from optimism to the crisis of imminent war. Yet in perspective the later Khrushchev era, from 1959 to 1964, was one of increasing direct negotiations as well as sharpening confrontation between the United States and the Soviet Union. Individual issues like the reunification of Germany and the Berlin problem still defied solution, but the habit of consultation became firmly established all the same. Its culmination was the treaty banning atomic testing of military weapons which the United States, the Soviet Union and later almost all other nations save France, China and Albania signed in 1964.

This increasingly frequent intercourse had far-reaching effects on the attitudes of the élites in both countries. For one thing great mutual interest in each other mushroomed in the United States and in the Soviet Union. Secondly, the ideological confrontation in the international field was beginning to mask an undogmatic market-type competition in the offer not only of ideas, but of concrete goods and services to third countries. These in turn bid up their support and played off one bloc against the other. One prominent American sociologist has analysed this period as a bi-polar international system, with both leading countries bidding for support – not unlike the electoral competition in a two-party state. Finally tacit recognition was given to the unalterable fact that both the Soviet Union and the United States were there to stay; the policy of each country had to be shaped accordingly. In the United States the unqualified condemnation of totalitarianism, which had reached its height in the early 1950s, now tended to wither away and the Soviet Union began to be regarded as undergoing a period of liberalization and evolution – in fact becoming not unlike the United States itself. It was now claimed that an inevitable logic of industrialization must sooner or later make all nations alike. In the Soviet Union no such ideological concessions were openly made, though Khrushchev himself was the first to stress the enormous technological achievement of the great rival and to urge Russians to emulate the best scientific and technological advances of capitalism. This in turn resulted in a new form of diplomacy: technical contact between scientists, technicians, writers and professional bodies of all kinds. Meetings between Russian and American professionals became more frequent. It was tacitly understood that major ideological questions would not be raised; there was usually a pained silence all round when somebody broke this convention. Even the prospect of much more tourism both ways began to seem feasible.

Naturally this personalization of diplomacy had its disadvantages and dangers. The benefit of traditional diplomacy is precisely its routine, impersonal nature which acts as a calming brake on politicians. On the Soviet side Khrushchev's personal voluntarism tended to commit the Soviet Union to attitudes the full consequences of which could not always be foreseen. Old habits died hard on both sides; beneath the apparent open-handedness of negotiations and meetings between the American President and the Soviet Chairman of Ministers a vast bureaucratic apparatus in both countries continued to operate in a climate of ideological conflict. Military, especially missile, planning was still firmly based on the view of the other as the certain enemy. The Berlin problem – a city divided between two groups of hostile occupying powers, each sponsoring an increasingly independent and antagonistic German government – reached crisis point once more in 1960. But much more serious was the Cuban missile crisis of October-November 1962, when the world for the first time teetered on the brink of a nuclear war. The Soviet version of these events will probably not be known for a long time, and it would be pointless to make guesses here. But the Chinese, who by this time were busy drawing up a bill of indictment against Russian 'revisionism', chose to characterize the policy of Khrushchev's government as a mixture of adventurism and capitulation. Spelled out, this meant that the risks taken by the Soviet government in supplying and installing missile sites in Cuba, right in the centre of America's most sensitive sphere of influence, was a dangerous provocation. But the Soviet capitulation before American threats, and the willingness to dismantle and withdraw the missiles, was an even more unwarranted concession to imperialism. The ill-advised and badly concluded venture became strongly associated with the style of Khrushchev's politics, and provided the first concrete case for the Chinese argument that Soviet policy was objectively if not consciously supporting American imperialism. In the USSR there were still ears sensitive to this kind of charge.

If there was a complete reversal of Stalin's policy in international affairs, developments within the Soviet Union were much more cautious and tentative. Foreign and internal affairs had become almost completely divorced from each other, both structurally and in terms of perception – very much as in the West. This, too, formed an implicit part of the later Chinese definition of Soviet revisionism (the Chinese cultural revolution of 1966–7 was in this sense a deliberate return to the mentality of 'Fortress Yenan' of 1935, with domestic policy fully aligned to the supposed exigencies of 'foreign' isolation). Khrushchev's own ascendancy after 1953, when he became the Party's First Secretary, benefited his immediate supporters substantially. It has been suggested that his administrative onslaught on the enormous bureaucratic apparatus of the ministries in Moscow and the creation of Regional Economic Councils in 1957, were partly motivated by the fact that most of the opposition against him had come from the top management of these technical ministries. Certainly one of the subsidiary effects of the reform was to dislodge large numbers of well-installed civil servants from Moscow and shift them into the provinces, a move as bitterly resented as similar efforts in almost every country in the world. But as an explanation this view smacks of Kremlinology. More probable is the view that the enormously centralized control over all the minutiae of Soviet economic life was no longer feasible in an era of full industrialization. The solution proposed was in no sense a lessening of overall planning, but shifted the focus of planning to regional administrative bodies rather than Moscow ministries. It also enhanced the local Party grip. The Union Republics as such were only marginal beneficiaries of the measure, since the Regional Councils were not made fully subordinate to the governments of the Republics but to some extent co-ordinate with them. The object was to utilize the geographical proximity of factories supplying each other, and to rationalize the whole system of distribution. At the same time the government was as much concerned as ever to prevent the emergence of regional self-interest or a sense of regional economic autonomy; frequent warnings appeared in the press against attempts to use the new councils as a means of giving primacy to local as opposed to national interests.

The most sweeping changes of the period were concerned with agriculture. It had long been Khrushchev's pet interest; as far back as 1952 he had made the abortive proposal that collective farms should own their own tractors and machinery. This reform was carried out in 1958, and was followed by a sustained campaign to raise the standard of living, political participation and agricultural productivity of the rural areas. The reforms followed a lengthy assessment of the relative failure of Soviet agricultural policy and the growing fear that falling productivity in a situation of continued industrialization must sooner or later produce a grave food crisis. Khrushchev, never one to think small, toyed with the idea of agrotowns, nothing less than an attempt to industrialize agriculture completely by creating more or less urban conditions of living and work on the land. This remained a fantasy, but a vast attack was made on marginal and hitherto uncultivated grazing areas in the campaign of the 'Virgin Lands' of Kazakhstan and Siberia. This campaign had something of a Stalinist flavour though without either the Party's enthusiasm or the coercion of the peasantry. A few tentative expert voices who instead suggested more intense and efficient exploitation of existing high-yielding land, and a more rational planting of crops, were ignored or argued into silence. With unsuitable climatic conditions the scheme failed; Khrushchev lost face, but no heads were lost.

228

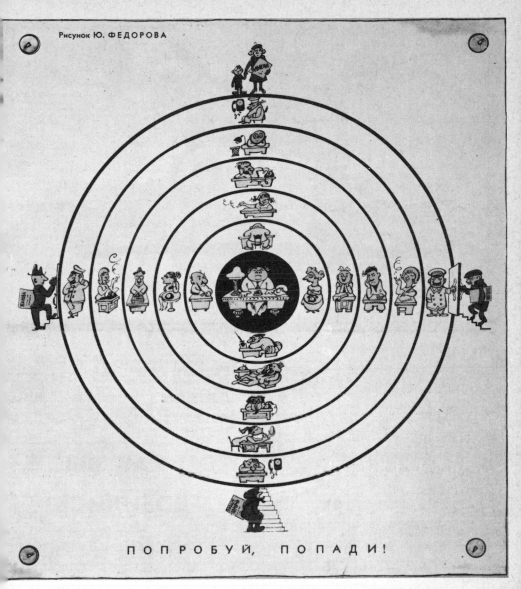

ПОПРОБУЙ, ПОПАДИ!

130 The attack on over-centralization. Caricature of everybody's total dependence on the man at the centre (1965). The woman at top bears a declaration, the man at left a complaint, the woman at bottom seeks help, and the man at right carries a petition

Khrushchev then took greater interest in raising productivity on existing farms. The process of amalgamating the smaller units of collective farms into larger ones had already been going on and was now deliberately accelerated. The number and acreage of state farms increased considerably at the expense of the collectives in the late 1950s. Prices for agricultural products were raised, prices for consumer goods were lowered. In 1962 a great campaign for the increase of chemical fertilizer production was started. This 'chemical industry campaign' was reminiscent of the old *sturmovshchina*; for weeks the press spoke of little else. Sensibly, the economic campaign was matched by a socio-political offensive. A huge effort was made at last to integrate the rural areas into the structure and life of the Party, and rural representation among those elected to Party and Soviet posts was raised significantly. Agricultural problems became all the vogue; the agricultural ministries and organizations suddenly became the focus of attention, and top-level Party meetings on the subject were enlivened by the determined questions, lectures and interruptions of the agriculturally minded First Secretary.

On 15 December 1958, Khrushchev said, 'In actual fact, as regards grain production, the country remained for a long time at the level of pre-revolutionary Russia.' He went on to give the following figures to support this statement:

SOWN AREAS, ACTUAL (BARN) CROP PER HECTARE, AND TOTAL CROP

	Grain-Area (million hectares)	Crop per Hectare (centners)	Total Grain Return (million poods)
1910–14 (average per year over present territory)	102·5	7·0	4,380
1949–53 (average per year)	105·2	7·7	4,942

'As you see, in sown areas, crop yield and grain returns, the country remained, in practice, at the same level as before the Revolution, though in numerical strength the population, and especially that of the industrial centres and cities, had considerably increased.' *Plenum of the Central Committee of the Communist Party of the Soviet Union, 15–19 December 1958*, Moscow 1959, p. 13

As early as September 1953, Khrushchev, in his report to the Central Committee, gave the following livestock figures (in millions):

	1916	1928	1941	1953
Large horned cattle:				
Total	58·4	66·8	54·5	56·6
Cows	28·8	33·2	27·8	24·3
Pigs	23·0	27·7	27·5	28·5
Sheep and goats	96·3	114·6	91·6	109·9
Horses	38·8	36·1	21·0	15·3

N.S. Khrushchev, *Measures for the further development of agriculture in the USSR*, Moscow 1954, p. 21

(*See tables in Appendix for information on present position of Soviet agriculture.*)

131 The balance between agriculture and industry has always been one of the major Soviet problems. Right, the rich wheatfields of a state farm in the Stavropol region ▶

132, 133 Non-conformist contemporary art. Left, *Suicide* by Ernst Neizvestny, one of the most interesting Soviet sculptors in the present generation. Right, *Foolish Kittens* by Oscar Rabin (1961)

The real area of liberalization was in the arts and literature. In his personal tastes Khrushchev was on the side of the Stalinist old guard – but the leader's personal tastes no longer had the full force of law. In the sciences the determination of the government to attain greater efficiency did not prevent Khrushchev, for instance, from continuing to support Stalin's pet geneticist, Lysenko, who was kept incongruously afloat for a few more years – an increasingly irrelevant piece of intellectual flotsam. In literature and the arts Khrushchev's frequent expressions of disgust were echoed and reinforced by official warnings and clamp-downs against any over-enthusiastic seizure of the right to criticize. A considerable number of writers and scholars who took the opportunity in the late 1950s and early 1960s to rewrite the past or criticize various aspects of the present found themselves officially attacked and often personally disadvantaged – in extreme cases carried off to lunatic asylums.

134 Soviet mass culture. The event for which this crowd have assembled in the Sports Palace of the Lenin Stadium in Moscow is a poetry reading, probably by the authors

'Spontaneity' was not permitted. The question of social responsibility – the only criterion familiar in a Soviet Union that had experienced twenty-five years of Stalinism – loomed as large as ever. But the frontiers of the definition, the area of the responsible and hence the permissible, were all the time being advanced. The role of testing these frontiers, of defending each new territory of permitted criticisms against officialdom, of stimulating or forcing the Party into stating a case, fell largely on the writers and artists. With the total impoverishment of Soviet philosophy, it was they who had taken over the Socratic function – at least until the day, if this should ever come, when the Party itself would take the intellectual lead. Instead of advancing and fertilizing new frontiers, the Party had for many years been exclusively concerned with a rearguard action, defending existing and established boundaries. The raising of fundamental intellectual questions was taboo. For the time being the Party would have much preferred to let such questions lie, and concentrate on problems of production and efficiency; it was reluctantly forced into making pronouncements in an area where it felt uncertain and at a disadvantage.

The importance of this situation cannot be exaggerated. Whereas economic and administrative reforms in the Soviet Union under Khrushchev had always been the result of official decisions, the new freedom in the arts and sciences tended to be the result of direct struggle and risk on the part of

135, 136 Contrasts in Soviet architectural taste. Left, the ornate palatial style of the Moscow Underground of the 1930s and, right, a recently built Underground station

individual authors. Some of these pioneers were Party members. The zig-zag line of the authorities during this period thus stems not only from the inter-Party struggles between 1953 and 1959, but also from the administrative and intellectual difficulties of defining accurately where the boundaries lay and, more crucially, the *meaning* of permissible change. Who could say what criticism was desirable, acceptable, excessive? What were the wider implications behind the overt texture of art and literature? Hence we find authors of relatively harmless books attacked and sometimes even put on trial, while others, like Solzhenitsyn (*A Day in the Life of Ivan Denisovich*) and Dudintsev (*Not By Bread Alone*), got away with critical discussion and massive sales. (It is not generally known, for instance, that satires at least as strong as those for which Sinyavsky and Daniel were sentenced to imprisonment in 1966 occasionally and with impunity appeared in Soviet literary journals – Bulgakov's piece in *Moskva*, for example.) The difficulties of the authorities were like those of commanders in a highly mobile war, where territory could not be held for good but where the enemy had to be kept at bay by an occasional armed retaliation of an exemplary nature. All the communist governments face this problem; and the most significant evidence of diversity in the socialist bloc is to be found in the entirely different definition of acceptable frontiers between, say, Poland and Hungary on the one hand, and the Soviet Union and the German Democratic Republic on the other.

Whatever the substance, Khrushchev's *manner* of making changes was irregular by traditional Soviet standards, and contrary to the deeply ingrained form of careful and cautious discussion (however formalistic such discussion had been under Stalin). As often as not, Khrushchev bombarded his colleagues in the Party Praesidium with unexpected proposals from distant corners of the land and even abroad. He had the disagreeable habit of sounding the opinion of his local hosts on ideas that might have occurred to him a short time earlier and about which his colleagues in the Praesidium knew nothing. Many schemes put forward by Khrushchev were never in fact put into practice – for example, the idea, which suddenly occurred to him during a visit to central Asia, that all central Asian Republics should form one super-unit for administrative and economic purposes. Others met considerable resistance even among those colleagues who had supported him faithfully in his struggles against the 'anti-Party group'. The attempt to apply modern principles of division of labour to the full might be something worth studying in the context of production. When applied to the Party itself, however, it was no less than a grave affront to the sacrosanct Leninist principle of an all-purpose political party. And yet Khrushchev seemed to have bludgeoned his colleagues into accepting this when in September 1962 he outlined a plan for splitting the Party into distinct agricultural and industrial sections, in order to make it conform to an economic pattern. Nor was Khrushchev free from occasional challenges to his leadership even after he took over the Chairmanship of the Council of Ministers from Bulganin in 1959. Kirichenko, an important member of the Praesidium, was mysteriously sacked in 1960, and there are still doubts about the genuineness of the illness which knocked Kozlov out of a very promising career in 1963.

Khrushchev was no ideologist but a pragmatic activist who took his Marxism largely for granted – and dug industriously in Lenin's collected works whenever he felt the traditional need for theoretical justification. His over-riding passions were agricultural improvement and commitment to industrial growth. It was in these terms that he saw socialist competition with the capitalist world, the final victory over the United States, the triumph of communism. At the Twenty-First Party Congress in January 1959 he made extravagant promises about the economic future, both in terms of consumption and in the context of comparison with the United States. At the Twenty-Second Congress the new programme of the Communist Party, which had not been touched since 1919, provided a cautious but nonetheless determined projection into a fully communist future. Though circumstances forced him to give way and increase the military estimates after the U2 incident and the fiasco of the Paris Summit, his commitment to lower defence costs and greater consumption was re-established in the course of 1963. The following year he was speaking openly of making consumer goods and agricultural investments the top priority of the next Five Year Plan, at the expense of heavy industry. He was willing to pin his reputation on the success of these policies. But the facts were against him. From 1958 onwards Soviet industrial growth began to slow down significantly. Having been slightly over 10 per cent per annum for over a decade it fell to $7\frac{1}{2}$ per cent in 1964 and seemed to be dropping further. Moreover the decline, in spite of all efforts, was particularly marked in consumer industries: a mere 2 per cent growth in 1964. Figures apart, the press bristled with complaints (naturally of individual rather than collective failures) and Khrushchev himself was not slow to pick up the waves of this dissatisfaction on his many travels.

ANNUAL AND PERIOD GROWTH RATES OF SOVIET GROSS NATIONAL PRODUCT AND OF SELECTED SECTORS

Annual rates for GNP		Sector	Average annual rate	
Year	Rate		1950–8	1958–64
1958	9·4	Industry	10·9	7·8
1959	4·9	Construction	13·2	5·8
1960	5·2	Agriculture	5·7	1·5
1961	6·2	Transportation	12·2	9·3
1962	5·1	Commerce	4·0	6·0
1963	2·6	Services	2·4	4·4
1964	7·9	GNP	7·1	5·3

From New Directions in the Soviet Economy, Part IIA and IIB, United States Government Printing Office, Washington 1966

Many reasons have been adduced for his fall, most of them *ex post facto*; the Kremlinologists failed significantly on this occasion. The surface causes are implicit in the earlier description of the man and his era. But at the same time he was a shrewd politician and his colleagues knew how dangerous it was to sell him short. It would not be easy to remove him. Beneath the immediacies of politics in the Party Praesidium, Khrushchev had, of course, alienated and annoyed many of the administrators and Party officials who had been directly affected by his reforms: civil servants sent into the country, agricultural experts hauled over the coals and subjected to a torrent of contradictory changes, the armed services with a vested interest in a rich flow of military expenditure, the Party traditionalists for whom the priority of heavy industry in any Soviet investment programme was sacred. With the terror a thing of the past, they had all looked forward to a spell of personal security and a more predictable future. At a more profound level, there were the basic diehards who questioned Khrushchevism as a whole – the idea of a half-way house in the retreat from Stalinism. There was no obvious logic about the particular position for which Khrushchev had settled, and he was unable or unwilling to attempt any full-scale Marxist-Leninist justification. He was concerned to emphasize the return of Party control over policy and administration in the Soviet Union, but at the same time was not prepared to enable the Party to articulate a genuinely collective policy from the bottom up. He had raised Soviet prestige throughout the world by an assertive and interfering foreign policy but had confined decision-making largely to his own initiative. The very unpredictability in foreign affairs which he helped to bring about tended in turn to require a Khrushchev-type direction of diplomacy. Above all, his insistence on rational and efficient working seemed to be in flat contradiction to his own tendency to interfere in everything and make decisions off the top of his head. In the end the policies he advocated were not in accord with his manner of executing them. He became something of an anachronism in the post-Stalin Soviet Union; what was wanted now was the benefits of Khrushchevism without Khrushchev.

He fell smoothly, silently – and comfortably – into a dignified retirement. In the second half of 1964 a majority of his colleagues seem to have decided that he must go. Such a decision had initially still to be put into effect in a conspiratorial manner; the tactical dice were strongly loaded in favour of the ruling incumbent. Khrushchev was summoned at the last minute from vacation in the Crimea to a meeting of the Praesidium on 13 October 1964. His previous tactic of appealing to the larger Central Committee had also been carefully anticipated and blocked, and a few days later he was duly outvoted in the larger forum. But if the mechanism of his removal smacked of the old and careful Stalinist preparation, the effect was strictly new. The attacks on Khrushchev in the press following his fall were short-lived and on the whole muted, and for the next few years Khrushchev could be seen by journalists on odd occasions cheerfully enjoying, or perhaps not enjoying, his retirement. Except for Adzhubei, his son-in-law and latterly his Ambassador Extraordinary, there was no purge of any kind.

With the fall of Khrushchev it has ceased to be possible to identify Soviet policy with any one person. Hence Kremlinology has lost its value as well as its point (its practitioners have learnt Chinese instead). Khrushchev's basic policies could as easily be carried out by a collective leadership as by an individual; his was not a system of terror and total insecurity. An early attempt was made to undo some of the less popular aspects of Khrushchev's policy. The slanging match with China, to which he had latterly devoted considerable energy and much venom, at first became muted. A genuine attempt appears to have been made to use the change in leadership in order to achieve a rapprochement with the Chinese. By 1965, however, the tyranny of facts had reimposed itself on both sides, and the public round of denunciations was back in full swing. Khrushchev's successors did not display his personal relish for journeys abroad or direct meetings and confrontations with foreign leaders – although the French and British press did their best to make a 'personality' out of Kosygin, Chairman of the Council of Ministers, during his visits in 1966 and 1967. But the essentials of contact between the Soviet Union and the United States, the basis of economic competition and peaceful co-existence, were maintained intact. The ebullient and personal style had gone, the basic direction of policy remained the same.

In the domestic sphere, too, the early review of policy by the new leaders soon led to a return to the basic Khrushchev line. Some of his reforms were quickly undone; most notably the regional economic councils, established in 1957 and redrawn in 1961, were abolished at the end of 1965. Planning as well as execution became centralized in Moscow once more. But this was not a return to Stalinism. As we shall see in the next chapter, the real beneficiaries of the December 1965 reforms were not the top planning and administrative staff, but the individual factory or combine manager. The Party reorganization on industrial and agricultural lines was quickly abandoned. As against this the commitment to economic growth, rational production and increased consumption was not only maintained but quietly stepped up – without the boastful trumpetings of previous years.

The defeat of a group and its particular line, followed by the effective adoption of the policies of the defeated, had long been common practice in the Soviet Union. It had always required elaborate, often tortuous justification on ideological grounds. This time the changeover was made smoothly, in personal terms, without any attempt to raise problems of deviation. What can we deduce from all this for the future?

VII SPECULATION

The fiftieth anniversary of the October revolution fell at a singularly un-dramatic moment in an otherwise exciting half-century. The speeches, articles, parades and meetings all stressed the continued relevance of the revolution as much as its historical significance. But this question of con-temporary relevance cannot be begged; it must be examined on its own merits. The very problem is a measure of the enormous progress and change which the Soviet Union has undergone in fifty years – the celebration of a distant, exciting and risky past contrasted with the stability and assurance of the present.

What is the achievement as a function of the past? Politics and social life are finally in balance, in harmony even. (There are a few people who predict severe social upheavals, if not disintegration, in the Soviet Union; we shall have more to say about them later on.) The Party is no longer in control of so many separate institutions, guiding or forcing them into a purposive direction; instead it incorporates these institutions and reflects them. Occa-sionally there are signs of resentment that institutional decisions are taken without consultations with the formal organs of the Party. Because those making the decisions are senior Party members, the views of the Party are felt to have been adequately taken into account, and the formal channels safely dispensed with. Personal careers at every level of distinction are ir-revocably bound up with Party life; so are all manifestations of professional and group interests and demands. In turn, the professional and technical aspirations of the educated strata who really run the complex industrial society of the Soviet Union strongly influence the overt policy formulated and carried out by the Party. Though the Communist Party in the Soviet Union is and will continue to be an essentially political instrument, and the top leadership is still recruited from among those pursuing a full-time political career, the days are over when political considerations simply overrode all technical ones. Social consensus is therefore no longer created by a small and autonomous political élite enforcing its own views and decisions on and through the Party, but is rather a two-way process generated within the Party which in turn effectively permeates and organizes every walk of life. In *this* respect the withering away of the state can now be considered a long-term

137 Premier Kosygin during his visit to London in February 1967 – tired, cautious and unspectacular compared to his predecessors

possibility rather than a utopian dream. Already a number of activities like sport have been 'socialized' into self-administration. More important is the growth since 1959 of socialized law enforcement – Comrades Courts and Volunteer Squads (*druzhina*) to take over the problems of controlling social delinquency. The Party will gradually take the place of the retreating state organs of enforcement – but the Party as an institution of popular participation, not of political control from the top. Administration and regulation, hitherto considered the classic preserve of the state, of its institutions and its bureaucracy, will increasingly be carried out through a form of self-regulation expressed by this consensus, which in turn finds expression through the organized Party. When we consider the promises that Soviet society will move, within a finite period, towards a state of full communism, we must assess this not in terms of any disappearance of regulation and control, but of their institutionalization in an even broader form – that of a growing Party made up of all the leading elements of an entire society.

Will this make the Soviet Union more or less conservative in a social sense ? It is an intriguing problem. A state bureaucracy may or may not innovate; it has done so in the last two decades in France, and failed to do so in England. Normally an autonomous state and its institutions have the possibility of innovating or conserving, depending on their own view of what is desirable and of their place and function in society. Social control based on an institutionalized consensus, on effective public opinion, hardly ever innovates, and is nearly always conservative. This suggests a conservative orientation for the future Party-suffused Soviet society. But there is a strong counter-tendency – especially in the short run. For Soviet social tradition over the last thirty years has itself been strongly conservative. The relaxation of Stalinist control has brought strong demands or at least a desire for change, which writers and artists have forcibly expressed in the last decade. In the extreme case of Yugoslavia this reaction has all but engulfed the formal organs of control and challenged the basic ideology. It may well be, therefore, that initially the switch to self-regulation will also produce some explosive demands for innovation in the short run. Perhaps the best prediction that can be made is to emphasize the strong economic and technological – as opposed to cultural, intellectual or humanistic – cast of Soviet professionalization. This would indicate a tendency to concentrate innovation in the economic and technical sectors; with these professions satisfied, the social consensus is likely to be conservative in other areas, and to contain demands for more radical innovations there.

In any case, all this means more Party influence, not less. These developments will all be Party-sponsored and take place initially within its senior

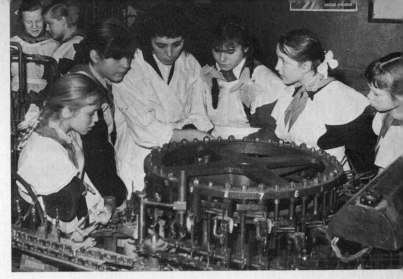

The USSR places
great emphasis on
technological education.
Pupils of the Yaroslav
Galan school in Lvov
are shown visiting
an electric-lamp plant

ranks. The nature of the Party has changed considerably during the course of
fifty years – from a small revolutionary élite to a rigidly disciplined instrument of mobilization and action; from a hierarchical dictatorship of cadres
to a membership of over ten million embracing all those who have attained
positions of power, prestige and responsibility. The relatively faceless men
who now sit in the Kremlin and in the top positions of state and Party are the
product of this new social phenomenon. Undoubtedly there will still be
conflict. But it will be a conflict of interests, organizations and attitudes based
on a consensus about social values and goals, not – as in former times – a
naked struggle for power, with the victor obliged to enforce uniformity in
the teeth of strongly marked differences over the interpretation of the
common ideology. The kind of consensus which exists in large sections of
American and British societies as a result of several centuries of common
national experience and the pressure of social integration has been created in
and through the Soviet Party within fifty years. The Soviet achievement has
compressed time into a dense and weighty mass of experience. It is no wonder
that this still weighs heavily on the Soviet individual today. He has little
sense of leisure as a period of doing nothing.

The process of creating a cohesive society has been accompanied by
thirty-five years of large-scale and rapid industrialization. The two processes
of social integration and economic industrialization went hand in hand. It is
probably true that without the Stalinist period of industrialization the fusion
between a revolutionary Party of Marxist ideology and the society which it
sought to transform could never have taken place. But equally the process of
industrialization created some of the greatest difficulties for integration;

243

hence the ubiquitous vigilance, the police terror, the labour camps. With all its appalling suffering and tragic waste, full industrialization and social integration could not have been attained by other means in the time. Was Stalin really necessary? Yes. Those who concentrate on the surface and formal structure of totalitarianism, and accordingly discover similarities between Nazi Germany and the Soviet Union, forget or ignore the fundamental differences. Soviet 'totalitarianism' arose in order to initiate and complete a process of industrialization and social homogenization, its extremes and excesses were a degeneration of an originally self-imposed discipline, while Nazi totalitarianism was a voluntaristic imposition of the racial quirks and international ambitions of a small gang of extremists who

139 Twice a year, on May Day
and on the anniversary
of the October revolution,
the Soviet Union displays
some of its military strength.
Left, the parade of tanks
through Moscow's Red Square
on the Forty-fifth Anniversary
of the October revolution, 1962

promised an ambitious and frustrated nation a cheap way out of its troubles, and whose final holocaust engendered neither social advance nor even major social change, except the physical annihilation of many millions of people. The Communist Party of the Soviet Union transformed Soviet society, while the Nazi Party of Germany transformed the world without changing German society appreciably.

If Lenin could come back and stand in Red Square with the Soviet leaders to review the parade, what would he think? Would he approve, or would they have to get rid of him in the same way in which Dostoevsky's Grand Inquisitor threatened the returned Christ? On the surface Lenin might well be appalled. A merciless critic of revolutionary verbiage unmatched by revolutionary feeling or actions, he would find the solid and comfortable tributes to the revolutionary past, the strident claim for present relevance, hideously unbecoming to such well-established bureaucrats in double-breasted suits and resplendent uniforms, controlling a vast and complex society which they have integrated into the international system, on speaking and visiting terms with the major imperialist powers but at loggerheads with the revolutionary cotton-overall régime in Peking. He would be disagreeably struck by the air of self-sufficiency and self-regard in this new Soviet Union, which appears to have abdicated the front-line leadership of the ever-continuing battle with imperialism to a poorer, still newer communist régime in the East. What would there be to talk about with the new Soviet generation of technocrats with their sophisticated machinery, their emphasis on consumer production and distribution, their formalistic tributes to his own work and ideas? Where is communist equality, which he strove so hard by writing and example to instil in his colleagues in their early struggle against the old, deeply ingrained manifestations of social inequality and privilege? Where, for that matter, are these colleagues now?

But Lenin was also a man of great vision and self-appraisal. Much that he would have found unfamiliar and repulsive in the atmosphere has followed directly from his own policies and decisions. The roles and attitudes of those who lead a powerful state for whom survival is no longer a problem, must inevitably be quite different from those of the heroic and determined strugglers of the early 1920s. As the Soviet Union has grown stronger and more complex, so the interest in its own affairs increases at the expense of the old neurotic worries about historical contradictions in the enemy camp. Knowing Lenin, one would suppose that, rather than contrast his successors with himself, he would be much more likely to measure them against the great master, Karl Marx. And here he would find gaps in Marx's system of ideas – many of the same gaps he himself already experienced in his own attempts to adapt Marxism to a philosophy of political power. For the situation has long outgrown Marx's widest frame of reference. Even so, Lenin might consider the two major implications of Marx's vision of socialism fulfilled: the absence of private property other than that for personal use, and the continued and deeply imbued belief in the correctness of dialectical materialism as a guide to thought and action. These two features are the sheet-anchor of Soviet society, and tie it directly to its ideological and historical base. It is therefore worthwhile to analyse the Soviet achievement a little further in this regard.

Whatever similarities of organization and process full-scale industrialization imposes on all societies involved in it, the distribution of capital ownership and the criteria according to which production decisions are made do distinguish industrial societies in important ways. It is no doubt true that in an age of increasing specialization and technical sophistication managers, engineers and scientists find a common language across ideological barriers. In this respect the West and the Soviet Union obviously have grown more alike – in the sense of having more in common. Even in capitalist countries the direct influence of ownership on production is growing increasingly vague and tenuous as the vital strata of management are interposed between owners and workers. Power and wealth have become disparate dimensions. Many observers have lumped these facts together as the development of bureaucracy common to all industrial countries. The fact that economic competition for scarce resources has outpaced their production has led to an increasing amount of planning in the West. Though the philosophy of planning is entirely different between East and West, this too provides points of possible dialogue. But beneath these similarities lurk a number of crucial differences. Because success in the Soviet Union cannot ultimately be expressed in terms of possessions (however great the differentiated scale of rewards between the educated and the unskilful), the basic approach of Soviet management is entirely different from that in the United States. To put it crudely, cost and money are an insignificant part of Soviet cosmology. The ladder of advance in the Soviet Union must remain on a dimension of public and interdependent scales of power, while that in the United States is directed more towards self-sufficient and personal scales of wealth. The relationship of individuals to politics and society is thus much more integrated in the Soviet Union than in the United States, the area of private choices correspondingly smaller.

The edges of this distinction tend to become blurred as increasing attention is paid in the Soviet Union to the satisfaction of consumer demands. But in the first place the Soviet leadership intends to continue to determine the nature of this demand. Khrushchev was all for filling the kitchen pot, but very much against the choking of Russian roads with individually owned cars. The provision of social services – whether in the strict sense of medical, nursery and housing facilities or in the wider context of culture – is more strongly emphasized as part of consumer rewards than in capitalist countries. Above all the whole apparatus of planning focuses productive effort on some future benefit instead of subordinating it to the consumer demands of here and now. Planning will continue to be sacred in the Soviet Union as the only rational way of making economic decisions, carrying them into effect, and ensuring that the resultant product reaches its destination. Econometrics and input-output matrices are regarded as tools for controlling change, not merely for predicting it. As society becomes more complex and the consumer more demanding as well as sophisticated there will be more planning, not less.

Secondly, there is a contextual gulf. Soviet citizens see their situation as very different from that of other countries. The notion of a 'state of society', and the attainment of personal satisfaction through a generalized attainment by society as a whole, plays a vital part in the Soviet Union. Anti-social behaviour and attitudes are much more sharply defined. In the West the boundary between public and private is sensitive and much attention is focused upon it; the private sector is an area within which room for individual action is left 'vacant'. By definition everything that is not illegal is permitted. In the Soviet Union the opposite is true. There has been a hesitant but noticeable retreat from legal sanction, coupled with greater reliance on social prohibitions, to enforce the collective social view of right and wrong. A society nearing the stage of communism is, as we have noted, characterized by a growing consensus. The law does no more than put teeth into the enforcement of the social consensus against deviants. The struggle for delimitations of the frontiers of the permissible, which was discussed earlier in connection with writers and artists, is not concerned with individual rights, but with the right to define social norms and the tussle about who shall define them. Human nature being what it is, this retreat from Stalinist methods of enforcement has, of course, produced an apparently startling amount of social (not political) deviation. Soviet newspapers abound with complaints against parasites, drunkenness, undisciplined youth and economic crimes such as fraudulent conversion of public property to private profit. But perhaps the significant aspect of this is not the apparent failure of the relevant Soviet policies, and the corresponding irrelevance of talk about communism, but the fact that public denunciation and appeals to social conscience have multiplied as a form of collective response to the retreat of the formal agencies of law enforcement. Deviation, like disease, is as much a function of awareness as of 'fact'.

The other important factor which differentiates Soviet élites from those in other countries is the full internalization of Marxism. This may not resemble the sophisticated structure of Marx's own thought; it is not difficult to lampoon Soviet thinking as a caricature and vulgarization of Marxism – *idiotnost*. But obviously any complex view of the world must change considerably in the process of adoption by hundreds and thousands of people, and in its application to the management of a vast society. The great majority of Soviet citizens are convinced that their world view is more scientific, more accurate and in every way superior to that of other people. This is no longer

140 Industrialization produces some similar social problems in every environment, especially with the relaxation of strict control. This Hungarian cartoon, reprinted in *Krokodil*, 1965, is entitled 'Individualists'

a matter of debate but – as far as they are concerned – a proven fact. The tendency of Soviet citizens to be more approachable, the growth of communication between members of the same profession across national boundaries, and the fact that there has been a general *détente* in the ideological warfare between capitalism and socialism, are not due to any decline of ideology in the Soviet Union (or in the West for that matter), but to the irrelevance of debate about these matters. Stalin's pedagogical monstrosities of over-simplification have had their effect – one can legitimately ask whether the equally monstrous efforts of Mao will have a similar effect in due course. That is why the things people talk about in 1967 are quite different from those that concerned them in 1922. We may reasonably assume that a man of Lenin's intellectual stature would understand all this. But – leaving aside the sense of unfamiliarity – would he approve and endorse those invoking his name today? In spite of the substantial achievements, the answer might still be no.

For one thing, Lenin would be disagreeably assailed by the strong smell of nationalism which has developed as a by-product of Soviet achievements. Domestically the hard facts and figures of Russification are undeniable. The demands of integration, the higher access to education by the specific Russian nationalities and the economic development of the peripheral regions of the Soviet Union, have all contributed to a layer of 'Russianness' superimposed on the official policy of equality of cultures, languages and races. Many of these developments have no doubt been inevitable, but not perhaps their complacent incorporation into official thinking and ideology. Anyone as sensitive to pretensions of national or cultural superiority as Lenin could not ignore the somewhat artificial and folksy nature of the support of local cultures, contradicted by the institutionalization of the Russian language and Russian attitudes as the only acceptable path to a career. The most obviously underprivileged group of Tsarist times has once more become the apparently most underprivileged group today – the Jews. Their high proportion in the arts, literature and the sciences has significantly not been matched by a corresponding presence in the administrative positions of the Party. Next door, in Poland, where once an extreme anti-nationalist version of communism originated, he would find things even worse – a 'Partisan' group of national communists steadily weeding out Jews from all positions of trust and power. And all this not merely at the top – for ethnic and cultural prejudices raise profound echoes in receptive societies. One assumes that Lenin would arrive at the fiftieth anniversary celebrations armed with his usual knowledge of what foreign communists were writing; he could not have helped noticing the references to Soviet discrimination against Jews, the strictures on decades of Soviet arrogance towards foreign communists. This, after all, was where he had left off, early in 1923.

These features of nationalism are matched by a disagreeable identification of revolution with the health and wealth of the Soviet Union *tout court*. It would not take Lenin long to disentangle the problems of communist discipline from the concomitant but ideologically separate overtones of nationalism on both sides in the dispute between the Soviet Union and China. The very idea of a struggle or conflict between two established power centres for the interpretation of communist orthodoxy would certainly be more alien to Lenin than it is to the present leaders of the Soviet Union. On this score he would certainly side with Brezhnev and Kosygin, who inherited polycentrism willy-nilly from their predecessor. But the accompanying and underlying stress on national rights, the dispute about frontiers coupled with the assertion of spheres of influence and control over regions acquired by Russia at a time of Tsarist imperialism, would make Lenin uncomfortable, if not exceedingly angry. This was the reason why he fell out with Stalin before his death, and attempted to ensure Stalin's removal from his post of great power as General Secretary. The present leaders have followed in the footsteps of Stalin and not in his own. There is a clear break between internal and external policies. In foreign policy, 'socialism in one country' – a formulation to cover a temporary period of stabilization in the enemy camp – has led to the transformation of the Soviet Union from the epicentre of world revolution to just another big power. The attitudes of independence and self-reliance on the part of the other communist states and foreign Communist Parties can be interpreted not only as a desirable liberation from Stalinist uniformity and control, but as a necessary reaction to Soviet failure to provide adequate support. The Soviet Union has lost interest in foreign countries except in the traditional bourgeois sense of big-power international politics.

Lenin envisaged communism as a form of political communion, and the Party as its organized expression. Until social conditions permitted, the Party must not lose itself in the larger amorphous society. A communist had to be instantly distinguishable from all others by his outward behaviour and his inner values. The present Soviet leaders do not conform to this pattern. Neither Lenin nor, for that matter, most of his contemporaries in the Russian Social Democratic Labour Party or outside it would recognize their successors immediately as communists according to the elemental criteria of personal experience. Apart from anything else, a considerable effort would be required to accept Kosygin, Brezhnev and Podgorny as the direct descendants of the Bolsheviks who saw their precious Soviet state through its turbulent but exciting infancy.

One wonders, for instance, what Lenin would make of the present emphasis on the collective. For Lenin this was a Party concept, based on the conviction that the sum was greater than its parts. In the Soviet Union today the meaning of the word collective is simpler and coarser, and has acquired an institutional context. The emphasis on collective action thus means that people identify themselves not as individuals but as members of a work group, factory, professional group or team, as well as a Party organization. Where newspaper reports of police proceedings in England state a name and an address (or lack of it) as a primary means of identification, the Soviet equivalent is the collective which, as it were, constitutes the individual – rather than the individuals constituting the collective. Is this the self-liberation which was the cause, product and justification of Marxist revolution?

Standing on the reviewing platform, Lenin would find himself in a quandary. Undeniably impressed by the visible effects of Soviet achievement, the obvious permanence of the socialist Soviet Union, he would be made personally uncomfortable and apprehensive by the atmosphere of a society of which he was a founding father and in which he was now a guest. The whole climate would appear extremely conservative. Though not himself especially interested in art and literature, Lenin died at a time when education, science and the arts were still in the throes of spectacular experimentation. The limits then had been no less than the frontiers of human capacity. Now experiments are no

Industrialization also produces many similar answers – like high-rise buildings.

longer designed to test the limits of the possible, but the area of the permissible; and these are still defined in the main by amended yet recognizably Stalinist criteria. We may suppose that Lenin would hurl questions at those surrounding him, and that they would reply vigorously in explanation and self-defence. And here the real sense of disillusion would set in. For what would Lenin have to talk about with this present Soviet leadership – other than ornamental references to the past and revered principles of Marxism? The difference between one for whom concrete achievement must be the expression of ideology, and those for whom ideology is necessarily the explanation of concrete achievements, is very great. If a sense of achievement is ultimately related too closely to physical objects, to statistics, even to facts, no dialogue can be really fruitful or stimulating.

Stalin now joins the parade, paroled from the uneasy conspiracy of relegation. His problem is much simpler. The changes since 1953 have, of course, been far less than those since 1924. The visible and concrete achievements of the Soviet Union over the last fourteen years are logical and to some extent predictable extensions of 1953. Stalin is perfectly at home in the atmosphere of the Soviet Union today. Certainly he would cavil at the extent of liberalization, the indiscipline or chaos in the international movement, the dismantling of the control apparatus. All these would seem to him to be policy failures which could and should be instantly corrected, given a

This Moscow housing estate was built in 1962 to meet an acute housing shortage

return to his own system – the means for which he would probably still find at hand. Stalin would shake his head at the unpredictable example of Khrushchev, and regret that the imminent purge of 1952 had not been carried through. He would warn the assembled Politburo of the dangers of their present path. We may suppose that his own nature and lack of imagination would preclude him from assigning the right weight to the unconscious changes that have taken place since his death. In his view, social processes were best initiated from the top downwards. Given the required amount of pressure and control, the rest of society could be made to adapt easily enough. In short, Stalin finds himself in exactly the opposite situation to Lenin. He is familiar with and approves of the basic climate, strongly disagrees with the present leaders and their policies – and is ready to make short shrift of them.

The fictional reappearance of Lenin and Stalin at the October celebrations is useful in enabling us to confront the state of the Soviet Union with its own past. But we are not interested only in assessing the sum of Soviet achievement, but also in drawing conclusions for the future. Contrary to the loudly proclaimed views of historians, prediction is not dangerous or reprehensible – it may merely prove to be wrong. With the present type of analysis it is almost mandatory to try and predict. What, then, may we expect from the Soviet Union in the future?

Some of the answers are already implicit in the foregoing argument. The commitment of the Soviet leadership to greater emphasis on consumer production is not likely to change unless there is an urgent threat of war. The Soviet consumer will undoubtedly continue to be substantially better off than he has been in the past. His rate of betterment will appear (and will be made to appear) extremely favourable in comparison to Western countries, for the industrial basis of a high expansion rate of consumer goods exists. No

BASE WAGE DIFFERENTIALS IN THE SOVIET UNION, 1963

(U.S. dollars per year, before taxes)[1]

Statutory minimum, rural areas	$360
Statutory minimum, urban areas	400
Collective farmer (1962)	574
State farm worker	586
Office typist	588
Textile worker	679
Construction worker	746
Machine tool operator	746
High school teacher	824
Steel worker	872
Coal miner	1,092
Physician, M.D.	1,260
Lawyer	1,376
Average for all workers and employees	1,445[2]
State farm manager	3,530
Technician	3,724
Engineer (oil industry)	4,238
Master foreman (machine-building)	5,028
Doctor of science, head of department in a research institute	5,730
Factory director (machine-building)	6,240
University professor	7,070
Cabinet minister, republic government	9,125

[1] Roubles convert into dollars at 1:1·11 ratio.
[2] Total wages received, *including bonuses*. All other figures in the table do not include bonuses.

Sources: V. F. Mayer, *Zarabotnaya plata v period perekhoda k kommunizmu* (Moscow: Ekonomizdat, 1963), pp. 141–4, 157–60. U.S. Department of Agriculture, Foreign Agricultural Economic Report No. 13, *Soviet Agriculture Today: Report of 1963 Agriculture Exchange Delegation* (Washington, D.C.: December 1963), pp. 38–43. B. Sukharevsky, 'Rabochiy den i zarabotnaya plata v SSSR', *Kommunist* (Moscow), no. 3, February 1960, pp. 22 ff. A. Volkov, 'Sokrashchenny rabochiy den i uporyadochenie zarabotnoy platy', *Kommunist* (Moscow), no. 13, September 1960, pp. 28 ff. E. I. Landin, *Realnaya zarabornaya plata i dokhody trudyaschikhsya* (Minsk: AN BSSR), pp. 58, 67. *Annual Economic Indicators for the USSR*, materials prepared for the Joint Economic Committee, Congress of the United States, 88th Cong., 2d sess. (Washington, D.C.: Government Printing Office, 1964), p. 66.

From Oxenfeldt and Holubnychy, *Economic Systems in Action*, Holt, Rinehart and Winston, N.Y., 1965 doubt attempts will be made to orient this era of relative plenty in the usual direction postulated by Soviet thinking. Compared to other countries, the Soviet Union will place heavier emphasis on social services as opposed to private ones; public instead of private transport, collective rather than individual holidays, educational rather than purely escapist forms of entertainment. Above all, and in spite of the deliberate inequality of rewards that is a built-in condition of every modern industrial society, the accent on social *distribution* rather than private *acquisition* will always limit inequality at levels lower than those tolerable in Western societies – however grey and uniform the resultant social patina.

But one of the consequences of opening up the Soviet Union to ever more information from abroad is that the Soviet public will tend increasingly to regard other countries as its reference for purposes of comparison and less and less its own past. This will provide a constant challenge to Soviet policy, and will act as a factor towards international rather than internal homogenization. There will be a demand for more cars and roads to go with them, so that official policy, if it is to oppose such demands, will have to give explicit reasons and state its case – to put up or shut up. In this field, as in many others, we may see a form of contained conflict between demands expressed by leading groups of professionals institutionalized within the Party. Professional groups of producers, influential by virtue of their attainments and skills in the process of production, will tend also to govern the form of consumption patterns – a factor which makes for an essentially middle-class approach. (The Soviet consumer as such is as ill-organized and voiceless as consumers in any other industrial economy.) In this respect, therefore, the notion of convergence between Soviet and, say, American society has considerable justification. By the same token the Soviet Union will be increasingly inapplicable as a norm for China or the developing countries, and have less to offer these countries as an example. Part of the Chinese complaint against Soviet revisionism is that it tries to have the cake of heading an international revolutionary movement and eating it too – through raised consumption.

All this has important secondary consequences. Since 1960 problems of efficiency and the best means of assessing it have been in the forefront of technical and political discussion in the Soviet Union. The mainly quantitative factors of the Stalin era are giving way to more selective, qualitative criteria. It is often claimed that this change has been imposed on the Soviet Union by 'market' forces. As quantities of shoddy and therefore unsaleable goods have accumulated in the shops, rejected by more affluent and discriminating consumers, Soviet planning has been forced to alter its approach by the weight of hard economic fact. This is partially true. But from within the productive process there has also been a long-suppressed but now noisy gallop towards economic rationalization. Economics and its practitioners in academic and planning positions are determined to achieve the same status for themselves and their subject as natural scientists and technologists. Already in the early 1960s men like Trapeznikov, Nemchinov and Libermann (with whom the whole process has been over-emphatically associated) have been advocating new methods of planning, incentives and costing to enable the Soviet economy to assess its achievements more rationally and cheaply than hitherto. The notion of profit has indeed come back – not as an incentive for investment or basic economic activity, but as a means of quantifying the elusive factor of success. There has always been a low-grade form of accounting (*khozraschet*) in the Soviet Union which has included an item of profit. But whereas under Stalin profit was a planned amount of residue, of pygmy status compared to the fulfilment of physical output targets, it is now becoming a refined notion of measuring the success of one enterprise or group of enterprises against another – a universal standard by which efficiency might be compared. Though in no sense a return to any notion of a capitalist economy, it has all the same represented an important and far-reaching change in Soviet thinking. Capital is ceasing to be allocated as a political gift carrying no price or cost in the economy, and is becoming a dependent variable which can be calculated like any other scarce resource – through a differential rate of interest. Prices, in turn, are being liberated from their total and artificial dependence on planning decisions. A thing used to be cheap or expensive because the planners made it so, and resulting imbalances throughout the whole process of production and exchange had to be corrected by allocation procedures which accentuated rather than corrected distortions. Now prices are approximating towards an expression of value in terms of relative cost and demand. At this time of writing, the reformers have the bit between their teeth. The concrete application of their ideas is, however, still in an experimental stage in a limited number of textile and other works (textiles are the historical laboratory of industrial societies). The innovators are not without enemies who consider the very notion of profit as ideologically subversive, and regard the factory manager's growing area of decision-making as a menace to the centralized structure of Soviet planning.

What will be the social consequences of this new version of NEP? As we have seen, the Khrushchev era was significant for the attempt to regionalize industrial planning, bringing about a great deal of administrative change at the top, and reducing the heavily centralized apparatus of planning and administration in Moscow. But there was a return to a system of central ministries when the Regional Economic Councils were abolished at the end of 1965. Ultimately this may prove a far greater break with the past than the creation of the Councils. For it has been accompanied by an entirely new emphasis on managerial decision-making at factory or plant level. Far from re-establishing the full Stalinist system of central planning and allocation, of which the manager was the mere executant, the re-creation of central ministries has been combined with a reduction in the purely routine aspect of their activities. In the long run the notion of profit as a measure of and reward for efficiency must logically be accompanied by greater leeway for those actually running the industry and making the profits. This has various consequences. For one thing, it will greatly increase the status of management, and probably also the rewards available to managers. For another, it may help to solve the intractable problem of centralization; with greater elbow-room at plant level, the desire to migrate to the centre at Moscow may be reduced. Coupled with the policy of improving the educational and cultural facilities in the provinces, some of the singular dreariness of provincial life which has bedevilled Russia since the eighteenth century may finally be dispelled. Industrial towns in the south and centre of the Soviet Union, as well as Siberia, may become not only large but interesting places to live in. Experiments like the university city of Akademgorod near Novosibirsk suggest a set of priorities for the creation of new urban environments in which the pioneering community of scientists is replacing that of shock-workers or conscripted labour as a means of opening up the peripheral areas of the Soviet Union. Thus the future may be one in which political recentralization proves to have been coupled with genuine social decentralization.

142 The eastern provinces are being developed apace, but in a more balanced fashion. This 1964 construction in the Krasnoyarsk territory is part of an industrial and housing complex near the Yenisey River

The modernizing and integrating tendencies of the Khrushchev era can well be illustrated by the situation of Soviet trade unions and the relations between labour and management in general. Right from the start trade unions never had any genuine wage bargaining functions, and their potential role as an institutional opposition to Party control, with possible perspectives of workers' control over industry, was firmly scotched after 1921. During the Stalin era they were merely executive organs of control: the Party's specialist labour organization. In the 1950s, however, the unions developed a role which, if not independent, at least became specialized and necessary. They assisted in settling labour disputes and fixing wage rates – not by bargaining, to be sure, but by advising and reporting. In this way they served as an important channel of communication between industry and government and Party, particularly the planning sections. In addition they have become the primary organization for administering the social security services which, as has been pointed out, are based almost exclusively on place of work. In this way they have come after all to institutionalize and represent the interest of members, and have been integrated into a society in which such institutional representation is not only possible, but increasing. Once more the rule to which we have already referred applies: Party views are served not only by specific reference to Party organizations, but through the fact that union channels *are* functional Party channels within their sphere of interest. Currently the unions are under pressure to take a more rather than less independent line on matters in labour questions. Naturally this is not the result merely of a general relaxation, but evidence of the Party's specific desire to improve labour relations – and hence productivity. As yet the unions are industrial only, and the 35 per cent of the total labour force in collective farms are not unionized at all. It may well be that this lacuna, deeply embedded in the ideology and structure of Soviet government, may be one of the great obstacles which prevents productivity on the land and in industry being matched both in terms of organization and attainments.

The incessant emphasis on agricultural production and improvement under Khrushchev has not disappeared with his retirement. Though the current leadership acts less dramatically and unpredictably, Soviet policy continues to be directed towards agricultural improvement. Two out of five plenary sessions of the Central Committee since the beginning of 1965 have been devoted to agricultural problems – without any flamboyant *sturmovshchina*. It must be remembered that in spite of the immense rate of industrialization and urban growth during the last fifty years, almost half the population of the Soviet Union still lived in villages at the end of 1961, and 35 per cent of the work force was engaged in agriculture. Neither the increase in productivity nor the rate of growth which distinguished the industrial sector until the beginning of this decade, has been remotely matched in agriculture. The fact that the standard of life on the land has improved, and that the Party is exerting more influence in, and recruiting more members from, the agricultural sector, is evidence of relative improvement in this forlorn area of society; but there was by 1964 nothing like any overall attainment of equivalence with the industrial sector. At least three times between 1960 and 1966 the Soviet Union imported large quantities of grain from abroad; only a good to exceptional harvest permitted self-sufficiency. The gross output of agricultural production was planned to increase by 70 per cent during a seven-year plan initiated in 1958. Actually it rose 14 per cent. The new leadership plumped for orthodox incentives: lower taxes, continuously higher prices for farm products and finally an important departure from precedent in guaranteeing monthly pay for members of collective farms who had had, ever since collectivization in 1929, to rely on the often slender dividend distributed to each member from the collective's profit at the end of the year. This measure was adopted by the Twenty-Third Party Congress in the spring of 1966. But the structural and productive imbalance of the industrial and agricultural sectors remains probably the Soviet Union's most crucial problem today – at a time when world food supplies generally are in excess of (industrially) effective demand. Instead of Khrushchev's claims that the Soviet Union was on the verge of challenging the United States' level of farm production, the best estimates (nett of waste and exaggeration, and assuming average harvests) suggest that production in 1970 is likely to approach no more than double the overall figures of 1953 when things were just beginning to move, and to remain at a level of about 65 per cent of United States output.

This is essentially a problem which is beyond mere technical remedies. In every other highly industrial country, between 10 and 20 per cent of the population produces more than enough food for the rest – assuming suitable and sufficient farm land, which the Soviet Union certainly possesses. Rural depopulation will have to be accelerated again unless industry can be much more effectively carried into the countryside, and there is little sign of this in either policy or substance at present. Secondly, the industrial base on which modern farming flourishes does not yet exist in the Soviet Union. Agriculture cannot thrive on left-overs, but depends on the gearing of chemical fertilizer, machine and vehicle industries and, above all, on the production of consumer goods which farmers want to buy. Thirdly, the technological problems of large-scale farming have eventually to be assigned a priority in the socio-political decision-making process similar to those already existing in the industrial field. The contradiction of Soviet agriculture has been a combination of mistrust for the farmers as a socio-political group with a basic lack of incentives on the one hand, and a belief that the problem of scale can better be tackled in terms of overall acreage rather than intensity and efficiency of exploitation. Since 1917 Soviet agriculture has been trapped between an incentive-less Scylla and the Charybdis of ineffective planning and policy. All attempts to break out of the dilemma have alternated between a 'Khrushchev' type of adventurism and excessive conservatism. Neither has seriously altered the structure or the ideological concept of Soviet agriculture since the collectivization drive of 1929. In the next few years the relationship of agriculture to industry, and the whole problem of agricultural production and organization, is likely to be tackled in a much more thoroughgoing manner; further industrial advance depends on it absolutely. Such changes may have substantial social and economic consequences which are difficult to foresee at present; will we read of over-consuming and under-producing 'welfare' collective farmers? This is the area in which the most dramatic changes may be expected to take place.

After 1929 foreign and domestic Soviet policy ceased to be meaningfully interdependent, except at the very high level of abstraction implied by the concept of 'socialism in one country'. Under Khrushchev and his successors the two spheres have become more closely integrated again – though not in accordance with any Leninist perspectives. The commitment to peaceful co-existence, with all its implications, is a major change in Soviet thinking, with many domestic consequences. For one thing, it relates Soviet achievement, and the Soviet evaluation of it, directly to that of other countries, particularly the United States. While Stalin used to make occasional comparisons with the United States, mainly for the benefit of foreign journalists, his actions were all taken with a view to isolating the Soviet Union from the outside world. The present tendency has been to increase contact. Khrushchev advocated the idea that it was possible to borrow foreign practices without adopting the ideology that went with them, and this propensity to import has since moved from the purely technological and scientific to a much wider intellectual plane.

There has been a corresponding shift in ideology to accommodate these new developments in practice. Facts have become sacred; they have been almost completely divorced from speculation. The era of a vulgarized Marxism kneading reality with grotesque generalizations (Stalin equated reality with intellectual *grotesqueries*) has given way to a Marxism of no speculation at all. Few commentators have picked up this crucial paradox: a society which professes the *predictive* historical philosophy *par excellence* refusing absolutely to indulge in any predictions or suppositions at all – and not because of duress. Marxist science has ceased to be the inevitable of tomorrow and become the concrete of today. True, this makes the increase of interaction with the foreign ideologically bearable, but it is more than that – a cultural revolution almost, the product of forced industrialization with the overt pressure removed, a social consensus of concreteness instead of an enforced silence.

An example that may lead to interesting developments in the future is the recent revival of Soviet interest in the social sciences, and the adoption of many of the techniques of social self-monitoring which have been developed in the West. Soviet social scientists certainly see themselves as providing the concrete facts on which future policy may be based; they are encouraged in this belief at the highest level. Whether the attempt to differentiate very firmly between concrete fact-finding and its ideological implications can in the end be maintained is doubtful. The very demand for facts with a view to better policy-making must relate those facts to an eventual judgment on the policies themselves. The British myth of an administrative civil service totally uninvolved in political policy-making is hardly likely to be perpetrated in a Soviet Union guided by a highly policy-conscious Communist Party. So far the areas of sociological inquiry have been limited particularly to education, work satisfaction and leisure. In Poland, however, there is growing up a strong school of more directly political attitude research, in Czechoslovakia an interest in measuring and comparing cultural levels in different social strata, all of which may eventually find their way also into the Soviet Union. The pace of professional liberalization and the commitment to empirical research is not set today by the Soviet Union but by other People's Democracies like Poland, Czechoslovakia and Hungary. The Soviet Union is no longer even typical of the state of social research in the socialist countries. This relative backwardness has not yet officially impinged on Soviet consciousness, but may well do so soon. There is, moreover, a relationship between this growing interest in factual research as a basis for decision-making and the renewed emphasis on collective leadership. The higher status of facts accords organizationally with a collective leadership in which competing claims for policies thrown up by different areas of interest and control are sorted and transformed into policy. That, at any rate, is the intention.

In short, the present situation suggests increasing future integration of the Soviet Union into an international system at various levels: the official level of the United Nations and formal diplomacy, the secondary level of increasing professional contact with corresponding groups in other countries, and beyond this the resultant cultural and ideological consequences of greater knowledge and reflection of what happens outside the Soviet Union. All this takes place in a series of concentric circles: the immediate one of the Soviet Union itself, with its diverse and as yet culturally unequal nationalities; next the People's Democracies, with whom contact is most frequent and easy; then the wider one of the United States and the West, at a similar level of industrial, technological and intellectual development; and finally the widest area of the truly international system including every sort of country with regard to which a distinctive attitude and set of policies will develop in the Soviet Union. Not only has Soviet diplomacy penetrated to every corner of the globe (as I write an officially accredited journalist has been offering economic assistance to the Fiji Islanders), but Soviet analysis of foreign countries has also become geographically all-embracing in the last few years, whereas it had previously been distinctly parochial.

It would be wrong to characterize the greater openness of the modern Soviet Union to the outside world as one-way. Quite the contrary, the significant feature of Soviet participation in the international system is the amount of information about the Soviet Union that is being diffused throughout the world. Apart from any tangible benefits of aid to developing countries during the Khrushchev era, there emerged the much less precise but probably more important notion that the Soviet experience might be directly relevant to the attainment of developmental goals in those countries. The whole concept of planning, nowadays so firmly anchored in almost all developing nations, springs directly from what they regard as the quintessence of the Soviet experience – even if what, in the Soviet Union, was a forced and extremely painful process of social and economic modernization has, in the course of international diffusion, been transformed into an apparently simple panacea the benefits of which can be automatically obtained by the creation of a planning department, ministry or commission. Equally important has been the model of the single party as a means of mobilizing the inert periphery of society – the idea that a determined group of men organized in such a party with a distinct philosophy of action can effectively act as the purposive vanguard for social change. All this, together with the technical achievements of conquering space and the impressive build-up of modern armed forces second to none, has given the Third-World image of the Soviet Union a specially glamorous polish. Yet the Soviet Union in 1967 offers a contradictory example to developing countries. Though its achievements are a desirable goal, there is growing doubt as to the relevance of its means. Developing countries today do not have the power to force their societies up the steep path of rapid industrialization, and the language of the contemporary and industrialized Soviet Union does not apply to their current problems. In some ways Third-World leaders find a common language more easily in China ('the Soviet Union and the United States can teach us how to build advanced factories, but the Chinese can show us how to mend our leaking roofs', said Nyerere); in others their own education and culture keep them attuned to the gentler melodies of the West. But none can afford to ignore the Soviet experience or achievement.

It is, oddly enough, via the Third World that Soviet experience has made its most profound impact on the West. In the early 1950s inquiring minds in the United States and elsewhere, other than those already sympathetic to socialism, were becoming conscious of the fact that the Soviet achievement had to be taken seriously. They began to regard it as a quicker but disagreeable alternative path to their own modernity and industrialization. Since then the impact of the Soviet model on developing countries has been studied more closely. The failure in those countries of so-called democracy based on the Western model has underscored the potential of the Soviet experience in reaching what is today probably the most universally accepted aim of all societies – full-scale industrialization and modernity in the shortest possible time. It is here, in the comparative evaluation of achievement rather than in any acceptance of Soviet ideology, that we must search for the origin of recent Western reappraisal of the Soviet Union and its immediate history. The process is not complete. The reports of technical and scientific delegations to the Soviet Union have made it clear that there is an increasing interest in the concrete and detailed achievements of Soviet technology. The time will probably come when the Soviet Union will sell not only its advanced industrial products in an increasingly attentive world market, but also the know-how that goes with it. From this to the possibility of Soviet investments abroad is perhaps not such a very long step – the Japanese overcame almost as fundamental social and ideological barriers against foreign investment. The whole notion of peaceful competition at least implies this possibility; and the key-in-hand construction of steel mills in India in competition with British and American consortia is already a first step to post-construction management – which in turn is first cousin to foreign investment.

The growing element of diplomatic competition, which Khrushchev initiated with such spectacular fireworks, is also being developed in a calmer atmosphere. As a result, the Soviet Union is breaking out of traditional and well-recognized roles. Whereas previously the progressive desire for change was almost wholly aligned against American imperialism (so that since the United States supported a ubiquitous *status quo*, the Soviet Union must support almost any event or conflict that might help to change it), these predictable roles are now breaking down. Recently the USSR has at times been as anxious to preserve the *status quo* as the United States. In 1965 the Soviet government deliberately and successfully took over the peacemaking function to end the India–Pakistan war, which neither the United States as a committed partisan of stability nor Great Britain as chairman of the Commonwealth could carry out effectively. For the first time the new Soviet diplomacy was in action at Tashkent as a neutral third party not directly involved in a dispute.

ʻIn the present situation there are new problems arising out of the growing emphasis on national sensitivity. ʺThe general acceptance of polycentrism in the communist world enhances national factors in the relationship among its members. ʻThe period of political and economic domination by Moscow came to an end in the mid-1950s. Even though the Soviet Union suppressed the Hungarian revolt and contained the danger of similar action in Poland, these events did not reverse the process of loosening the relationship of the neighbouring governments with Moscow. But they changed its direction; the impulse towards more independence came from above, from the ruling parties, not from below *against* them.ʺ The year 1956 saw probably the last, not the first, direct Soviet interference in the affairs of her 'socialist' neighbours.ʺSupra-national planning for the socialist bloc as a whole, based on a rational division of tasks and specializations, continued formally until the early 1960s, and was officially abandoned only when the Rumanian government revolted openly against its allocated role of raw-material and agricultural producer. Recent research has, however, made it clear that in practice the Comecon was quite ineffective after Stalin's death in integrating the peripheral socialist economies with the Soviet Union. If anything, the common Marxist perspective made them similar and competitive. For Russia's communist neighbours the logic of the Soviet model made absolute industrialization mandatory. Tactically this pursuit of a similar and internationally 'unplanned' path was made much easier once the split between the Soviet Union and China introduced an element of internal competition within the bloc. Thus we have a familiar Western spectacle repeated in the East: Soviet technicians half-heartedly prospecting for oil in Poland under bilateral agreement while the Soviet Union is flooding the world market with surplus oil from the new wells in Siberia as well as the old ones in Georgia. Poland is willing to pay over the odds for the sake of developing its own oil industry on an uneconomic scale.

It is perhaps inevitable that these problems should spill over into a more specifically political context. Memories are long when the devil drives, and frontier questions previously considered as settled were suddenly raised anew – like the Soviet annexation of Bessarabia from Rumania after 1945. A resurgence of nationalism has swept eastern Europe as a whole in the last few years. In Rumania and more recently in Poland recent years have witnessed the emergence of power groups of a quite new type within Party and state. Almost without any specific programme, not concerned with any ideological issues, they represent inchoate nationalist ambitions within the Party and help their supporters to positions of power within Party and state. In some ways they are a form of national socialism in its literal sense – anti-Russian, anti-Semitic, anti-foreign, anti-intellectual – associated in Poland with General Moczar, the Minister of the Interior, and the so-called 'Partisans'.

In Yugoslavia the resurgence of Serb, Croat and Slovene self-consciousness as national entities with distinct and competing interests has already endangered the cohesion of the federal state, leading to unprecedented experiments and reforms to circumvent it – to such an extent that in the eyes of the Soviet Union Yugoslav communism is disintegrating in a series of spectacular experimental explosions. Yet it is only the greater concessions to national sovereignty and autonomy at the expense of inter-Party discipline and cohesion in these last years that have enabled a workable relationship between the Soviet Union and Yugoslavia to survive. While Khrushchev still talked to the Yugoslavs in a Marxist canon – albeit a more tolerant one, in which criticism and approval alternated – the new Soviet leadership has tended to treat the Yugoslavs as outside the communist bloc altogether. Relationships have been put increasingly on a state-to-state basis. Whatever interest the Yugoslav experiments have, they are unlikely to make much impact on their socialist neighbours and especially not on the Soviet Union – that is, if the Soviet Communist Party can prevent it.

Political polycentrism, competition and even occasional conflict only reflect the fundamentally unimpaired social diversity of the socialist bloc. Given time, the Stalinist system of control might well have succeeded in shaping these societies in a uniform pattern based on a Soviet model – except that, as we have already noted, Stalin was not primarily interested in that kind of uniformity. But fifteen years was not nearly enough, and the deeply embedded ethnic and cultural differences were pushed below the surface only temporarily. This diversity is in fact reflected not only in the basic social institutions, but also in a good deal of specific legislation. One example will suffice. The law on abortion varies widely in socialist countries. Abortions are legal in the Soviet Union, Czechoslovakia and Hungary. (In the Soviet Union the only period when they were proscribed was briefly in 1924, and between 1936 and 1955, at the height of Stalinism.) They are strictly forbidden in the German Democratic Republic and in 1966 were prohibited in Rumania. Similarly the process and facility of obtaining divorces varies considerably from country to country.

Easily the most dangerous and bitter conflict within the socialist 'bloc' is the Sino-Soviet split. Underlying its ideological polemics is an increasingly deliberate elaboration of national issues and symbols. The search for ammunition on both sides has thus brought to the surface a whole number of questions about frontiers, spheres of influence and sovereign rights. National postures, once evoked, have a habit of displacing other issues; it is difficult to envisage where this re-structuring of the Sino-Soviet conflict may lead – especially when a frontier of over two thousand miles is involved. One of the problems posed by polycentrism among the People's Democracies, and made much more acute by the Sino-Soviet split, is the need to evolve adequate procedures for disputes between socialist states – for which there is absolutely no ideological basis. Inter-Party relations are one thing – secret, informal, consensual or openly in conflict – but cannot meaningfully be related to, or duplicate, diplomatic relations between sovereign states. There is simply no precedent for such problems; and this accounts for much of the violence of the polemics. This remains a major unsolved problem, and the form of its eventual resolution is exceedingly hard to predict – state-to-state, purely Party-to-Party, or what kind of balance between them?

If competitive co-existence vis-à-vis the United States has coincided with conflict with China, in which ideological and nationalist motivations are almost inextricably entangled, the deductions that might have been drawn for the future have been both confused and tested by the war in Vietnam. For the Soviet Union the conflict presents many problems. Its immediate national interests are not involved. Soviet passivity has handed the Chinese endless amounts of rope with which to hang themselves – a temptation the Chinese have carefully resisted. In one sense the Vietnam war has entered, and has been made to accommodate itself to, the Sino-Soviet dispute. Both the USSR and China claim to be assisting the Vietcong to the maximum and accuse the other of hindering their respective efforts. Yet at the same time the war has put both the Sino-Soviet conflict and Soviet–American relations into a state of suspended, purely verbal animation. It can neither resolve the Sino-Soviet split nor widen it. In the last resort the long-standing and deeply ingrained Soviet view of the world as divided into capitalist, socialist and neutral nations must align the Soviet Union with the North Vietnamese and China. The whole concept of co-existence is based on the assumption that there will be no basic challenge to the existence of either bloc. So far the Soviet Union has spoken of the potential American threat to the socialist bloc in Asia rather than of the present existence of such a challenge. There has still been some room for manœuvre between China and the USSR for influence over the Vietcong and North Vietnam, without any risk of total commitment for either. If, however, such a global challenge were to be perceived by the Soviet Union, through the danger of escalation of the Vietnam conflict into a direct military clash between China and the United States, this picture could alter radically. An American war with China would involve Soviet interests directly, since it would probably feel itself threatened too – as a communist rather than as a national or territorial entity. Soviet interests and the interests of communism would quickly become identified as one and the same. For the perception of interests does not take place in a vacuum of unadulterated rationality, but in a cloudy plasma of experience, habit and ideology. This is where the computers in the Pentagon are likely to miscalculate.

It is of course impossible to predict the actual outcome of the Vietnam situation; for purposes of glimpsing into the likely next fifty years of the Soviet Union it has arbitrarily to be ignored. In conclusion we return therefore to the problem of convergence. The increasing interpenetration of ideas, structures and processes between socialist and capitalist countries has already been heavily stressed. Many observers believe that the logic of capitalism, as of communism, in the twentieth century is dictated by the broad social and economic considerations of advanced industrialization, that both types of societies will move towards each other, and finally attain a similar social structure. Others draw the opposite conclusion from the same set of facts. What they insist on calling the uniquely rigid bureaucracy of the Communist Party cannot accommodate the social logic of advanced industrialization and will not yield to it; there will be severe social upheavals as industrial technocrats with their supporting workers and unreconstructed, conservative *apparatchiks* clash head on. At worst (or best?) the communist system will disintegrate. I believe this to be a compound of error and wishful thinking (and a failure to study sociology). The odds are rather on a continuation of the process of convergence – with important qualifications.

We have seen the West turning increasingly to state management and state capitalism. *Par contre* the tendency towards greater autonomy for the Soviet professions and enterprises suggests that the Party leadership in its narrower role of a dogmatic political instrument will cease to be the prime locus for decision-making in the Soviet Union. In this regard, therefore, the notion of convergence makes sense, and will undoubtedly continue. On the other hand, it is necessary to recall that ideologically the two types of society start from very different premises. Increasing state capitalism in the capitalist countries is to be controlled, and ultimately managed, by a system of elections in which alternative policies represented and shaped by alternative élites, or groups of élites structured by party organization, compete for the all-important electoral vote. This helps to disguise the fact that in the West the actual role of the elector in decision-making is decreasing all the time. In the Soviet Union there is no likelihood whatever of a similar form of alternative control relying on the persuasion of voters. Participation will take place within the single Party; as long as and precisely because the Party consists of the leading and most qualified groups of society, Party control of the state will be viewed as equivalent to social control. Though participation among lower strata will in sum be no greater in the Soviet Union than in the West, it will continue to be regarded as taking place through action and discussion and not through elections. Men participate in the manifold processes of social and political life through membership of the all-pervading Party or the local Soviets or other collective bodies instead of choosing between contenders to represent them in office. The guarantee of a vote; or membership of a collectivity of action: who can say which offers the more promising or effective means for the masses to make their influence felt?

Soviet society has now openly accepted the idea of social and professional domination by the competent and qualified. The Soviet schooling system is more selective in its stress on ability than almost any other. The British, for instance, currently look to the educational system as a means of redressing social imbalances. The Soviet system – believing as it does that social imbalance has already been removed by fifty years of Soviet government – selects the best qualified for higher schooling without fear of institutionalizing any existing social privileges. The effectiveness of this argument may be questioned, but not its cognitive consequences. Soviet analysis of its own educational system shows clearly that certain groups have easier access to educational facilities than others. Inequality between individuals and social groups (*not* classes) is freely and even officially admitted in the Soviet Union. But it is characterized as due to human rather than social endowment, an inequality of skill not background. And the claim is partly though never wholly true. If middle-class behaviour is to be measured in terms of the desire to achieve and a strong emphasis on formal education, then the Soviet Union is as bourgeois as the United States – certainly in the increasingly cynical view of the younger generation.

The Soviets' view of their society identifies social power with political power, and political power as wholly anchored in the Party – a Party consisting of the best qualified and most able members of society. An élite, in other words. When the present generation of Party leaders is superseded, the successors may for the first time be technocrats with different professional experiences but with identical schooling in the Soviet Marxist ideology, while Western politicians will in a sense be the very opposite, politicians whose professional experience has been in politics but whose schooling and background may differ considerably. The paradox is that the more politics become distinct from other social or professional activities, the more politicians will become professionals. The more directly politics represent and incorporate all other forms of social activity, the easier the access of non-political professions to positions of power. In this regard the Soviet Union may yet come to be a model for the future technocratic or professional democracy which faces us all.

But this is a long way off. As the Soviet Union celebrates fifty years of revolution, fact-fascinated, it continues for the time being to be primarily backward-looking and to regard the future as an extrapolation of the past. There is growing public awareness of problems to be solved, but they are problems with which people have been familiar, often painfully, for some time. Even so, the self-confidence of fifty years of concrete achievement will certainly stiffen the ideological conviction of certainty and rightness inherent in Marxism-Leninism.

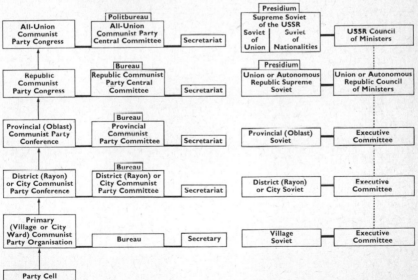

BASIC STRUCTURE OF THE COMMUNIST PARTY OF THE SOVIET UNION				BASIC STRUCTURE OF THE SOVIET GOVERNMENT		

269

Leningrad
Petrozavodsk
Archangelsk
Naryan-Mar
Dud
Salekhard
Tallinn
Riga
Vilnius
Minsk
Yaroslavl
Syktyvkar
Khanty-Mansiysk
Moscow
Gorky
Perm
Lvov
Kiev
Kharkov
Saransk
Kazan
Izhevsk
Sverdlovsk
Kishinev
Saratov
Ufa
Rostov
Tomsk
Krasnodar
Omsk
Nov
Majkop
Batumi
Ordzhonikidze
Groznyy
Yerevan
Tbilisi
Gorno
Baku
Nukus
Alma Ata
Ashkhabad
Tashkent
Frunze
Dusanbe
Khorog

143, 144 Map of the USSR in 1967, and comparative sizes of the USSR, the US and the UK

USSR
USA
UK

snoyarsk
Bratsk
sinsk
Irkutsk • Ulan Ude
Kyzyl

Yakutsk

Lena

Kolyma

Indana

Amur

Birobidzhan

Vladivostok

1 RSFSR
2 Ukrainian SSR
3 Belorussian SSR
4 Uzbek SSR
5 Kazakh SSR
6 Georgian SSR
7 Azerbaijan SSR
8 Lithuanian SSR
9 Moldavian SSR
10 Latvian SSR
11 Kirghiz SSR
12 Tadzhik SSR
13 Armenian SSR
14 Turkmen SSR
15 Estonian SSR

0   500   1000 MILES

Major nationalities of the USSR
Population (000) at the census of 1959

Russians	114,588	Germans	1619
Ukrainians	36,981	Chuvash	1470
Belorussians	7829	Latvians	1400
Uzbeks	6004	Tadzhiks	1397
Tatars	4969	Poles	1380
Kazakhs	3581	Mordovians	1285
Azerbaijanians	2929	Turkmen	1004
Armenians	2787	Bashkirs	983
Georgians	2650	Kirgiz	974
Lithuanians	2326	Estonians	969
Jews	2268	Udmurts	623
Moldavians	2214	Mari	504

From I. Dewdney, *A Geography of the Soviet Union*; Pergamon Press 1965

Soviet Population by Republics—1959 census (million)

Russian Republic		117·5	**Belorussian Republic**		8·1
of which: Russians	97·8		of which: Belorussians	6·4	
Tatars	4·1		Russians	0·7	
Ukrainian Republic		41·9	**Uzbek Republic**		8·1
of which: Ukrainians	31·9		of which: Uzbeks	5·0	
Russians	7·4		Russians	1·1	
Kazakh Republic		9·3	**Georgian Republic**		4·0
of which: Russians	4·0		of which: Georgians	2·6	
Kazakhs	2·8		Russians	0·4	
Ukrainians	0·8		Armenians	0·4	
Azerbaijan Republic		3·7	**Tadzhik Republic**		2·0
of which: Azerbaijanians	2·5		of which: Tadzhiks	1·1	
Russians	0·5		**Armenian Republic**		1·8
Moldavian Republic		2·9	of which: Armenians	1·6	
of which: Moldavians	1·9		**Turkmen Republic**		1·5
Ukrainians	0·4		of which: Turkmen	0·9	
Lithuanian Republic		2·7	Russians	0·3	
of which: Lithuanians	2·2		**Estonian Republic**		1·2
Latvian Republic		2·1	of which: Estonians	0·9	
of which: Latvians	1·3		Russians	0·3	
Russians	0·6				
Kirgiz Republic		2·1			
of which: Kirgiz	0·8		Grand Total		208·8
Russians	0·6				

Population Growth, Russian Empire and USSR, Great Britain and USA †

Russian Empire and USSR			Great Britain			USA		
Date	Total pop. (000)	Annual inc. %	Date	Total pop. (000)	Annual inc. %	Date	Total pop. (000)	Annual inc. %
1724	20,300		1801	10,648		1790	3,929	
1897	111,916	0·8	1901	37,000	2·5	1900	75,995	(
1914*	145,000	1·5	1911	40,831	1·0	1910	91,972	2·1
1926	147,028	(	1921	42,769	0·5	1920	105,711	1·5
1939	170,467	1·3	1931	44,795	0·4	1930	122,775	1·6
1940*	192,900	‡	1938**	46,208	0·4	1940	131,669	0·7
1950*	200,000	1·1	1951	48,854	0·5	1950	150,697	1·4
1959	208,800	1·7	1959**	50,578	0·4	1959	178,153	1·7

* End of year estimates. ** Mid-year estimates. All others are census figures.
† Frontiers as in each year. The Russian figures for 1897 and 1914 exclude Finland, Poland, Khiva and Bukhara. The US figure for 1959 excludes Hawaii and Alaska.
(Increases cannot be accurately calculated owing to frontier changes, war losses, etc.
‡ Increase due to territorial changes.

From Oxford Regional Economic Atlas, The USSR and Eastern Europe; Oxford University Press, 1963.

Production of Selected Goods in the USSR

Product and unit	1913	1921	1928	1933	1940	1945	1952	1963
Industrial								
Electric power, bill. kwth.	2·0	0·5	5·0	16·3	48·3	43·2	119·1	412·0
Crude oil, mill. tons	9·2	3·8	11·6	21·5	31·1	19·4	47·3	206·1
Coal, mill. tons	29·1	9·5	35·5	76·3	165·9	149·3	300·9	532·0
Steel, mill. tons	4·2	0·2	4·2	6·9	18·3	12·2	34·5	80·2
Machine tools, 1000 units	1·8	0·8	2·0	21·0	58·4	38·4	74·6	183·0
Turbines, mill. kw.	—	—	0·04	0·3	1·2	0·2	3·4	11·9
Locomotives, units	477	78	479	948	928	8	439	2162
Trucks, 1000 units	—	—	0·7	39·1	136·0	68·5	243·5	414·0
Tractors, 1000 units	—	—	1·3	73·7	31·6	7·7	98·7	325·0
Grain harvesters, 1000 units	—	—	—	8·6	12·8	0·3	42·2	82·9
Excavators, 1000 units	—	—	—	0·1	0·3	—	3·7	17·9
Fertilizers, mill. tons	0·09	—	0·1	1·0	3·2	1·1	6·4	19·9
Timber, mill. cu. meters	67·0	6·5	61·7	173·3	246·1	168·4	291·4	352·7(a)
Cement, mill. tons	1·8	0·06	1·8	2·7	5·7	1·8	13·9	61·0
Consumer								
Automobiles, 1000 units	—	—	0·1	10·3	5·5	5·0	59·7	173·0
Washing machines, 1000 units	—	—	—	—	—	—	4·3	2282·0
Bicycles, 1000 units	4·9	7·7	10·8	125·6	255·0	23·8	1650·4	3352·0
Cameras, 1000 units	—	—	—	29·6	355·2	0·01	459·1	1432·0
Radio sets, 1000 units	—	—	—	29·0	160·5	13·8	1294·5	4802·0
Television sets, 1000 units	—	—	—	—	0·3	—	37·4	2474·0
Cotton fabrics, bill. meters	2·7	1·5	2·7	2·7	3·9	1·6	5·0	6·6
Leather shoes, mill. pairs(e)	60·0	28·0	58·0	90·3	211·0	63·1	237·7	463·0
Sugar, mill. tons	2·2	0·06	1·9	1·4	2·8	0·5	4·1	6·2
Canned food, billion cans	0·1	0·1	0·1	0·7	1·1	0·6	2·1	6·4
Alcohol, mill. decaliters	55·2	10·2	23·3	38·8	89·9	26·5	89·1	184·0(b)
Agricultural								
Grain, mill. tons	86·0	36·2	73·3	69·1	95·5	75·0(d)	82·5(c)	138·0(b)
Cows, mill.	28·8	24·8	29·2	19·0	27·8	22·9	24·3	38·3
Hogs, mill.	23·0	13·1	19·4	9·9	27·5	10·6	28·5	40·8
Vegetable oil, mill. tons	0·5	0·03	0·5	0·3	0·8	0·3	1·0	2·2
Fish caught, mill. tons	1·0	0·3	0·8	1·3	1·4	1·1	2·1	4·7
Freight transport, bill. t/km	126·0	42·3	119·5	218·3	407·4	374·6	877·6	2300·0

a 1962   b 1961   c 1953   d Approximately   e Factory production only.
Note: Data for 1921, 1928, and 1933 refer to the USSR in pre-World War II frontiers, which enclosed a territory about 3 per cent smaller than that in 1913, 1940, and the remaining years.
Sources: *Narodnoe khozyaystvo SSSR v 1958 godu* (Moscow 1959); *Narodnoe khozyaystvo SSSR v 1962 godu* (Moscow 1963); *SSSR v tsifrakh v 1963 godu* (Moscow 1964).

From Oxenfeldt and Holubnychy, *Economic Systems in Action*, Holt, Rinehart and Winston, New York 1965

Comparative growth rates of gross national product[1]

(Annual averages)

Country	Aggregate		Per capita	
	1950–58	1958–64	1950–58	1958–64
USSR	7·1	5·3	5·2	3·5
France	4·4	5·4	3·5	4·0
West Germany	7·6	5·8	6·4	4·6
Italy	5·6	6·1	5·0	5·4
United Kingdom	2·4	3·9	1·9	3·1
Japan	6·1	12·0	4·8	11·0
United States	2·9	4·4	1·2	2·7

[1] The annual average rates of growth shown in the table may reflect considerable dispersions around the averages for particular years. The extent of dispersion can be seen in the following tabular presentation of annual rates of increase in GNP from 1958 to 1964.

Country	1958	1959	1960	1961	1962	1963	1964
USSR	9·4	4·9	5·2	6·2	5·1	2·6	7·9
France	2·5	2·8	7·3	4·3	6·3	4·3	5·3
West Germany	3·5	7·1	8·9	5·8	4·1	3·2	6·6
Italy	4·4	7·3	6·8	8·3	6·0	4·8	2·9
United Kingdom	1·0	3·6	4·5	3·3	·2	3·5	5·4
Japan	−·1	18·3	13·0	15·8	6·9	8·3	13·9
United States	−1·2	6·7	2·5	1·9	6·1	3·4	4·8

United States and Soviet Union: Yield per acre and production of major crops, 1964

Crop	Unit	Yields per acre United States[1]	Yields per acre USSR[2]	USSR as percentage of US	Unit	Production United States[1]	Production USSR[3]	USSR as percentage of US
				Percent				Percent.
Corn, grain	Bushels	62·6	27·8	44	1,000 bushels	3,583,780	[4] 362,186	10
Wheat	do.	26·3	12·6	48	do.	1,290,650	[4] 2,120,843	164
Rye	do.	19·5	12·1	62	do.	33,318	[4] 503,910	1,512
Oats	do.	43·1	19·1	44	do.	880,095	[4] 268,687	31
Barley	do.	37·9	20·4	54	do.	402,895	[4] 1,093,110	271
Grain sorghum	do.	41·1	([5])		do.	491,884	([5])	
Rice, rough	Pounds	4,096	1,725	42	1,000 short tons	3,657	426	12
Cotton, lint	do.	517	647	125	1,000 bales	15,180	8,200	54
Soybeans for beans	Bushels	22·8			1,000 bushels	701,917	[4] 9,186	1
Sunflower seed	Pounds	([5])			1,000 short tons	([5])	[4] 6,145	
Peanuts harvested for nuts	do.	1,569	([5])		do.	1,102	([5])	
Flaxseed	Bushels	8·6	([5])		1,000 bushels	24,406	([5])	
Sugarbeets	Short tons	16·8	8·8	52	1,000 short tons	23,389	89,500	382
Sugarcane, for sugar and seed	Tons	36·6			do.	25,053	([5])	
Sugar production					do.	[6] 6,501	[7] 7,700	118
Tobacco	Pounds	2,067	989	48	1,000 lbs.	2,227,347	[8] 405,646	
Fiber flax	do.	([5])	194		1,000 short tons	([5])	381	
Potatoes	Hundredweight	185	109	59	1,000 hundredweight	239,403	[9] 1,845,250	771
Sweet potatoes	do.	84	([5])		do.	15,284	([5])	
Vegetables		([5])	125		1,000 short tons	18,789	21,494	114
Citrus		([5])	([5])		do.	7,669	([5])	
Grapes		([5])	([5])		do.	3,489	2,898	83
Total fruits		([5])	([5])		do.	[10] 18,891	10,466	55
Hay, all kinds	Short tons	1·72	·06	34·9	do.	116,100	[9] 37,030	32

[1] Area harvested. Crop Production, 1965 Annual Summary, U.S. Department of Agriculture (USDA), Statistical Reporting Service (Washington D.C. Dec. 20, 1965). pp. 41–43, 51
[2] Derived
[3] Narodnoe khozyaystvo, SSSR v 1964 (Moscow 1965).
[4] USDA estimate
[5] Not available
[6] Continental beets and cane, including Hawaii, Puerto Rico, and Virgin Islands for 1964–65. World Agricultural Production and Trade, USDA, Foreign Agricultural Service (Washington, D.C. June 1965), p. 8.
[7] From domestic beets only
[8] Government purchases (procurements)
[9] Perennial and annual grasses only
[10] Excludes berries. Fruit Situation, USDA, ERS (Washington, D.C. January 1966), p. 29

7-year plan in agriculture: Objectives and performance, 1958, 1964–65

Item	Unit	1958 actual	1965 plan	1964 actual	1965 actual
1 Gross farm output	1958=100	100	170	113	114
2 Crops	1958=100	100	([1])	119	107
3 Animal products	1958=100	100	([1])	106	123
4 Gross farm output per capita	1958=100	100	156	102	102
5 Crops	1958=100	100	([1])	108	96
6 Animal products	1958=100	100	([1])	96	110
7 Marketed output	1958=100	100	([1])	126	([1])
8 Marketed output per capita[2]	1958=100	100	([1])	100	([1])
9 Grain output, official[3]	Million tons	134·7	153–172	152·1	120·5
10 Grain output, adjusted, USDA	do.	115·0	([1])	115·1	98
11 Raw cotton output	do.	4·4	5·7–6·1	5·3	5·7
12 Sugarbeet output	do.	54·4	76–84	81·2	71·5
13 Sunflower output	do.	4·6	([1])	6·1	5·4
14 Flax fiber output	Thousand tons	438	580	346	443
15 Potato output	Million tons	86·5	147	93·6	88·0
16 Vegetable output	do.	14·9	30–32	19·5	17·0
17 Fruit and grapes	do.	6·6	13·9	9 5	([1])
18 Meat output[4]	do.	7·7	16·0	8·3	9·9
19 Milk output	do.	58·7	100–105	63·3	72·4
20 Eggs output	Billion	23·0	37·0	26·7	29·0
21 Wool output	Thousand tons	322	548	341	356

[1] Not available.
[2] Urban population only.
[3] Net of corn other than grain corn. Soviet statistics on grain output are believed to be exaggerated and this may also be true of sunflower and some other products. In the more important case of grain, we also show an adjusted series.
[4] Slaughtered weight, including offal.

274

United States and Soviet Union: Agricultural resources

Item	Year	Unit	United States	Soviet Union[1]	USSR as percentage of US (%)
Population	1964	Millions	[2]192·1	227·7	119
Civilian labor force (work experience)	1964	do.	[3]85·1	[4]116·0	136
Annual average employment	1964	do.	[2]70·4	[4]103·4	147
Agricultural labor force (work experience).	1964	do.	[3]7·1	[4]46·5	655
Annual average employment in agriculture.	1964	do.	[3]4·8	[4]39·1	815
Farm share of total labor force (work experience).	1964	Percent	8·3	40·1	
Farm share of total employment (annual average).	1964	do.	6·8	37·8	
Sown cropland	1964	Millions of acres	[5]306	526	172
Sown cropland per capita	1964	Acres	1·6	2·3	144
Tractors on farms	Jan. 1, 1965	Thousands	[6]4,625	1,539	33
Motor trucks on farms	do.	do.	[6]2,925	954	33
Grain combines on farms	do.	do.	[6]990	513	52
Agricultural consumption of electricity	1964	Billions of kilo-watt-hours.	[7]29·9	18·4	62
Use of commercial fertilizer in terms of principal plant nutrients:					
Total	1964	1,000 short tons	[8]8,131	5,500	68
Per acre of sown area	1964	Pounds	59	21	36

[1] Narodnoe khozyaystvo, op. cit.
[2] Statistical abstract of the United States, U.S. Bureau of the Census (Washington, D.C. 1965), p. 5
[3] Monthly Labor Bulletin, No. 48, U.S. Department of Labor (Washington, D.C., January 1965)
[4] U.S. Bureau of the Census preliminary estimates
[5] 59 crops planted or grown. Crop Production, op. cit., p. 43
[6] Changes in Farm Production and Efficiency, USDA, Economic Research Service (Washington, D.C., July 1965), p. 22
[7] Estimated from average consumption in June. Agricultural Prices, USDA, SRS (Washington, D.C., November 1965), p. 23
[8] Changes in Farm Production and Efficiency, op. cit., p. 27.

The Soviet 7-year plan: Objectives and achievements, 1958–65

Item	Unit	1958 (actual)	1965 (plan)	1965 (actual)	Per cent fulfill-ment	Actual increase as percent of planned
1 National income	1958=100	100·0	162–165	157·0	95–97	88–92
2 Capital Investment a	Billion rubles, 7 years	b 122·0	c 194–197	240·0	122–124	157–164
3 Workers and employees	Million persons	54·6	66·6	76·9	116	186
4 Sown area	Million hectares	195·6	(1)	209·1	d 107	(1)
5 Population, total	Million at mid-year	270·0	225	231·0	103	133
6 Population, urban	do.	98·0	108	123·0	114	250
7 Industrial output, total	1958=100	100·0	180	184·0	102	105
8 Industrial output, "A"	do.	100·0	185–188	197·0	105–106	110–114
9 Industrial output, "B"	do.	100·0	162–165	160·0	97–99	92–97
10 Gross farm output	do.	100·0	170	114·0	67	20
11 Retail trade turnover	do.	100·0	162	159·0	98	95
12 Housing construction, urban	Million cubic meters, 7 years	~b 286·0	650–660	557·0	84–86	72–74
13 Housing construction, rural	Million houses, 7 years	~ b 3·8	7	3·5	50	e–9

a State and cooperatives.
b 1952–58.
c Excluding the value of project making work.
d Percent increase over 1958 (there was no target in the published version of the 7-year plan).
e Decline of 0·3 million instead of increase of 3·2 million.
[1] Not available.

From New Directions in the Soviet Economy, Part IIA and IIB, United States Government Printing Office, Washington 1966

BIBLIOGRAPHICAL NOTE

Works on the Soviet Union are legion, even in English. Readers unfamiliar with the literature but fired with a desire to read more (if such exist) are recommended the following, bearing in mind the necessarily idiosyncratic nature of any such selection.

There is, curiously enough, no good full history of the Soviet Union. E. H. Carr, *A History of Soviet Russia* (seven volumes, London 1950 onwards), has at present reached six volumes, taking the story from 1917 to 1926. Two further volumes are in preparation to bring the story to 1928–9. This work is outstanding, vastly comprehensive yet extremely readable. Thereafter the period is not covered on such a scale.

The best short perspective of Russia before 1914 is the recent book by Lionel Kochan, *Russia in Revolution, 1890–1914* (London 1966). The intellectual history of the pre-revolutionary period is still most perceptively covered by Edmund Wilson, *To the Finland Station* (latest edition, London 1962). On the revolution itself N. Sukhanov, *The Russian Revolution* (latest edition, New York 1962), the account of a participant and historian, is still the most valuable. John Reed, *Ten Days that Shook the World* (first published in 1919; latest edition, London 1961), captures the frenetic atmosphere in which millions of words poured from all directions to the confusion of all concerned. Trotsky's own account of the revolution is valuable and fascinating; so, of course, are his other retrospective works, *The History of the Russian Revolution* (second edition, London 1965), *My Life* (latest edition, New York 1960), and *The Revolution Betrayed* (London 1937).

There are several biographies of Lenin. David Shub, *Lenin* (latest edition, New York 1955), is short and adequate but dated. Louis Fischer, *The Life of Lenin* (London 1965), is more recent and comprehensive, and concentrates on the person. Adam Ulam, *Lenin and the Bolsheviks* (London 1966), is the most recent contribution by a learned and acute, if slightly 'superior', scholar of the Soviet Union. A dull but competent summary of Lenin's main political ideas is Alfred G. Meyer, *Leninism* (latest edition, New York 1962). Anyone wishing to look at Lenin in the raw should concentrate on *What is to be Done* (1902), *The State and Revolution* (1917), *Imperialism, the Highest Stage of Capitalism* (1916), and *Left Wing Communism: An Infantile Disorder* (1920), to be found in the collected or selected works published in English.

Stalin is less well served. The best and most perceptive biography, although now somewhat dated, is Boris Souvarine, *Stalin* (New York 1939, originally *Staline. Aperçu historique du bolchevisme*, Paris 1935). Isaac Deutscher's *Stalin* (latest edition, London 1961) hovers uncertainly between the desire to be a literary masterpiece and an attempt to do Stalin justice as an historical figure. Deutscher's biography of Trotsky is, however, a model of its kind, and can be recommended for the man and the period – though it necessarily ceases to be immediately relevant to the Soviet Union after 1929. Of recent writing on Khrushchev, Mark Frankland, *Khrushchev* (Pelican 1966), is a useful short introduction.

The best way to study the later Soviet Union is through books dealing with special aspects. A vital document of the period is Stalin's own *Short Course of the History of the CPSU (B)* (originally published in English in Moscow 1939), and the collection in two volumes entitled *Problems of Leninism* (latest edition, Foreign Languages House, Moscow 1947, first published in English in London 1940). Merle Fainsod, *How Russia is Ruled* (second edition, London 1963), is a modern and the most comprehensive analysis of the system of government and party (also contains a useful bibliography). Fainsod has also edited the party archives of the Smolensk region, captured by the Germans, and later appropriated by the Americans, in *Smolensk Under Soviet Rule* (London 1958), which provides a fascinating insight into the mechanics of the Soviet government during the 1920s and early 1930s. Leonard Schapiro, *The Communist Party of the Soviet Union* (London 1964), is a scholarly work somewhat distorted by the author's strong prejudice, but invaluable on party history. Kremlinology at its subtlest is represented by R.R. Conquest, *Power and Policy in the USSR* (London 1961), and *Russia After Khrushchev* (London 1965).

Outstanding for comprehensive and comprehensible analysis of the Soviet economy is A. Nove, *The Soviet Economy* (second edition, London 1965); M. Dobb, *Soviet Economic Development since 1917* (revised edition, London 1966), is a Marxist account which analyses the economic development of the Soviet Union in its own terms. An interesting Marxist critique of the Soviet Union is Tony Cliff, *Russia: A Marxist Analysis* (London 1964). Anyone familiar with orthodox economic theory will find P.J.D. Wiles, *The Political Economy of Communism* (Oxford 1962), an idiosyncratic but highly intelligent analysis of Soviet economics. The subject of trade unions is best studied in a book by Emily Clark Brown, *Soviet Trade Unions and Labour Relations* (Cambridge, Mass. 1966). Finally, facts and figures can be got most easily from G. Warren Nutter, *Growth of Industrial Production in the Soviet Union* (Princeton, New Jersey 1962). The figures themselves have been seriously questioned; the most recent overall view of Soviet industrial achievements is Norman M. Kaplan and Richard H. Moorsteen, 'An Index of Soviet Industrial Output', *American Economic Review*, L, 3 (June 1960), pp. 295–318. A more detailed report may be found in 'New Directions in the Soviet Economy', Studies prepared for the Sub-Committee on Foreign Economic Policy and the Joint Economic Committee Congress of the United States, IIa and IIb (Washington, D.C. 1966). This also includes a survey of agricultural performance. Naüm Jasny, *The Socialized Agriculture of the USSR* (Stanford, California 1949), is the most reliable general account up to the date of its publication. A more recent work dealing specifically with the role of the Machine Tractor Station is Roy D. Laird, D. E. Sharp and R. Sturtevant, *The Rise and Fall of the MTS as an Instrument of Soviet Rule* (University of Kansas 1960).

The best introduction to social problems in the USSR is a collection of reprinted articles and essays, Alex Inkeles and Kent Geiger, *Soviet Society* (London 1961). This is now unfortunately a little out of date and no more recent work of similar scope has yet been published. A useful collection of studies on the change of Russian society between the late Tsarist period and the end of Stalinism is C. E. Black (ed.), *The Transformation of Russian Society* (Cambridge, Mass. 1960).

There is no shortage of specialized literature on particular aspects of Soviet life. Readers interested in the literary scene in the Soviet Union can also turn to a variety of somewhat pedantic and highly 'politicized' analyses of modern Soviet literature, but perhaps the most interesting comment can be found in the essays and articles of a man who stands half-way between East and West, Mihajlo Mihajlov, *Moscow Summer* (London 1966). This is not an attempt to analyse trends, but a personal comment of someone who feels directly involved (and went to gaol twice in Yugoslavia for expressing his feelings).

A short and now somewhat dated history of the Comintern is Franz Borkenau, *World Communism: A History of the Communist International* (New York 1939), and Borkenau, *The Communist International* (London 1938). More recent work on the Third International has mostly been detailed research of particular areas or problems.

Foreign affairs are dealt with in Louis Fischer, *The Soviets in World Affairs* (New York 1960), and Alvin Z. Rubinstein (ed.), *The Foreign Policy of the Soviet Union* (New York 1960). Relations with other socialist countries are analysed in Z. K. Brzezinski, *The Soviet Bloc* (Cambridge, Mass. 1960) – though the interpretation is tinged with antipathy. Special attention to the origins of the Russo-Chinese conflict is paid in Benjamin Schwartz, *Chinese Communists and the Rise of Mao* (Cambridge 1951), and Robert C. North, *Moscow and Chinese Communists* (revised edition Stanford 1962). More recent studies are D. S. Zagoria, *The Sino-Soviet Conflict* (latest edition, Princeton 1962), and D. Floyd, *Mao Against Khrushchev* (latest edition, London 1966).

On the Second World War Alexander Werth, *Russia at War, 1941–1945* (London 1964), is outstanding and comprehensive.

Since the nationality problem is of such crucial importance, however, reference should be made to Walter Kollarz, *Russia and Her Colonies* (New York 1952), and (for the early period) Richard Pipes, *The Formation of the Soviet Union* (Cambridge, Mass. 1964).

Most of these books are substantive pieces of research or analysis. Few of them (except Reed and Trotsky) shed much light on 'what life was like for the ordinary citizen'. For this the memoirs of participants or victims are best. Victor Serge, *Memoirs of a Revolutionist* (London 1964), is outstanding for the early period. The notorious Victor Kravchenko, *I Chose Freedom* (second edition, London 1949), is a highly spiced account in which the uninitiated are led to a private peephole into the Kremlin. W. G. Krivitsky, *I Was Stalin's Agent* (London 1939), was the first of the secret police revelations by a senior defector. From within the party hierarchy, a confessional picture of life in the 1930s is given in the anonymous *The Letter of an Old Bolshevik: A Key to the Moscow Trials* (London 1938). A luridly tragic account of the sufferings of a German Communist at the hands of both Russian and German secret police is Margarete Buber-Neumann's *Von Potsdam nach Moskau: Stationen eines Irrweges* (Stuttgart 1957). And, of course, the most fascinating participant picture is Khrushchev's own version in 'The Crimes of Stalin', speech given at a session of the twentieth Party Congress, 25 February 1956, United States Department of State, Washington, 4 June 1956 (reprinted in *Soviet Society*, pp. 263–99).

A mine of information exists in the major Soviet novels. Since those published in English and accorded acclaim are almost invariably critical of past or present aspects of Soviet life, a recommended list must give a distorted picture. But Boris Pasternak's *Doctor Zhivago* (London 1958), uniquely evokes the early period of the Soviet Union in a way no other book has done.

LIST OF ILLUSTRATIONS

281

283

INDEX AND WHO'S WHO